Family Mobility

Family mobility decisions reveal much about how the public and private realms of social life interact and change. This sociological study explores how contemporary families reconcile individual members' career and education projects within the family unit over time and space, and unpacks the intersubjective constraints on workforce mobility.

This Australian mixed methods study sampled Defence Force families and middle-class professional families to illustrate how families' educational projects are necessarily and deeply implicated in issues of workforce mobility and immobility, in complex ways. Defence families move frequently, often absorbing the stresses of moving through 'viscous' institutions as private troubles.

In contrast, the selective mobility of middle-class professional families and their 'no-go zones' contribute to the public issue of poorly serviced rural communities. Families with different social, material and vocational resources at their disposal are shown to reflexively weigh the benefits and risks associated with moving differently. The book also explores how priorities shift as children move through educational phases. The families' narratives offer empirical windows on larger social processes, such as the mobility imperative, the gender imbalance in the family's intersubjective bargains, labour market credentialism, the social construction of place, and the family's role in the reproduction of class structure.

Catherine Doherty is a Senior Research Fellow in the Faculty of Education at Queensland University of Technology. She works in the sociology of education with an interest in mobile populations and educational markets. As well as this project, she has published research on international students in higher education, and international curriculum in secondary schools.

Wendy Patton is a Professor and Executive Dean in the Faculty of Education at Queensland University of Technology, widely published in theoretical approaches to career studies across different populations in terms of age, socio-economic background and employment experience. She is currently the Series Editor of an International Career Development Book series by Sense Publishers.

Paul Shield is a Senior Research Fellow in the Faculty of Education at Queensland University of Technology with expertise in quantitative methodologies. He has contributed to major systemic reviews of educational reform and a wide variety of educational studies.

Changing mobilities
Series Editors: Monika Büscher, Peter Adey

This series explores the transformations of society, politics and everyday experiences wrought by changing mobilities, and the power of mobilities research to inform constructive responses to these transformations. As a new mobile century is taking shape, international scholars explore motivations, experiences, insecurities, implications and limitations of mobile living, and opportunities and challenges for design in the broadest sense, from policy to urban planning, new media and technology design. With world citizens expected to travel 105 billion kilometres per year in 2050, it is critical to make mobilities research and design inform each other.

Elite Mobilities
Edited by Thomas Birtchnell and Javier Caletrío

Family Mobility
Reconciling career opportunities and educational strategy
Catherine Doherty, Wendy Patton, Paul Shield

Forthcoming:

Changing Mobilities
Monika Büscher

Cargomobilities
Moving materials in a global age
Edited by Thomas Birtchnell, Satya Savitzky and John Urry

Italian Mobilities
Edited by Ruth Ben-Ghiat and Stephanie Malia Hom

Family Mobility

Reconciling career opportunities and educational strategy

Catherine Doherty,
Wendy Patton and Paul Shield

Routledge
Taylor & Francis Group

LONDON AND NEW YORK

First published 2015 by Routledge

2 Park Square, Milton Park, Abingdon, Oxfordshire OX14 4RN
52 Vanderbilt Avenue, New York, NY 10017

Routledge is an imprint of the Taylor & Francis Group, an informa business

First issued in paperback 2019

British Library Cataloguing-in-Publication Data
A catalogue record for this book is available from the British
Library

Library of Congress Cataloging-in-Publication Data
Family mobility : reconciling career opportunities and educational
strategy / edited by Catherine Doherty, Wendy Patton and Paul Shield.
    pages cm – (Changing mobilities)
    1. Migration, Internal–Australia–Social aspects. 2. Educational
sociology–Australia. 3. Occupational mobility–Australia–Social
aspects. 4. Student mobility–Australia–Social aspects. 5. School
choice–Australia. 6. Work and family–Australia. I. Doherty,
Catherine Ann. II. Patton, Wendy, 1957- III. Shield, Paul.
    HB2135.F36 2014
    304.80994–dc23   2014003125a

ISBN: 978-0-415-71412-9 (hbk)
ISBN: 978-0-367-86865-9 (pbk)

Typeset in Times New Roman
by Wearset Ltd, Boldon, Tyne and Wear

To professionals working in rural and remote communities.
To military families.

Contents

List of figures   x
List of tables   xi
Acknowledgements   xii

1 The family in more mobile times   1
The mobility imperative 2
Thinking about family as process 4
Thinking about projects and strategies 8
Thinking about career and work 10
Thinking about educational strategy 13
Coming from another angle 16
Thinking about mobilities from Australia 17
Thinking personally 18
An overview 20

**2 Work/family/education articulations in space with mobility
systems**   23
Space and place as interactive context 23
Motility as a prerequisite 26
A case for viscosity 28

3 Making sense of mobility in family narratives   34
Thinking through narrative 34
Capturing family narratives of mobility 37
Mobility in the orientation 40
Mobility as complication 42
Mobility as resolution 43
Mobility in the coda 45
Re-placing family life 46
Moving emotions 53
Moving stories 55

4   Seeking continuity in circumstances not of our choosing   57
Military families research to date 59
Education systems and their institutional contradictions 60
Managing space and time 63
House or school first? Acquiring motility strategies 65
The educational complications of institutional discontinuities 69
Accumulating troubles in learning trajectories across space 87
Low viscosity settings 79
Protecting the future by manufacturing continuity 81
Accommodating spouse career aspirations 87
Waxing and waning motility 91
Conclusion 94

5   Optimising location in circumstances of our choosing   97
The optimising circuit 100
Variations on a theme 108
Counter-narratives 119
*Professionals and institutional solutions to their selective
    mobility 126*
Conclusion 129

6   Movers and stayers   132
Introducing the sampled professionals 132
Introducing the constructs 135
Measurement models of the constructs 138
*Characteristics and attitudes of the more motile and mobile
    professionals 143*
Reasons behind the decisions for moving and staying 145
The social trajectories of family relocations 149
Conclusion 150

7   Mobius markets   152
Demystifying the mobius 153
The social limits to credential society 154
Credentials for exchange value 156
Credentials for use value 159
Professional currency on the mobius market 161
Professional families moving in the mobius market 164
The interplay of factors in moving/staying 166
Conclusion 169

8   Professionals' public/private dilemmas in rural service   171

Professional families and rural communities: a recursive
    im/mobility problem 171
Professions and the public good 172
Public/private dilemmas for teachers in rural and regional
    communities 174
Case 1: Public service at private cost 176
Case 2: Professional allegiance and private choice 177
Case 3: Professional insider knowledge in private choices 178
Case 4: Private risks in public service 178
Reconciling neoliberal and public good value sets 179
Conclusion: the private limits to public service in small
    communities 183

9   Families moving on to get ahead   186

Mobility as a lens on family 187
Family as a lens on mobility 189
Family mobility as a lens on career/work studies 190
Family mobility as a lens on educational markets 192
Family mobility as a lens on the mobile society 195
Family mobility as a lens on workforce mobility policy 195
Conclusion 198

**Appendix 1: Original item sets for their corresponding
constructs**   200

Bibliography   202
Index   215

Figures

3.1   Example excerpt from a family orchestration score   39
6.1   A single-factor tau model for public good (standardised
      estimates)   139
6.2   A single-factor tau model for neoliberalism (standardised
      estimates)   141
6.3   A single-factor congeneric model for location range
      (standardised estimates)   142
6.4   A higher-order congeneric measurement model with two
      factors for motility (standardised estimates)   142
6.5   Shifting IRSAD scores over the past family relocations   149
8.1   Locations in survey's hypothetical scenarios   180

Tables

3.1	Labov and Waletzky's narrative structural sections	36
4.1	Early years schooling nomenclature and starting ages by Australian state as at 2010	70
6.1	Respondent profession by highest educational qualification	134
6.2	Respondent profession by annual family income	136
6.3	Item set for the construct 'public good'	139
6.4	Item set for the construct 'private good'	140
6.5	Item set for the construct 'neoliberalism'	140
6.6	Item set for the construct 'location range'	141
6.7	Item set for the construct 'motility'	143
6.8	Significant predictors for motility	144
6.9	Model summary – dependent variable: motility	144
6.10	Significant predictors for number of moves	145
6.11	Model summary – dependent variable: number of moves	145
6.12	Rankings of the overall importance of factors in the two most recent moves	147
6.13	Scores and rankings of the factors behind decisions to stay	148
7.1	Mean difference in the age of the oldest child at the time of the most recent move	166
8.1	Spearman's correlation between 'neoliberalism' and 'public good'	173
9.1	Cross-tabulating motility and viscosity	197

Acknowledgements

There are two research projects behind this book. The first study of military families was generously funded as a Queensland University of Technology Vice Chancellor's Postdoctoral Fellowship. The second study of professional families was generously funded by the Australian Research Council. We appreciate this enabling support.

We are also very grateful to the various agencies that helped us make contact with potential participants and respondents across our various categories. These include the Defence Community Organisation, The Queensland Police Service, RHealth, The Queensland Teachers Union, The Queensland Nurses Union, Australian Medical Association Queensland and the Local Government Association of Queensland.

Our work across the past few years has been ably assisted by hard-working research assistants whose contributions across the different phases have been invaluable. Thank you to Barbara Rissman, Rowena McGregor, Carly Lassig, Michael Mu, Marian James, Michele Moon and Megan Kimber. We would never have got this far without them.

The idea for a book in this series came from John Urry when the Centre for Mobilities Research at Lancaster University hosted a brief visit from a rather nervous Catherine Doherty. Thank you to John for the idea, to Monika Büscher and Peter Adey for seeing worth in our proposal, and to the anonymous reviewers for their valuable feedback. The same rather nervous Catherine Doherty also visited Margaret Archer at l'Ecole Polytechnique Fédérale de Lausanne. We have benefited greatly from Professor Archer's generous guidance around reflexivity, life projects and critical realist metatheory.

Finally, we would like to express our thanks to the interview participants for sharing their mobility stories with us, and to the survey respondents for taking the time to answer our many questions. It is people like you who keep social science on its toes.

Chapter 1

The family in more mobile times

It's really tricky trying to work out if for [daughter's] sake we stay here for her to do a high school … it's really tricky. We just haven't come to that decision.

(Louise, military family, two parents, three children)

Well, wherever we go obviously he's going to have work because the army put us there. Hopefully I'll have work wherever we go and the only thing we get a choice in is what the kids do. We don't really get to choose where we live, we don't get to choose how long for but at least we get to choose where the kids get to be.

(Julie, military family, two parents, three children)

All families are mobile in various ways on different scales, but some families are more mobile than others. Some families have mobility thrust upon them, while others have great capacity to be mobile but choose not to. The same could be said about members within families. This book explores the strategy, choices and concerns behind differently textured mobilities that families with school-aged children undertake in their household relocations. More particularly, this book explores how different families reconcile priorities around career opportunities and educational strategy in their mobility decisions over time and space, and what broader social effects flow from these private decisions.

This book contributes empirically and theoretically to the 'new mobilities' paradigm in sociology, which makes visible how 'issues of movement, of too little movement or too much, or of the wrong sort or at the wrong time, are central to many lives and many organisations' (Sheller and Urry 2006: 208). The concept of mobilities here is purposefully plural, refracted and diverse, embracing spatial, virtual and imaginary movements of people, objects, ideas, images, information and matter across space or electronic networks, at different paces and on different scales. Urry's (2000a) manifesto for a sociology that foregrounds mobility reclaimed a more geographic meaning of mobility from its common metaphoric usage in sociology. In this way, mobility is 'understood in a horizontal rather than the vertical sense' (p. 3) of social mobility. This paradigm's research agenda is interested not only in understanding the movements of people and objects as social and cultural phenomena, but also the second-order consequences of such mobility for places 'located in the fast and slow lanes across the globe' (p. 207). Mobilities by their selectivity, pace, presence and absence contribute to the ongoing social construction of places, their reputations and their viability (Massey 1993). In this book, we are particularly interested in one sort of mobility – the important, high stakes and large-scale event of relocating the family home; that is, re-placing family life in a new location. This book examines how private decisions made within families about moving on can produce both solutions and troubles within the same family, and then solutions and troubles as public issues if a locality fails to attract the professionals it needs.

Social theory has been tracking how social relations are increasingly consti-tuted and transformed while on the move, as opposed to contained within stable, fixed and bounded societies. For example, Appadurai's (1990) concept of '-scapes' explained globalisation as accelerating, disjunctural flows of people, technologies, ideologies, media and finance. Bauman in his 'liquid modernity' (2000) thesis pointed to the social and economic advantages of 'travelling light' for advantageous mobility in the late twentieth century. Urry (2000a) critiqued mainstream sociology for reifying sedentary society and overlooking the social interconnections and transformations produced by the various mobilities of people and things.

The mobility paradigm is equally interested in immobility as both choice and circumstance: 'It is not a question of privileging a "mobile subjectivity", but rather of tracking the power of discourses and practices of mobility in creating both movement and stasis' (Sheller and Urry 2006: 211). 'Spatial autonomy', the capacity to control the timing and placing of one's mobility and move to 'optimal environments' (Weiss 2005: 714) has become a valuable asset:

> We might say that unforced 'movement' is power, that is, to be able to move (or to be able voluntarily to stay still) is for individuals and groups a major source of advantage and conceptually independent of economic and cultural advantage.
>
> (Urry 2008: 491)

Others less well resourced are differently 'placed' in their restricted capacity either to pursue opportunities elsewhere or to resist enforced movement. In this way, the mobilities paradigm responds to the complexities implicated in the growing press of a 'mobility imperative' in a more fluid social world.

The mobility imperative

Population mobilisation has become an attractive policy goal for nations, organi-sations and corporations to protect economic competitiveness and to foster

productivity, flexibility and responsiveness. Strategies of economic regionalisation have scaled up labour markets by reducing barriers to movement to allow
people and businesses to pursue opportunities elsewhere. Governments increasingly court skilled immigration to recruit just-in-time human capital, rather than
grow their own (Connell 2010). A report by PriceWaterhouseCoopers (2010),
Talent Mobility 2020, projects a significant change in the ecology and flow of
global talent as workers from emerging markets increasingly compete for global
opportunities. Other prospective studies of worker mobility have highlighted the
need to recognise that the worker is typically part of a family, and that greater
recognition of the 'family effect' (Shortland 2012: 51) needs to be factored into
securing, deploying and retaining mobile talent. While technological affordances
may reduce some pressure on the need for long-term relocation, the PriceWaterhouseCoopers report suggests it will not 'erode the need to have people deployed
on the ground' (p. 5). In this vein, Florida argues that success in 'the new global
competition for talent' lies in a nation's ability to mobilize, attract, and retain
human creative talent' (Florida 2005: 3).

Urry (2000a: 5) understands this tactical shift by employers through the distinction between 'gardening and gamekeeping metaphors'. Gamekeeping policies offer 'carrot' incentives to encourage inward mobility. As an example, the
'Connecting People with Jobs' initiative by the Australian Commonwealth government in 2010 offered AU$6000 to unemployed workers with families to relo-
cate into areas with better employment prospects, and a subsidy for their
employer. Similarly, a 'Relocations Grants Scheme' in 2011 offered metropolitan homeowners AU$7000 to offset removal costs and encourage them to buy
into smaller centres, with the hope of stimulating regional investment. Business
advocates have equally touted 'stick' solutions in public debates, for example
advocating that welfare entitlements be reduced if unemployed workers refuse to
relocate to sites with labour shortages. While such policies may target the individual worker, relocating will implicate their family unit.

Despite such efforts, family mobility has proven less amenable to social engi-
neering than policy makers might hope. There is a widespread reluctance to relocate households with school-aged children, and some evidence that moving
house is detrimental to schooling outcomes (Voight *et al.* 2012). This normative
default is responsible for other innovative responses to the mobility imperative
by families and employers such as long-distance commuting and 'fly-in fly-out'
or 'drive-in drive-out' arrangements (Haslam McKenzie 2010) which involve
one parent working away from the family home over intensified rosters. Such
'workable solutions' to the mobility imperative exact a considerable cost at the
micro level of family relations. At the macro sociological scale these solutions
have also raised concerns about their reinvigoration of an asymmetrical, gendered division of labour in the home (Schneider and Limmer 2008; Meil 2009).
Here, we align with Costas' (2013: 1468) argument for a less celebratory, more
ambiguous and contradictory version of mobility that recognises the 'stickiness'
and frictions associated with movement. Such friction can eventuate within

families (Abraham *et al.* 2010; Coulter *et al.* 2012) on a micro scale, and between public and private concerns at a macro scale, therefore warrants further enquiry to understand how family relocations become thinkable and doable, on whose terms, and at what cost.

This book takes a novel approach in exploring families' mobility decisions not in separate, analytically partitioned domains of work, family and education, but rather as the messy lived nexus of competing priorities that must be temporarily reconciled within family units, with regard to the structure of opportunities offered in each locality. In later chapters, we will explore this nexus through the experiences and narratives of two specific groups of families who display markedly different patterns and logics of mobility. The first group are the families of military personnel in the Australian Defence Forces (ADF). This career path requires frequent relocations across Australian states, as well as extended absences of the serving member on active service or training. These hyper-mobile families pursue ordinary lives in the extraordinarily circumstances of frequent and repeated family relocations in circumstances not necessarily of their choosing. The second group belong to doctors, nurses, teachers and police working in rural and remote Australia, and the larger pool of such professionals who more typically avoid such settings. The capacity of these qualified professionals and their reluctance to move to 'hard to staff' localities has created an ongoing challenge for these communities to support viable services. By focusing on these purposefully contrasting patterns of family mobility, and exploring both their associated private troubles and public issues, we exploit the mobility paradigm to expose how families work across time and space in these more mobile, individualised and marketised times.

Our framing requires a more dynamic, processual definition of family, an explicit approach to projects and strategies, a less individualist concept of 'career', and more consideration of families' strategies in educational markets. In this chapter, we prepare these conceptual tools, before outlining the book's lines of enquiry more fully. We draw from different literatures but seek to show where and how their various lines of enquiry converge and intersect to build a rich dialogic social science capable of addressing complexity.

Thinking about family as process

Families are intriguing social collectives – ubiquitous yet variable, dynamic yet anchoring, resilient yet fragile, limiting yet enabling. A one-size-fits-all definition of family as a core sociological concept and social institution is becoming increasingly elusive. On one hand there has been radical but uneven change in social scripts around fertility, gender roles and marriage and how they play out in families, while, on the other hand, there are differences between what people think family should be and how it is actually lived (Gilding 1997; Edin and Kefalas 2005; Evans and Gray 2005; Hodgson 2008). There has been a proliferation of family forms that include children (such as nuclear families, single-parent families, extended families, 'blended' or step-families, same-sex couple families, adoptive families) alongside a pragmatic thinning of the concept's empirical operationalisation. Surveys tend to use 'family' and 'household' as interchangeable common-sensical terms left to respondents' interpretations.

We would highlight the distinctive relational bonds and uniquely dense and intense intersubjectivity that distinguishes the family from other social collectives. The complex emotional, biological, legal and economic bonds that can hold members together also decentre the individual in a mesh of intimate rights and responsibilities. When families think about moving, the force and nature of these bonds becomes evident. This book is about how families manage their mutual rights and responsibilities when contemplating a move. Following Crossley, we understand intersubjectivity to be that which decentres the individual in forming and maintaining a collective 'us':

> intersubjectivity is the fabric of our social becoming.... It is what holds us all together in an identifiable group or unit ... 'fabric' conjures up an image of multiple overlappings and intertwinings, organised and arranged in different ways, sometimes becoming disorganised. It connotes a sense of unity and strength which is achieved by way of this overlapping. No thread is either strong or significant on its own but the intertwining gives it strength and form.
>
> (Crossley 1996: 173)

The overlapping and intertwining in families implicates a mesh and intersection of public and private domains. Sherif-Trask (2010) reviews the progress of theory of families from the idealised functionalism of early sociology through feminist and postcolonial critiques of the hegemonic form naturalised and privileged by Western scholarship. Despite the contested status of the concept and its lived complexities, for Sherif-Trask, families are 'the arena where macro- and micro-forces come together' (p. vii). Berger (2002) describes a symbiosis between 'modern society', being the urban industrialised West, and the 'modern' family, being the conventionalised two-heterosexual-parents-plus-children nuclear family. In response to politically motivated claims that the family as an institution is under threat, Berger highlights the protean dynamism of this nuclear family form and its capacity to absorb and adapt to major change in the moral fabric. For Berger, like Sherif-Trask, the family is an institution that crucially integrates private realms and public concerns, particularly around the protection and socialisation of children. For Sherif-Trask (2010) and others (for example, Boulding 1983), families are where social change originates, and for Berger (2002: ix), it is a resilient social building block, 'far less fragile than it has been commonly assumed'.

For our purposes, the public/private family can be understood as both the primary generative institution and the institution of last resort that acts as a shock absorber to mitigate the impact of external structural forces on its members through private solutions: 'It is in the institution of the family where the most basic dimensions of human life intersect and sustain each other – the biological with the social, the material with the normative, the symbolic with the transcendental' (Berger 2002: 80). This framing foregrounds both active and reactive processes undertaken within families to promote individual members' life chances, while protecting and promoting the collective unit at the same time.

However, not all theoretical accounts of family are about united strength and coherence. Some writers have argued that the inherent tension between the individual and the family collective is mounting as a result of greater consumerism and women's changing status given greater workforce participation, improved fertility control, and access to no-fault divorce. Lesthaeghe (1995) identified 'the second demographic transition' across the 1980s in Western societies that, by his account, redefined marriage on more conditional grounds related to the self-fulfilment of the adults involved. Such trends might suggest that it will become harder for families to manage and accommodate their members' individual needs and wants.

Beck and Beck-Gernsheim (2004) offer another perspective on the relation between individual and family. Through their thesis of 'institutional individualization' and its 'individualization of the family' (p. 500) they argue that the social flux of globalisation plays out in intimate settings, with families sailing into uncharted seas under less adherence to traditional scripts and more active choice and flexibility around how life is to be lived. Restructured social institutions 'such as the labor market and citizenship, the education system, the legal system, social security' (p. 502) are granting 'risky freedoms' (p. 512) and placing more onus on the individual to exercise choice. Under these rubrics, 'risks are distributed so that they are no longer borne by the state and economy but shifted on to individuals and families' (p. 502). What could once be taken for granted must now be explicitly negotiated on an ongoing basis. These authors call for new questions to be asked in family studies around what holds people together in the absence of inherited scripts and how families negotiate their risky freedoms. Our interest in families' deliberative processes, priorities and concerns around relocation contributes in this space.

When it comes to reconciling public and private, individual and collective concerns, new social norms have already prompted much enquiry into 'work/life' balance and 'work/life' strain within families (for example, Drago 2007; Baxter and Alexander 2008). Such research has attended to time and its allocation in the domestic division of labour (for example, Sullivan 2006). Time has also featured in studies of family relations across life-course phases (for example, Elder and Giele 2009). However, the dimension of space is rarely considered in family studies. This blind spot is perhaps understandable, given that the spatial 'togetherness' of family members is perhaps the social unit's defining indicator and core motive at key child-rearing phases, so central it has been taken for granted. However, the mobility paradigm would argue that both spatial mobility and immobility as life circumstances, and their social consequences, need to be accounted for (Urry 2000a; Sheller and Urry 2006).

Holdsworth's (2013) recent book purposefully addresses this blind spot. She scans British and European research from both family studies and mobility studies to show how the fields might enrich each other. In contrast to the common assumption that mobility endangers the family unit, Holdsworth's theme is that mobility is necessary for family relations. Her focus is on how families have always generated a variety of mobility practices on different spatial and temporal scales which are intrinsic to the formation, maintenance and dissolution of family units. She highlights the relationality, interdependence and social meanings achieved through mobility: 'closeness and belonging are experienced through mobility, rather than despite it' (p. 6). She is also interested in how not all parties are equally autonomous when it comes to family mobility. She addresses the tensions created between individual and collective mobilities, and how 'mobilities and immobilities are intertwined' (p. 28), implicating class and gender differences. Similar to our frame on family as process, Holdsworth rejects both overly structural and overly atomistic concepts of family and adopts a definition of family 'as verb': 'family practices are continually in the process of (re-)creation' (p. 13). Holdsworth then poses the paradox that makes family relocations such intriguing and telling events:

> On the one hand, mobility is a strategy that many parents use to maximise children's current and future prosperity, yet at the same time mobility is popularly portrayed as undermining childhood.... Having children is therefore ultimately equated with putting down 'roots'.
>
> (p. 69)

In the sociology of the family/work interface, there is an understandable fascination with more experimental modes of mobile living and concern about their social impact. Empirical work has tracked the emergence of new spatial arrangements for family households precipitated by work demands or opportunities. Levin (2004) describes the 'new family form' (p. 224) of 'living apart together' and its mobilities. Van der Klis and Karsten (2009) consider the gender imbalance of 'commuter families', which 'enable parents to seize distant work opportunities and preserve solid local roots for family life' (p. 341). Schneider and Limmer (2008) highlight the growing demand for job-related mobility of various scales in Germany and its impact on family and community life, while Meil (2009) focuses on what job mobility means for the division of labour in the family home. Haslam McKenzie (2010) documents the emergent 'fly-in fly-out' family form in remote Australia, whereby typically the male partner works in a remote location with little social infrastructure over a compressed working period, returning to the family home for breaks. Luck and Ruppenthal (2010) compare the 'mobility culture' (p. 44) of different European nations and birth cohorts. By focusing on job-related mobility that takes the worker from the family home, these studies implicitly demonstrate how much importance can be placed on maintaining residential stability for children in family deliberations, enough to exclude a family move.

This literature as such fails to account for those families that forego such stability in order to remain together while on the move for work purposes. Taken together, these different sociological fields also fail to account for the conundrum at their intersection: that is, how the immobility/stability typically valued for children can at times be set aside in the pursuit of educational or career opportunities. To this end, the book explores two different types of families in Australia with what could be considered problematic degrees of mobility – one experiencing too much for private purposes, the other too little for public purposes.

By exploring mobility histories, strategies and plans, this book will understand the family as both a generative and a responsive social institution to make evident its processes for accomplishing being together across time and space. Where Holdsworth (2013) reviews the variety of mobilities families perform, we are more particularly interested in the high stakes life event of family relocations. While the school commute, the family holiday and the extended family visit can become habitual practices, family relocations are major mobility events that bring explicit and careful deliberation to the surface, and reveal what is at stake for members and their relationships.

Thinking about projects and strategies

From Archer's research programme on life concerns, reflexivity and social mobility, we borrow the concept of reflexive projects to conceptualise the role of strategies and plans in the construction and mediation of social realities. For Archer (2007: 4):

> 'Reflexivity' is the regular exercise of the mental ability, shared by all normal people, to consider themselves in relation to their (social) contexts and vice versa. Such deliberations ... form the basis upon which people determine their future courses of action – always fallibly and always under their own description.

With this power of reflexivity, humans devise 'projects' which Archer explains as 'any course of action intentionally engaged upon by a human being ... to promote our concerns; we form "projects" to advance or to protect what we care about most' (p. 7). In this frame, a family is marked as a group of individuals whose projects are allowed to legitimately impinge on each other, or who seek to share and harmonise their projects, while negotiating gender roles, fertility, workforce participation, child-rearing, education and the domestic division of labour. For many families with school-aged children, such core business would typically relate to furthering career and education projects, nested within a meta-project of living life together.

Archer works within a critical realist metatheory, which understands social realities to emerge through a complex, layered ontology operating within an open system, such that causal forces at one layer in their combination produce emergent properties at the next. To put this another way, the product of a combination of elements will be more than the sum of its parts and different in its essential nature. In this frame, we can understand the family to realise emergent properties that are more than the sum of its individual members and different in their social substance. The family, as a social reality, though reliant on its members for its existence, is something more than these individuals, and this 'something more' exerts a social force of its own. Forming a family changes things for the individuals involved, and will decentre them in a new network of overlapping rights and responsibilities. Crossley draws out this intersubjectivity underpinning families' collective projects:

> plans are not necessarily the properties of individuals. They can be formed between individuals, as an irreducible property of a couple.... In these situations it is not I who decide what to do, nor you. It is we who decide ... it constitutes a complex interactive situation, which cannot have been planned as such by either side, but within which a plan is formulated.
>
> (Crossley 1996: 81)

Archer further explains that the outcome of any project will depend on both actors' actions and the social environment, in terms of how external parties and institutions can either enable or constrain the project's progress and outcome. Attention to this agency/structure interaction can account for both successful and unsuccessful projects, foreseeable and unforeseeable problems. As families 'make [their] way through the world' (p. 5), they will be 'reading' and assessing both the opportunities and constraints of different locations in terms of furthering career and educational projects. This constant iterative work is family in progress. Further, Archer's definition highlights the dependence on 'fallible' readings of the world – making judgement calls to the best of one's ability, with no guarantee that all factors in the strategising are accurately understood or predicted. Our empirical focus on mobility brings much of this deliberative work to the surface, where readings of risk, opportunity, decisions, dilemmas, choice and priorities have to be explicitly assessed and renegotiated.

Archer's work concentrates first on individuals' projects, but in a later book (2012) she explores how young couples seek to 'dovetail' their projects in order to establish a life together. Connell (2003) also developed the idea of projects, but in this case 'family projects', being 'coherent and persisting patterns of action which link the present with some imagined future' (p. 239). As a collective, a family's effort to dovetail or 'harmonise' (Beck and Willms 2004: 67) members' projects will require negotiations and adjustments, with perhaps delays, sacrifices or compromises for some, then ongoing reflexive work of monitoring outcomes and revising strategies, to make things work optimally for them as a social unit. Family mobility or immobility can emerge as a strategy in this way.

Thinking about career and work

Like 'family', the term 'career' carries common-sense meanings that we need to trouble. The term 'career' has been criticised for its Western middle-class focus and the lack of its applicability across other cultures and settings. More recently, the term 'work' has been adopted to provide a less conceptually and culturally compromised term that is more inclusive. Understanding career and human behaviour in the domain of work has largely been the realm of psychology and it is really only in the last twenty years that more sociological understandings have informed the literature. This section will provide a brief summary of the background literature, then outline our approach to 'career'.

In everyday terminology 'work' typically refers to the domain of life in which people, paid or unpaid, provide labour towards the outcome of a service or a good; 'job' refers to a specific work position which may be permanent full-time or part-time and in a particular role or organisation; while 'career' refers to the sequence or collection of jobs held over an individual's life. In Western societies, 'career' has traditionally been conceptualised as a linear sequence of 'jobs' which follow a vertical trajectory in status and remuneration. Arthur *et al.* (1989) described career as 'the evolving sequence of a person's work experiences over time' (p. 8), while Nicholson and West (1989) recommended 'the more neutral term "work histories" to denote sequences of job experiences and reserve the term "career" for the sense people make of them' (p. 181). Richardson (1993, 2000) suggested that career is a limited and irrelevant concept and subject to a middle-class bias in perception and ideology. She proposed that the focus should be on how people construct their own meaning of work in their lives, and suggested that we should use the terms 'work', 'jobs' *and* 'career' in any discussion thereof.

More recently Richardson and Schaeffer (2013) have argued that the common-sense connection between paid work and career is an artefact of the rise of capitalism. Constructing unpaid work or care work as 'work' challenges many social precepts in a capitalist hegemony. These authors proposed a dual model of working that addresses both market work and unpaid care work, emphasising that there are two kinds of work, and that both are equally important:

> this new model challenges the prevailing discourse regarding how most people talk about and experience the work in their lives, that is, as career, and proposes that they talk about and experience this part of their lives as market work instead of career. It also proposes a second domain of work, that is, unpaid care work that most people, at least at this point, are not

likely to talk about or experience as work at all. What we are proposing then is a radical reconfiguration of how people talk about and experience essential components of their lives having to do with the work they do.

(Richardson and Schaeffer 2013: 25)

Blustein (2001, 2006) has also challenged the conventional language and understanding of work and career, acknowledging that the majority of women and men have limited choice in the work they undertake to support themselves and their families. He has proposed a more inclusive frame on working which corrects the limited way the field has addressed issues of gender, social class, family background, cultural characteristics and their impact on career development. Even for those with the privilege of choice, these factors will impinge on the range of alternatives.

Psychologists have referred to work as a means through which individuals 'implement a self-concept' (Super *et al.* 1996: 139). Writers in the organisation development field have referred to careers as 'individual expressions of identity' (Inkson and Elkin 2008: 76). It is these views that have been subject to criticism, with assertions that the term 'career' implies choice and privilege while disregarding structural constraints, and that much work does not afford such a subjective sense of career and identity. Many individuals pursue work for survival and this work may not contribute to any more than need fulfillment, as opposed to building a personal and public identity and fulfilling a 'calling'.

In addition to these reconceptualisations, much of the social context of work has been changing, rewriting previous understandings of career processes. These contextual factors include political, economic, technological and demographic changes to the nature and structure of work and employing organisations (see Inkson 2007 for a comprehensive summary). The emphasis and agency in the emerging twenty-first-century career has shifted from the organisation to the individual, as reflected in new notions of 'protean' (Hall 1996; Hall and Las Heras 2009) and 'boundaryless' careers (Arthur 1994; Arthur and Rousseau 1996; Sullivan and Arthur 2006). The concept of protean career refers to the notion that, in order to adapt and survive in a changing world, the individual needs to be self-generating: that is, protean. This understanding displaces the notion of a linear or vertical career. It recognises flexible and idiosyncratic career sequences. In addition, it embraces all aspects of an individual's life as relevant to career, placing the individual at the centre of career, with organisational and occupational contexts as their stage. This version of career is closely related to the concept of the boundaryless career (Arthur and Rousseau 1996), which emphasises how career is now about an individual organising, not organisations, in the intersection between self-organising and social phenomena (Littleton *et al.* 2000). In this vein, Sullivan and Arthur (2006) note the importance of what they term 'physical' (actual movement across jobs and organisations, through to countries) and 'psychological' mobility (a mobile mindset) for successful negotiation of boundaryless careers in the twenty-first century. Though these authors use a different vocabulary, we would highlight the resonance between these ideas and the individualisation thesis of Beck and others outlined above. Both highlight the growing role and play of the agent's reflexive strategy in the face of the contextual contingencies in an increasingly unpredictable and open system.

Building on this background, Richardson and Schaeffer (2013) have emphasised that, as work was equated with jobs in the market economy, so 'work and family became embedded in our minds and experience as two separate spheres of life' (p. 26). However, a more relational, intersubjective lens would emphasise the necessary interface between adults, work and relationships in multiple ways. The demands of market work and care work both impact and influence personal decisions and vocational decisions. In mobility research, Bonnet *et al.* (2008) are similarly interested in the occupational and mobility outcomes of family negotiations, the possible conflicts encountered, and the processes of adjustment and compromise in the way family lives unfold. They arrive at a cognate concept of 'family career' to encapsulate the trajectory achieved over the historical series of occupational negotiations of constraints and opportunities within a family.

While much of the literature in this area has focused on work/family conflict and stress for both women and men in managing competing roles, empirical studies overwhelmingly suggest that women remain more likely to change their career paths and forego workplace opportunities because of family responsibilities (Schultheiss 2009). Although governments in many Western countries have implemented key policy levers such as family leave, child-care support and flexible work arrangements, these have been introduced more in connection with pressures for all citizens, women and men, to be economically independent. Schultheiss (2009) and Richardson and Schaeffer (2013) critique such policy, theory and research addressing the relationship between work and family as privileging paid market work over unpaid work, such as caring for children, ageing parents and other loved ones, especially at a time when care of the ageing is becoming a pressing social issue.

Metaphors of 'balancing', 'dovetailing' or 'harmonising' work and family projects carry a positive valence that can mask power inequities and conflict in the process and outcomes thereof. In this vein, Crompton (2006) argues that the term work/life 'balance' is a misnomer, because it suggests that some state of harmony is inevitably achieved between competing market work and care work priorities. She suggests a more neutral term of work/life 'articulation', which distinguishes between the practical arrangements made and work/life conflicts arising from combining work and family obligations (Crompton 2006). Pocock's (2005, 2003) work similarly highlights work/life 'imbalance' and work/life 'collision':

> many Australians live within a complex web of working and home life, where caring, reproduction and paid work jostle alongside each other in

their demands for time, energy and money. 'Home' and 'work' cannot be separated into a neat binary, into neatly gendered jobs. They cannot be 'balanced', since they are part of a seamless, messy whole: a conglomerate. Conventional categories of labour and economic analysis, which treat paid work as separate from home, life and the care that essentially underpins work, are hopelessly inadequate to the task of understanding this whole.

(Pocock 2003: 16)

These perspectives evidence the makeshift instability of temporary fixes. They draw attention to the ongoing process of making, then remaking, decisions as families grow through new phases with emergent pressures, hopes and demands. In this mix, we would highlight the increasingly important consideration of protecting and promoting all members' educational opportunities.

In this book, we conceptualise career as the relational series of workable solutions negotiated to both accommodate and facilitate interrelated individual and family projects. Decisions around paid work, unpaid work and education for all family members are understood to impinge on and interconnect with the market work plans and aspirations of both adults and children. These plans and aspirations are in turn interconnected with the broader context within which these projects unfold, including the structure of educational and employment opportunities in different places, which make mobility more or less thinkable and doable.

Thinking about educational strategy

In addition to the well-recognised need to achieve work/life articulation, this book will coin the phrase *work/family/education articulation* to foreground educational strategy and investments as equally compelling projects shaping family careers. We work together in a Faculty of Education, which may in one way explain our interest in how educational strategy contributes to family mobility. There are, however, more pressing reasons justifying this premise.

Teese and Polesel (2003) among others (for example, Hirsch 1976; Collins 1979) argue that the social stakes around educational achievements and credentials have been steadily rising:

As the relationship between employment and qualifications tightens, schools grow in importance, both for the weakest students – whose economic vulnerability can only be offset by success at school – and also for the strongest, whose economic claims must be asserted through high standards of achievement.

(Teese and Polesel 2003: 2)

The educational credential has become essential currency in labour markets, as entry to more and more occupations demands some level of formal certification. The sociology of education has documented repeatedly how families' responses to this credential pressure are strongly filtered by their social class. Connell's (2003) work mentioned above characterised the class difference in family projects around high schooling in Australia. By this account, middle-class family projects were shown to be planning pathways to further studies to sponsor professional career paths, while working-class family projects worked to a shorter horizon, hoping to keep the child productively engaged in schooling. Ball's (2003) empirical study of middle-class strategy in UK educational markets revealed both the anxiety and the 'regime of prudentialism' (p. 179) exercised around children's education: 'Investment in the child begins early and financial capital enables the buying in of services and experiences which play their part in making up the child as an educational subject' (p. 169). Lareau's (2003) ethnography of differently classed families in the US describes the contrast between the 'concerted cultivation' of middle-class childhood and the 'natural accomplishment' of working-class childhood. More specifically, sociologists such as Bourdieu (1986), Bernstein (1990) and Power *et al.* (2003) highlight the particular status and interests of the professional fraction of the middle class in their investments in the symbolic capital of educational credentials. This form of cultural capital cannot be inherited by the next generation, but can only be accrued by individuals through the same time-consuming educational investments. Thus any strategy for intergenerational reproduction of the professional parent's middle-class advantage will centre around education projects.

Since the 1980s, governments in many societies have been using neoliberal policies to promote marketisation of school and university sectors (Ball 1993; Apple 2001; Campbell 2007). Pursuit of these policies by governments have led families' educational decision-making to become more deliberately strategic. In the same way that neoliberal policies have restructured public sector services such as health, transport and telecommunications onto more competitive and privatised footings, educational sectors have been under similar pressure to diversify and compete. Under such market logic, the local school no longer serves as the default 'choice'. Rather, active and conscientious school choice becomes the mark of the 'good parent/citizen ... whose knowing participation in the market as an informed chooser of schools is supported by government' (Campbell *et al.* 2009: 4). This choice becomes one of those 'risky freedoms' (Beck and Beck-Gernsheim 2004: 512) which can foster aspiration and anxiety at the same time. It is, however, the middle classes who are most engaged as choosers and for whom the market competes.

Under these policy conditions, family relocation in metropolitan areas has been well documented as a popular strategy pursued by middle-class families to gain advantage in spatialised educational markets and in school catchment zones. In their introduction to a special edition of the *Journal of Education Policy* Butler and van Zanten (2007) speak to how 'residential strategies' (p. 4) are played in the UK, US and European nations. In this issue, Noreisch (2007) documents the phenomenon of middle-class families moving out of catchment areas with high social mix in Berlin while Poupeau *et al.* (2007) examine the growing phenomenon of school transfers by middle-class families in Paris. Geographers have also become interested in how school choice constructs place and space. Bell (2009) makes a distinction between a family's aspirational 'choice set' and the local 'geographic set' of potential schools to show how, in her Detroit sample, the convenience of a local school was not a high priority in family's decision-making. Elsewhere, Dougherty *et al.*'s (2009) econometric study linked housing market prices in Connecticut to the catchment areas of popular schools and Holdsworth (2013) alludes to the 'obsessions with house prices and school catchment areas' as 'part of the zeitgeist of twenty-first century urban life in the United Kingdom' (pp. 68–69). These studies indicate how much importance is being placed on school choice in family relocation deliberations – enough to warrant a timely household move, for those with the capital and capacity to move.

Ironically, families who move for other reasons can be poorly served by the managerial practices emerging around schooling markets. Waiting lists and booking fees privilege the immobile who know where they will be living. Catchment zones that are imposed by popular schools to manage enrolment pressure privilege local knowledge, which is not always accessible to new arrivals. Our point here is that educational marketisation has raised the stakes around family mobility, by increasing anxieties and aspirations around school choice. Families with school-aged children will be moving through spatialised educational markets and this becomes a major factor in their deliberations.

There is another aspect to educational markets that warrants attention to the educational projects of adults as much as children in family mobility. The emergence of a knowledge-based economy has advantaged the educated, skilled worker (Ehrenreich 1990), placing a greater premium on the role of educational credentials and their currency in structuring and governing the labour market. In the late 1970s, Collins (1979) warned of spiralling credentialism whereby access to more and more occupations has come to be restricted to, and governed by, the educationally qualified. At a similar time, Hirsch's (1976) analysis of positional goods argued that people profit from educational credentials in both absolute and relative terms – the first being the utility and quality of the knowledge accrued, and the second being 'the differential over the educational level attained by others' (p. 6). These trends have flourished under the more recent discourse of 'lifelong learning' (Bansel 2007). Bernstein (2001: 365) describes the current social condition as that of a 'totally pedagogised society' highlighting the knowledge economy's thirst for the renewable worker available for ongoing retraining and re-credentialing. This concept captures the ongoing pressure on adults to invest in formal education.

For this reason, we argue that consideration of educational markets should not be confined to matters of school choice, but should equally account for the market conditions in which the branded or certified graduate can profit from such investment. In Chapter 7, we develop the concept of 'mobius market' to capture the ongoing work of maintaining and updating credentials to maintain one's position and value in the credentialed labour market. This requirement for re-credentialing means families will often have a number of educational projects and investments underway that they need to manage and coordinate across generations, and access to further education or professional development for adults has emerged as a priority. However, it is not just individuals and families that invest in educational credentials.

Coming from another angle

There is considerable public subsidy underwriting the lengthy preparation of a professional workforce. This investment is justified through the ostensible public good of its outcomes: nations need qualified doctors, nurses, teachers and other professionals to service their populations. On this basis, a functionalist sociology of the professions has typically distinguished professions from other occupational categories on the basis of their ethic of altruistic public service (Sciulli 2009). More critical sociology of the professions questions the strength of this ethic in the face of personal interest, and would highlight the professions' unwarranted monopolies, self-interested socio-economic advantage, and place in 'the structure of privilege' (Collins 1990: 13). The professional is produced in limited higher education sites, typically in metropolitan centres, but their expertise is needed in all communities. This situation implies that post-qualification mobility constitutes an important, if implicit, part of the profession's service contract with the public that underwrite their preparation.

Our interest here stems from Australia's chronic problem in recruiting and retaining professionals to work in rural and remote settings – a public issue created by the relative immobility or selective mobility of some, which impacts on communities situated in Sheller and Urry's 'slow lanes' (2006: 207). It is not that professionals aren't mobile, but rather, there are certain spaces and places of high need where they choose not to live and work. This maldistribution of a society's educational capital has resisted generations of policy interventions and incentive schemes. Reports (Haslam McKenzie 2007; Scott et al. 2012) focus on workplace considerations such as conditions and remuneration, but also acknowledge the family nexus ruling these professionals' choices:

> Usually, the employment options for the 'trailing spouse' in remote communities are very limited: an important consideration given the shift to dual career families. The higher quality education resources in the larger population centres are another major reason why families often prefer to live in these centres. This is a particularly important consideration once children reach secondary school age.
>
> (Haslam McKenzie 2010: 367)

This twist, locating the professional career in broader family circumstances and considerations, brings us back to consider the tangled projects and priorities in family mobility decisions more closely.

Australia is not alone in this problem, nor is it isolated. The mobility paradigm makes visible 'a complex relationality of places and persons' (Hannam *et al.* 2006: 13). There is a global 'brain drain' of qualified professionals out of relatively disadvantaged communities towards more advantaged, from rural to urban (Voigt-Graf 2003; Wang and Gao 2013) and from global South to North in search of better opportunities for both self and family (Kline 2003; Marchal and Kegels 2003; Connell 2010). In short, a professional qualification that is recognised beyond national boundaries can facilitate movement. In this way we will argue in the next chapter that credentials and institutional processes for the recognition and equivalence of such professional qualifications across borders serve as a mobility system, enhancing and facilitating the portability of expertise and its associated status. To address the shortfall of professionals in the rural and remote health sector, Australia recruits doctors from elsewhere – most coming from the UK, India, Malaysia, Ireland, Sri Lanka, Pakistan, Canada, Iran, South Africa and Singapore – employing them on restricted conditions that can require years of service in 'Districts of Workforce Shortage' before granting them full registration (Health Workforce Australia 2012: 31). Meanwhile, young Australian teachers eschew country service and choose to travel to the UK or US to staff inner-city schools as a life adventure (Widegren and Doherty 2010). National investment in 'gardening' strategies through public investment in professionals' preparation does not guarantee a fixed workforce in a world that is increasingly exploiting 'gamekeeping' strategies. These flows implicate nations in each other's labour markets.

In this section, we have approached the mobility of professionals and their families from a different angle – looking from the other end of the telescope, so to speak – to make evident how private decisions made within the families of professionals can aggregate to produce social problems elsewhere. The maldistribution of professionals across rural and remote Australia thus implicates both local educational markets and global labour markets.

Thinking about mobilities from Australia

In his review of mobility research, Vannini (2010) notes its Eurocentric origins and bias to date. In contrast, this book explores the very different spatial conditions across Australia's large distances and sparse population as a telling contrast. Mobility theory can and should equally illuminate these very different spatial/social conditions.

By some accounts, Australia is considered a 'settler' nation, largely populated by immigrants whose families and forebears have at some stage made the choice to move in order to survive or to get ahead. However, others were forcibly moved here, such as convicts and indentured workers, or came here as displaced persons, such as refugees. Much Australian history in this sense is a history of family mobility by British, European, Asian and Pasifika populations over time, weaving the mobilities of advantaged and disadvantaged people together. By other accounts, modern Australia was forged through violent invasion and colonisation, displacing nomadic Aboriginal families from their ancestral lands, forcibly restricting and regulating their rights to mobility. The perseverance of Aboriginal and Torres Strait Islander populations in their fights to win back their land rights and reoccupy their land speaks to a powerful urge to reclaim mobility, place and space on their own terms. Twenty-first-century Australia encompasses and reflects these varied and opposed mobility histories, such that the map of Australia includes very different places across vast spaces – global cities, thriving regional hubs, shrinking rural towns and remote Indigenous homeland communities – all of which require viable services staffed by human service professionals.

Readers outside Australia may not appreciate the scale of Australia's landscape and how these dimensions amplify the risks and consequences of family mobility. Australia could accommodate the footprint of the UK 30 times over, but is home to only one third of its population. Australia has a similar land area to the US, but accommodates a population only 7 per cent that of the US. The estimated population density of Australia, 2008–2012, is 3 people per square kilometre of land, on a par to Iceland and desert nations in Africa, while that of the US is 34 and the UK is 257 (World Bank, http://data.worldbank.org/indicator/EN.POP.DNST, accessed 11 April 2013). Dots on maps of Australia's interior can indicate an isolated fuel station or a remote cattle station, not a well-serviced community. In fact, Australia's population is highly urbanised, the vast majority of people clinging to the coastline. Once beyond metropolitan centres, few assumptions can be made about high-frequency public transport linking localities that European readers might take for granted. A small population base with very low density makes this impossible. Nevertheless, there are people living and working out in these spaces who require the same human services as others living in metropolitan centres – in health, education and policing.

Thinking personally

We are ourselves part of the professional middle class we have been researching, and bring our own im/mobility histories and choices to the task. Our private histories weave very similar family, educational and career considerations to those we explored with our interviewees. My story (Doherty) follows a trailing spouse plot line. I shifted my career focus from sociology to teaching in the hope of joining my partner, who was working in forestry on a remote Aboriginal island at the time. I then fell into the trailing spouse role without much thought or protest, as did many female peers at the time, following his career trajectory through capital cities and regional towns while raising children. Some moves were by choice, but one was precipitated by a workplace restructure re-assigning my partner's job to a regional centre. Our final move to metropolitan Brisbane was hard on one child, who felt the loss of former friends acutely. I resolved to avoid further relocations, and we have now lived 16 years in the same house, the metropolitan setting offering rich career and educational opportunities for all family members. I now watch my adult children and their partners with interest, and am keen to see how they will decide whose work opportunities to follow when such issues arise. I doubt this next generation of professional women will be content with the trailing spouse role and suspect these negotiations are going to get harder, not easier.

The geographic tensions among family, education, career aspiration and education infrastructure have also shaped my career journey (Patton). As my small regional town did not provide university opportunities, I left home at the age of 16 to pursue my education degree – the first in my family to do so. After graduation as a secondary teacher, then a number of appointments in small rural towns, the motivation for further study and the lack of the study options then available by distance mode led to a career change and a move to the capital city of the state. My metropolitan location then accommodated ten years of part-time study to gain a second degree with honours and a doctorate, with a number of job changes. I have since chosen to resist major relocations and have remained as an academic in the same city. Although physically immobile (Sullivan and Arthur 2006) through my desire to stay close to my family, I remain highly psychologically mobile, with a mindset which is global and a pursuit of national and international developments via travel and through active connections with colleagues in my field.

Despite being somewhat older than my colleagues and a member of the postwar 'baby boomers', my family career (Shield) has been one of productive immobility. In a nutshell, I have grown up, gone to school, married a local partner, raised children and accessed a variety of educational opportunities and career opportunities, all while living within two adjacent inner-city suburbs of Brisbane. My own children attended the same high school I attended and were taught by some of the same teachers. After schooling, I pursued a science degree in physics at the local university. Not only did the study benefit my career but it also deferred the possibility of being conscripted to serve in the Vietnam War. There were not too many jobs available for an isotope physicist, so I then completed a one-year Graduate Diploma in Education and went teaching. Physics and mathematics teachers were in short supply and as a result I was not required to do country service, but was appointed to an inner-city high school where I stayed for ten years. I continued studying part-time, gaining further qualifications in Education, Applied Science and Computer Science, which led to a career change with ample career opportunities in the Department of Education, then in teacher education. I have now worked for Queensland University of Technology and its predecessor institutions in an academic role for nearly 30 years. In sum, I have had the privilege and advantage of ready access to further study, job markets and the peace of mind that comes with close family support, all in the same location.

Though our three histories contain a variety of circumstances, strategies and dispositions, they serve to exemplify the knot of projects and relational circumstances that mobility choices entail. They also demonstrate the gravitational pull of the metropolitan centre and its affordances. There is another story to be told on a larger scale that stems from our work as teacher educators in which we bear responsibility for preparing a professional workforce for Queensland, including the rural and remote communities therein.

Following the nation's demographic pattern, most young people prefer to be located close to the coast and in larger metropolitan locations. As such, there is a perennial shortage of teacher supply in rural and remote communities within Queensland and Australia more broadly. This shortage remains the case despite a number of financial and leave incentives, and internal structures whereby mobility within the state's public school sector facilitates career advancement. For example, an early teacher graduate could reasonably hope to be a principal of a small two-teacher school within three to four years, and then, with the necessary mobility and leadership across schools of increasing size, could expect to be a principal of a reasonably large metropolitan school within ten to 15 years.

Our faculty has worked with the major employers of teachers in Queensland to develop a number of proactive initiatives to encourage student teachers to spend some of their career in rural and remote communities. These initiatives include coordinating subsidies to encourage course placements in a rural/remote school; a programme offering a lifestyle taster by a week-long immersion in rural and remote communities; and a targeted final internship in a rural/remote school with the promise of a two-year teaching appointment there on graduation. Despite the attractiveness of this offer in a time when only a small percentage of graduates can expect to immediately achieve full-time ongoing employment, many students reject an offer to join this programme. Their reasoning is related to the contingencies associated with mobility. Young singles lament the potential reduction in social and family connectedness, while students with partners and children express concern about their family in terms of work and education opportunities. These concerns resonate with those in our own personal stories, and though sympathetic, we as teacher educators are left with the unresolved public problem that these private decisions create.

An overview

This chapter has carved out our particular focus within the new mobilities paradigm, and assembled a range of conceptual tools to think with. In this way our interest in family im/mobility dialogues with empirical and theoretical developments in family studies, work and career studies and educational sociology. We are interested in the family processes that, through reflexive strategy and making fallible readings of opportunity and risk, deliberate on spatial relocation to progress the suite of individual and collective projects underway in the family unit. We are interested in understanding how the intersubjectivity and care work that constitutes a family decentres and impinges on the individualist career. We have also highlighted the growing prominence of educational projects in response to the credentialism of the twenty-first-century labour market. We argued that 'work/life balance' is better conceived of temporary work/family/education articulations negotiated over time and space, as priorities and the weight of various intersubjective claims shift. We then related the private decisions made within families to a larger scale, to pose the question of how the im/mobility decisions of some might impact on others. Attention to mobility thus allows us to move between the scales of private solutions and public problems.

In Chapter 2, we turn to consider relevant theoretical tools from mobility theory, and theoretical treatments of space and place as the necessary and interactive backdrop to family relocations. We explore the concept of motility and then develop a companion concept of institutional viscosity to account for the structural effect of resistance or enablement offered by the various institutions mobile families pass through.

In Chapter 3 we consider narratives as a familiar and essential genre that can handle multiple people, projects, places and events over time and space in a consequential sequence that makes sense from the actor's perspective. We exemplify how we harnessed this affordance in the design of our interviews with families to capture their mobility histories, and how an analysis of the structure inherent within interview narratives can cast family mobility events in different lights.

Chapter 4 presents narratives from the 34 hypermobile military families we interviewed. Their stories tell of moving in circumstances not necessarily of their choosing, the passage through both sympathetic and intransigent institutions, and their search for continuities in the absence of stability. Parents narrate the private troubles their children accrue in their educational trajectories as a result of institutional discontinuities, and the stress and effort around re-placing other family members' projects. Different families cope in different ways, and motility is shown to wax and wane over mobility events.

Chapter 5 presents a parallel analysis of the 32 professional and non-professional families we interviewed in rural/remote Queensland, to understand the interpersonal and institutional conditions under which they were prepared to come and stay in these less popular locations. From the capacity of these professional families to choose the timing and placing of their moves, a number of patterns emerge from their narratives. Each pattern engenders its own complications within the family unit.

Chapter 6 shifts to a more quantitative analysis of results from an online survey of 278 professionals (doctors, nurses, police officers and teachers) with school-aged children sampled across Queensland more broadly, to understand what demographic factors, dispositions and attributes help explain dimensions of family mobility. We report how we built and tested constructs to measure motility, neoliberalism and adherence to a professional ethic of public service, then how these variables interacted to make family mobility more or less likely.

In Chapter 7, we pursue our interest in education as an intergenerational priority of increasing importance in families, middle-class professionals in particular, and explore how adults' projects of investing in further credentials, or maintaining the currency of these credentials can impinge on mobility decisions. We develop the concept of 'mobius market' to capture the never-ending work of staying connected to educational markets in order to invest and profit from credentials across family generations.

Chapter 8 turns the lens on the role of place, and the social construction thereof, to understand how the middle-class professional families view opportunities in rural or remote localities. We consider how the professional credential has become more a vector of private positional advantage, at risk of losing its historical ethic of serving the public good. We revisit interview and survey data to see how this tension plays out in families to better understand the public problem of the chronic absence of professionals in rural and remote settings.

Our final chapter reflects on the empirical journey taken, and the work/family/education articulations our mobility lens has illuminated. The book talks back to the fields of family studies, work and career studies and sociology of education, as well as mobility studies. This purposeful nexus allows us to trace the effects of policies in the educational domain in other aspects of life. We pull spatial and social senses of mobility together to ask how and why families might choose to move on to get ahead.

Chapter 2

Work/family/education articulations in space with mobility systems

Family relocation does not fall into the realm of streamlined transport and digital communications that have captured the attention of many mobility researchers (Vannini 2010). Nor is it the agile mobility of the untrammelled technologically augmented individual (Elliott and Urry 2010). As a high stakes mobility event with deep sociological implications, it is both more simple and more complex. It involves real bodies in large-scale intervals of real time across physical space, the clutter of household goods and pets, and the mundane but crucial detail of re-embedding a number of lives synchronously on multiple institutional fronts.

In the opening chapter we developed our approach to families through their intersubjective processes. This approach highlighted the work of reflexive projects and strategies in response to more fluid, individualised and marketised life-worlds. Similarly, our approach to career acknowledged the growing importance of the work/family interface and spiralling credentialism, hence our focus is on how the complex of work/family/education articulations impact on mobility decisions. In this chapter, we build on theoretical resources from the mobility paradigm to enrich our perspectives; first, on space and place as the necessary backdrop to family relocations, and second, to understand the attributes of systems and institutions, as well as resources and dispositions that make mobility more or less possible. We extend the ambit of choice in marketised society to include choice of residential location. We then consider how some people are in a better position to choose than others and some places are better positioned to attract such people.

Space and place as interactive context

Mobility entails movement across space; however, space is more than a back-drop to people's movement, or an inert expanse of landscape. Rather, spaces and the embedded networks of places are socially constructed, inscribed, infused and overlaid with meanings, reputations, histories and relations. Movement across space necessarily engages with these social layers of meanings and relations as much as with geographic distance, climate and topography. In turn, movements across spaces and through places will contribute to the ongoing social production of these meanings, reputations, histories and relations. Lefebrve (1991) argued the need to bring together the social, material, physical and mental constructions of space, describing three dimensions in the production of space – sensorily perceived space, discursively conceived space and experientially lived space (Schmid 2008). This multifaceted social sense of space can account for the effects of how space and place are read, for example:

- names of towns or regions accumulate connotations that create reactions in people who have never been there, but whose circulation of such reputations sustains these effects on those localities;
- a town or school that hosts a flow of mobile military families acquires a reputation that colours its relations with other towns or schools and informs families' choices;
- a school with a reputation for high quality attracts more enrolments and impacts on the local real estate market; and
- a private school changes its bus routes to redefine its spatial catchment.

These more phenomenological and interactive constructions of spaces will play a crucial role in families' mobility deliberations as they project themselves into spaces and places only 'known' and imagined through reputation and representations.

Massey (1993) similarly outlines a 'progressive' sense of place that understands place first in terms of the social relations and their differences that intersect there, and second through its relations to other places. In regard to the former, mobility is considered an important vector of social differences and their interaction. For Massey, places are constituted through a 'politics of mobility' (p. 63) which makes evident the advantage for some who can control their mobility, and its by-product of disadvantage for others who cannot. For Massey, these differential mobilities are interconnected phenomena that impact on place:

> not merely the issue of who moves and who doesn't … it is also about power in relation to the flows and the movement. Different social groups have distinct relationships to this anyway-differentiated mobility: some are more in charge of it than others; some initiate flows and movement, others don't; some are more on the receiving end of it than others; some are effectively imprisoned by it.
>
> (Massey 1993: 61)

This perspective underpins our interest in the selective mobility of middle-class professionals and their families, and the second-order effect on the receiving end of rural and remote communities that fail to attract them. It also legitimates our interest in the consequences of the military families' limited control of their mobility.

In the second aspect to a 'progressive sense of place' Massey argues that places should be understood not by reference to their internal properties and attributes, but rather by their relational and dynamic positioning within a network of places across multi-scalar space, 'in a situation of co-presence' (p. 66). In this way, 'here' is not just about being 'here' but equally about not being 'there' through 'a sense of place, an understanding of "its character", which can only be constructed by linking that place to places beyond' (p. 68). From Harvey (1993), we take the further premise that places increasingly exist in a relation of competitive tension. In this way, their co-presence is not benign. Rather, 'the differences between places to some degree become antagonistic' (p. 7). Such relations can produce 'winners and losers' (p. 7) in the competition for investment and population, thus inform efforts to re-make 'the way places are both represented and imagined' (p. 17) in order to better compete. As an example, we could point to an increasingly common ploy of featuring private schooling and its symbols in advertisements for new residential developments, projecting a middle-class imaginary over the raw landscape of blank blocks. This competitive effort could be understood as the 'gamekeeping' tactics outlined in Chapter 1, and the success of such effort to manifest in mobility. These ideas help conceptualise space as uneven, internally differentiated (Urry 2000b) by advantage and its shadow of disadvantage, but not statically so while localities actively compete with each other.

The everyday terms 'rural', 'remote' and 'regional' could benefit from reconsideration in light of this progressive, relational sense of place. Following Baum *et al.* (2005), we use the term 'regional' to broadly designate towns with more than 10,000 residents that act as service or industry hubs beyond metropolitan centres. The term 'rural' will describe communities and townships supporting a predominantly agricultural business, and 'remote' will refer to communities at a significant and formative distance from other population centres. These everyday terms are neither necessarily independent nor fixed properties of locations, given the decline of agriculture, the closure of services and transport links, and the emergence of new industries such as coal seam gas in previously rural districts. Nor are these categories internally uniform – rather, they include places marked by both 'opportunity and vulnerability' (Baum *et al.* 2005: 01.3). The characteristics of regional/rural/remote are also as much imagined as experienced attributes (Green and Letts 2007), invoked and reproduced in the social construction of these communities and categories. The underlying distinction between 'city' and 'country' carries a long history of layered social meanings, associations and imagining that has shaped how places are produced (Williams 1973). Rural, regional and remote categories are defined and realised ultimately in terms of their contrast to 'metro-centric' (Green and Letts 2007: 59) norms and expectations of service and amenity. It is still important to retain a sense of the experientially lived dimension of physical space and the brute force and scale of geographic distances between Australia's places. However, the same space or place can take on very different meanings and attributes for different people, and these subjective readings of place will carry much weight in mobility decisions and actions.

Harvey (1993: 5) observed that 'none of us can choose our moment in time … but we do have a range of choices as to location and such choices matter'. We would argue that these choices matter on both private and public scales, producing 'uneven spatial outcomes that have come to be reflected in the daily lives of people and across space in competing places' (Baum *et al.* 2005: 02.15). The power or capacity to choose one's locality emerges as an axis of social advantage, and the aggregated decisions of individuals and families in this regard shape the fate of localities, in terms of who comes, stays or leaves, and on what terms. The capacity of the spatially autonomous (Weiss 2005) to optimise their location can serve to pool such advantage in 'winner' places with the capacity to attract investment and talent, and pool its counterpart of disadvantage in other locations less able to attract the same, polarising life opportunities over time. In this way, a growing trend for welfare-dependent families in Australia to 'choose' to move beyond metropolitan areas in search of more affordable housing despite less prospects of work (Hugo and Bell 1998) can stigmatise a location over time (Healy and Hillman 2008). These families' mobility choices will be more 'structured' by their circumstances and resources than others, and their choices carry consequences for others.

This section has worked from a social conceptualisation of space and place to paint the necessary backdrop of socially differentiated spaces and competing places for family mobility. We now turn to the concept of 'motility' from the mobility paradigm to consider how individuals and families also bring differentiated resources and dispositions to mobility decisions.

Motility as a prerequisite

The variable of *motility* has much to contribute to an understanding of family mobility. Kaufmann developed the concept of motility to refer to the capacity, attitudes, resources and skills that make mobility possible: that is, its prerequisites. The concept thus summarises and gauges potential for mobility, rather than mobility events per se:

> motility is comprised of all the factors that define a person's capacity to be mobile, whether this is physical aptitude, aspirations to settle down or be mobile, existing technological transport and telecommunications systems and their accessibility, space–time constraints (location of the workplace), acquired knowledge such as a driver's licence, etc. Motility is thus constituted of elements relating to access (that is, available choice in a broad sense), to skills (the competence required to make use of this access) and appropriation (evaluation of the available access).
>
> (Kaufmann 2002: 38)

Under this definition, an individual or family unit could be considered to be highly motile if having access to the social and material means to contemplate moving, the skills and dispositions that make it thinkable and doable, and a will-ingness to take up such opportunities. Conversely, a family that lack the social and material means, without such skills and dispositions, or are reluctant to con-sider such opportunities, would be considered to have low motility.

This definition embraces both attributes of the agent (aptitude, aspirations, knowledge) and attributes of the contextual social infrastructure (transport and telecommunications systems, constraints). However, in the idea of 'appropri-ation', the agent becomes pivotal, appropriation being the volitional action taken by the agent to realise potentials inherent in both the individual and the systems. This conceptual bias towards agency, while mindful of structural context, is made more explicit later:

> actors are central in the mobility process.... Only by integrating the inten-tions of people and the reasons which make them mobile or which, on the contrary, leave them immobile will we succeed in attaining this goal. Getting past this confusion suggests redirecting the interest of researchers towards the aspirations and plans of those involved, as well as the things that motivate them, and their possible realm of action.
>
> (Kaufman 2002: 36)

Given this emphasis, we would argue that the concept of motility could be ana-lytically sharper and more valuable if confined to capturing the agentive dimen-sions that make mobility events more or less possible. Similarly it could benefit from a partner concept that refers to the contributions that institutional and social structures make in enabling or constraining mobility. Kaufman acknowledged the variable strength of structural conditions that lend themselves (or not) to mobility, 'from the structured and confined pole to the non-structured and infinite pole' (2002: 9). Nevertheless, at this stage, Kaufmann was more inter-ested in understanding the variable degrees of motility in how people exercise the 'degree of freedom' (2002: 43) at their disposal, re-describing motility as their 'movement capital':

> motility forms theoretical and empirical links with, and can be exchanged for, other types of capital ... movement can take many forms,... different forms of movement may be interchangeable, and ... the potentiality of movement can be expressed as a form of 'movement capital'.
>
> (Kaufmann et al. 2004: 752)

A further article (Flamm and Kaufmann 2006) sought to operationalise this more agentive concept of motility along the three definition axes of access, skills and appropriation, all of which in their explanation adhere to the agent. Using grounded theory with data from a qualitative study, the axis of access was unpacked and interpreted as a 'personal access rights portfolio' (p. 172). The axis of skill was considered 'first and foremost a question of accumulating experience' (p. 176), and the axis of appropriation involved habits, principles and personal evaluations of options. Similarly, Kesselring (2006) explored how various groups managed the 'modern mobility imperative' (p. 269). The paper offered three ideal types of mobility management – the centred, the decentred and the virtual. Again, though mindful of contextual conditions, the author was most interested in the 'individual share in mobility' and 'the actors' ability to influence their movement through time and space' (p. 270). Motility studies thus continued to privilege the agentive aspect in explaining social 'fluidification' (Kaufmann *et al.* 2004: 747).

Further work explored the interface between spatial mobility and social mobility in a more 'systemic' (Kaufmann *et al.* 2004: 752) approach, shifting the spotlight to include structural dimensions and dynamics: 'embedded actors are central to spatial mobility, as are specific contexts that delimit or make possible movement' (p. 749). The authors called for more consideration of 'the inter-action between actors, structures and context' (p. 749) in mobility research. The definition of motility was extended to describe the propensity of objects (as well as people) to be mobile through both horizontal and vertical social structures. It was not, however, clear how the notion of 'appropriation', embedded in the earlier definition of motility, might apply to inanimate objects. In what Archer might consider 'concept-stretching' (2007: 40), the dual focus conflating struc-ture and agency was encapsulated in an augmented concept of 'motility': 'we will argue that social structures and dynamics are interdependent with the actual or potential capacity to displace entities, that is goods, information or people' (Kaufmann, *et al.* 2004: 745).

While this interdependence makes everyday sense, the conflation fails to theoretically or analytically disentangle attributes of the 'specific contexts that delimit or make possible movement' (Kaufmann *et al.* 2004: 709) from actors' dispositions and resources. 'Motility' could be a more useful concept if restricted to matters of agency, but becomes analytically diffuse and omnivorous if it claims to account for structural conditions as well. Kaufmann *et al.* (2004: 748) themselves pose exactly the question that warrants the development of a partner concept to capture the role of structure: 'which contexts condition societal fluidi-fication and in what way?'

A case for viscosity

We propose a partner concept of *viscosity* as an additional tool for the new mobilities paradigm to capture this variable degree of resistance or facilitation offered by structural context. Urry's (2000a) manifesto for a new sociological method that could account for the social in movement across time and space sought to move beyond the traditional agency/structure binary underpinning sociology's default assumption of fixity. Much subsequent mobilities research has attended to what is new and changing, highlighting 'mobile culture', the sociality of transportation, and overtly mobile populations (Vannini 2010).

However, Urry (2000a) was equally intent on explaining the 'uneven reach' (p. 18) of networks and flows, and efforts to 'regulate' mobilities (p. 19). This would indicate the ongoing relevance of structural efforts or effects that mediate and mitigate mobility.

Within the mobility paradigm itself, Urry (2007) overlays Kaufmann's idea of movement capital with the concept of *network capital* 'in order to connect the mobilities paradigm to issues of socio-spatial inequalities' (p. 39). Urry's treatment differs, however, in that this concept aligns with his more structural concept of *mobility systems*, being 'the enduring systems that provide what we might call the infrastructures of social life. Such systems enable the movement of people, ideas and information from place to place, person-to-person, event to event' (Urry 2007: 12). The tandem concepts (network capital and mobility systems) allow a double-handled agency/structure analysis of 'life in a world that combines exceptional freedom ... and exceptional system dependence' (p. 15). However, not all mobility systems are equally efficient, and this concept could benefit from some comparative gauge of how effective they are in facilitating mobility. For example, the mail coach was an effective mobility system in its time, but air and rail systems eventually offered faster, more efficient mobility structures, which in turn have been eclipsed or augmented by electronic means. The 'fluidification' of society Kaufman refers to is in essence the lessening of viscosity, as new systems are devised to enable and speed up the movement of goods, information and people across space.

For this reason, a metaphorically cognate variable of *viscosity* may help to refer to the degree of resistance or enablement offered by structures to interact with agents' motility. It can analytically distinguish settings and systems that enable and support mobility (low viscosity) from those that make it difficult or impossible (high viscosity) and express relational degrees between settings (being more or less viscous). In physics, viscosity describes the degree of resistance fluids pose to the motion of submerged objects. High viscosity would indicate that the mobility of the object is impeded by the heavy, resistant nature of the fluid. In biology, the motility of an organism is mitigated by the viscosity of its environment; thus, the explanation of any observed mobility requires an understanding of both pre-existing conditions. To draw on these versions of viscosity metaphorically, moving through a low viscosity social context could be considered to be like swimming in water – relatively effortless, meeting little resistance or impediment. Conversely, moving through a high viscosity context would be like swimming through treacle – vexed, stressful and effortful. Costas (2013) similarly advocates for a metaphor and variable of 'stickiness' in mobility studies.

So what constitutes the institutional substance that offers resistance to the motile agent? Urry's (2007) concept of mobility systems speaks to transport infrastructure, cargo logistics and road networks which have an obvious relationship to the physical mobility of people and objects. However, the mobility of families and their need to re-embed lives in multiple institutions highlights the fact that people move through institutions and social infrastructure as well. Social institutions will have practices and systems that manage and regulate the flow of people through their services according to the pace and mode they normalise or legitimate. According to research on schooling for mobile populations, schools are typically 'predicated on permanently resident children attending the same school' (Kenny and Danaher 2009: 1, see also Henderson 2001, 2004). This finding would suggest an institutional default of high viscosity, with institutionalised entry and exit points at either end. It also indicates a paucity of routines and procedures to facilitate entry and exits elsewhere in their programme. In this way, irregular comings and goings are not anticipated. Indeed, they are considered institutionally bothersome or aberrant. The mobility paradigm makes this institutional viscosity evident.

The viscosity of an institution and its practices is not necessarily a fixed quality, but rather can be re-calibrated in response to the politics and priorities of the times. As another educational example, the Bologna Accord of 1999 set in motion a strategic process of radically reducing the viscosity of higher education institutions in Europe, to allow students, academic credits and staff to flow more easily across institutions (Robertson and Keeling 2008). More generally, many universities have pursued various strategies and processes of internationalisation to encourage the international movement of students and staff (for example Knight and de Wit 1997; Byram and Dervin 2008).

A further example of recalibrating the viscosity of educational institutions of particular interest to this project has been the recent development of a national curriculum in Australia (Australian Curriculum Assessment and Reporting Authority 2012) to replace the patchwork of eight distinct state curricula in use across the nation. Each state prescribed its own handwriting style, assessment regime and school entry age. The incongruence of these systems had posed a major structural impediment and deterrent to interstate family mobility. Family mobility played an important role in the political rhetoric surrounding the development of the national curriculum. Making the curricular templates for schooling on a national scale more considerate and supportive of mobile families was a palatable motive that could justify the federal government's controversial intervention in a state government domain. Within the state jurisdiction itself, the Queensland Education Department has developed a unique identifier for each student to allow consistent tracking and record-keeping regardless of school changes and mobility within the state. These efforts could be understood as strategies within the social infrastructure to lower institutional viscosity, making mobility more normalised and better supported.

In schools, viscosity may also be changing under the 'metapolicy' (Rizvi and Lingard 2010: 16) of neoliberal choice. Parents are now encouraged to exercise choice as to which school their children attend, and to change their choice of school if warranted. To this end, the Australian government has invested in a website (www.myschool.edu.au/) that profiles every registered school in Australia against a range of 'quality indicators' to resource parents' thinking. This institutional effort could be construed as an attempt to create a less viscous, more fluid market environment, under the logic that this competitiveness and customer mobility will force under-performing schools to address quality concerns. Similar thinking has informed public investment in family relocation pro- grammes to 'increase residential and educational opportunity for children' (Johnson Jr 2012: 132) from economically disadvantaged pockets in parts of the US, with mixed results. Informal family relocation within a city has emerged as a common strategy to secure the desired school choice under versions of such policy in many nations (Maloutas 2007; Noreisch 2007; Poupeau *et al.* 2007; Campbell *et al.* 2009; Dougherty *et al.* 2009; Lubienski and Dougherty 2009;). This work and other literature around the geography of school choice (Bell 2009; Taylor 2007) tends to unproblematically presume an urban or suburban popula- tion settled in one place with sufficient density and transport options to support multiple schools within daily reach. Our point here is that not all families live in such conditions. Nevertheless, they will still be exposed to choice policy, the dispositions it cultivates and its effects, both anticipated and unanticipated. The question we would add to this field is: how might school choice decide which town to live in or move to?

Distinguishing between agentive motility and institutional viscosity does not rule out their complex entanglement, but does separate out the structural con- straints/enablements for mobility which could be amenable to social policy. It also allows a more nuanced exploration of their interaction in two ways. First, it enables consideration of different 'match' scenarios for families in the cross- tabulation of high/low motility, and high/low viscosity. Second, it allows the impact of their interaction to be better understood across time. In Chapter 4, we follow these two lines of enquiry with reference to the hyper-mobile military families, to show how different degrees of motility and viscosity interact, then how a family's motility can wax and wane according to the viscosity of the insti- tutions they encounter across moves.

What of the professional families? How might concepts of motility and vis- cosity illuminate their selective mobility? We would argue that the *credentialism* in which these families have major stakes serves as a mobility system: that is, as social infrastructure that fosters and supports the portability of work experience, expertise and status, thus reducing viscosity and enabling mobility. Having a portable credential will contribute to an individual's motility – 'have degree, will travel', so to speak. However, this effect relies on the institutional structures being in place to recognise the value and status of the credential across borders. Credentialism is typically associated with 'vertical' social mobility; however, the state, national and international regulatory processes for the recognition of credentials create the conditions of possibility for 'horizontal' mobility without loss of status. With a credential and systems for its recognition in place, one's worth in the labour market need not rely on local knowledge and accumulated experience in situ, but rather on a certified body of knowledge that is considered relevant, portable and applicable anywhere.

As a federation, Australia's state and territory jurisdictions have historically managed the accreditation and registration of many professions. However, over time these processes are being up-scaled through the creation of national bodies such as the Medical Board of Australia and the Australian Institute of Teaching and School Leadership, to expedite mutual recognition across states or national registration protocols. These institutional efforts are essentially about enabling mobility. For example, the national registration scheme for health professionals was motivated by the goal to 'help health professionals move around the country more easily, reduce red tape, provide greater safeguards for the public and promote a more flexible, responsive and sustainable health workforce' (COAG Communique of 26 March 2008, quoted in House of Representatives Standing Committee on Health and Ageing 2012: 8).

Further afield, Australia, as a signatory to the Lisbon Recognition Convention developed by the Council of Europe and UNESCO in 2002, subscribes to an international protocol and processes for the recognition of overseas qualifications. Through the mechanisms of a dedicated office, Australia is able to welcome professionals that have been certified elsewhere such as nurses, teachers and doctors. The establishment of such social infrastructure, routines and protocols at national and international scales has reduced (though not eliminated) institutional viscosity to encourage a flow of skilled migration. Enabling this flow has been an important gamekeeping policy response to the problem created in rural and remote communities by professional families' selective mobility.

Employing institutions can manipulate and adjust viscosity tactically over time through systems of incentives and contractual obligations, to make either moving or staying more likely. The everyday coupling of 'recruitment and retention' in managerial discourse masks the fact that the former is about offering conditions that seek to fan worker motility, and the latter is about offering conditions that seek to dampen or repress that motility, at least temporarily. It refers to the 'keep' part of 'gamekeeping'. As an example, Australian health services actively seek to recruit overseas trained doctors to redress the maldistribution of professionals in rural and remote communities, but the Commonwealth Department of Health and Ageing imposes an initial requirement that they serve ten years in a district of workforce shortage before being eligible for full, unconditional registration. The department then applies a 'scaling mechanism' which reduces this period if the doctor serves in a more remote locality (House of Representatives Standing Committee on Health and Ageing 2012). In a similar way, the Queensland Police Service requires that officers serve in their present position and location for three years before being eligible to apply for promotion or positions elsewhere. These 'carrot' and 'stick' levers of incentive and obligation purposefully adjust the viscosity conditions to make certain mobility decisions more or less likely. However, these viscosity adjustments can only be one side of the mobility equation. The targeted professionals and their families will bring their degrees of motility into the mix, so any mobility outcome – be it mobility into or out of areas of need – will derive from how the variables of viscosity and motility interact.

This chapter has drawn together theoretical resources from the mobility paradigm and sociological treatments of space and place to inform our thinking about the role of the social landscapes and institutions in family mobility. Our discussion has purposefully traversed a variety of literature and moved the focus from workers and employment to family and schools, because it is the intersection of these sites and concerns that must be reconciled in families' mobility decisions. It would be naive of social science to restrict its understanding of such a multi-faceted social issue to the container defined by any single institution's boundaries. The next chapter outlines how we approached the two empirical projects behind this book through narrative interviews, which offered us the means to understand how each family constructed coherence across their mobility biographies.

Chapter 3

Making sense of mobility in family narratives

Thinking through narrative

The first chapter introduced our approach to family, projects and careers, then our focus on the complex reflexive decision-making within family units around mobility. Our discussion highlighted the variety of intersubjective considerations and institutional fronts implicated in any such decision, whether to stay or to move on. In the second chapter we conceptualised place and space as an inter-active canvas for movement, and explicated the concepts of motility and viscos-ity to analytically describe enablements and constraints on mobility at both the agentive and structural levels. We considered how credentialism serves as a mobility system that allows workers, professionals in particular, to carry exper-tise and status from one location to another, forcing employers to engage in 'gamekeeping' strategies in some locations to attract and retain such credentialed workers. This chapter will explore how place and mobility are important constit-uents of family narratives in which moving can feature variously as motivation, problem or solution in the crafting of a collective biography.

Narratives are powerful tools for both social actors and social science to make sense of experience. They select and weave people, places, time, motivations, actions and events together in a way that reveals how the actors themselves understand their options, read the structure of opportunities around them, then devise, enact and evaluate courses of action, for better or worse. In everyday life, the 'irrepressible genre' (Rosen 1988: 13) of narrative is a habitual way of making personal sense of the sequence, links and consequences between experi-ences or events involving people and places over time, through the motives, complications that arise and their resolution: 'Narrative gives us a ready and supple means for dealing with the uncertain outcomes of our plans and anticipa-tions' (Bruner 2002: 28). This textual capacity can thus accommodate and process Archer's (2007) conceptualisation of devising and revising life projects on the basis of fallible readings of opportunities. Narrative as a textual form does not just recount what was observed to happen, but also incorporates the feelings, hopes, reflections and evaluations of events with 'a dialectic between what was expected and what came to pass' (Bruner 2002: 15). Following Labov and Waletzky (1997), we understand narratives of personal experience to not just recount past events but also evaluate them, these functions shaping their conventional linguistic features. Narrative accounts thus convey the importance actors accord events, how they connect events and actions in causal sequences, how they appraise actions and apportion blame or guilt, and what moral they draw to fold back into ongoing everyday life (Labov 1997). Importantly, for the social scientist they offer access to the narrator's 'theory of the events' (Labov 1997: 409).

Using a large sociolinguistic corpus of English vernacular narratives collected in a variety of US communities, Labov and Waletzky's detailed analysis at clause level identified predictable stages evident across the collected narratives and the implicit rules governing their characteristic logic and sequencing. This structural analysis helps to 'unpack' and make visible the parts that 'construct the unity' (Riessman 2008: 81). For our purposes here, these stages are summarised and exemplified in Table 3.1.

In the exemplar narrative given in Table 3.1, the family mobility event featured as a resolution. It could equally serve:

- in the orientation, as a motivation in the given dispositions ('we wanted to move/stay');
- in the orientation, as an aspect of the contextual setting ('it happened around our third move');
- as a plot complication ('but then we had to move/stay');
- as a plot resolution ('so we decided to move/stay'); and
- in a coda reflection or moral to the story ('so if we ever have to move').

Not all oral narratives will fulfil all stages, the essential core of any narrative being the temporal sequence of complication and resolution. Narratives can also involve repeated cycles of complication, evaluation and resolution. However, a narrative of personal experience ultimately achieves more than a recount of past events:

> By here specifying that the experience must have 'entered into the biography' of the speaker, I distinguish narrative from simple recounting of observations as the events of a parade by a witness leaning out a window. It will turn out that events that have entered into the speaker's biography are emotionally and socially evaluated and so transformed from raw experience.
>
> (Labov 1997: 399)

Bruner (2002) similarly argues that such self-telling is part of the process of self-making, that the stories we tell of and to ourselves are of interest not as specious fictions but as constitutive textual truths on which lives are premised and lived.

Table 3.1 Labov and Waletzky's narrative structural sections

Stage	Description	Example
Abstract	Encapsulates the whole narrative by way of introduction	Our last move came at a tricky time.
Orientation	Orients the listener in respect to the context and setting needed to understand the events that unfold. Gives information on the time, place of the events of a narrative, the identities of the participants and their initial behaviour. Establishes the point from which the proposed chain of events flows in the narrator's interpretation.	Everyone was settled, I had work, the kids were happy at school, we had a lovely home, and another baby was on the way … all good, except my husband wasn't that happy at his work, and there weren't many other prospects for him in that town.
Complication	Reports a next event (or multiple events) in response to a potential question: 'and what happened [then]?' An event that disrupts or changes the circumstances established in the orientation, thus relies on temporal sequencing.	Then a good opportunity came up for him in the city.
Evaluation	A part of the narrative that reveals the attitude of the narrator towards the narrative. Reflects on the consequences of the event for the participants involved. Serves to mark the climax of the complication, prior to its resolution.	We thought long and hard, but figured it was now or never, despite babies and school.
Resolution	The portion of the narrative sequence that follows the evaluation, the 'point' of the narrative that resolves or terminates the complication in some way. Relies on temporal sequencing.	So we took the plunge. He took the job and we moved everyone holus bolus early the next year.
Coda	Returns the narrator's perspective to the present moment, connecting the past events to the present.	It was stressful at the time but it has all worked out well in the end and we have no regrets.

Note
Adapted from Labov (1997) and Labov and Waletzky (1997).

They help 'construct coherence' (Gubrium and Holstein 1998: 164). In this way, narratives of personal experience are more than data. The stories families tell of and to themselves produce their own truth effect and influence future deliberations and actions.

In this chapter, we use aspects of Labov and Waletzky's analysis of the structural elements of narratives to unpack the variety of ways family moves were storied by our interviewees, and how spatial options were constructed and juxtaposed in these narratives. In this way, structural analysis helps us understand the 'relation between meaning and action' (Riessman 2008: 89) and 'biographical disruptions' (p. 80) in family mobility. This enables us in later chapters to draw out the patterning across and between the narratives of military families who are typically required to move, and professional families who typically choose whether or not to move.

Capturing family narratives of mobility

The unique affordances of narrative to make sense of the 'temporal unfolding of human lives' (Polkinghorne 2007: 472) and to weave the story lines of multiple characters and places together informed our design for two qualitative studies of family mobility: one interviewing parents in 34 military families in 2009, the other interviewing 32 professional parents across regional, rural and remote Queensland in 2011. In both cases, the semi-structured interviews were designed to invite participants' narratives of how work, family and schooling choices interacted and articulated across their history of family relocations.

For the military family sample, 34 families with at least one parent serving in the Australian Defence Force (ADF) and one or more children in primary schools were identified in three towns across two states, with the assistance of the ADF's Defence Community Organisation and selected schools. These schools were selected from both the government and Catholic systems, on the basis of their high proportion of enrolments from ADF families. The parents in each family were asked to 'tell the story' about their family career to date and its embedded educational projects, from when the current household was established to the time of interviewing, across residential moves, school grades and career phases, then to give some sense of how they hope their story might progress in the future. Where possible both parents were interviewed, but more typically only the female non-ADF partner was available, given the frequent and lengthy deployments of the military partner. Occasionally children joined the conversation and contributed to telling 'our' story. The interviews took approximately an hour, ranging from 27 minutes to one hour and 17 minutes. They were audio-recorded and later transcribed. The 34 military families told of a total of 121 moves with children; 15 of these were within the same state, 95 interstate, and 11 international.

For the professional family sample, we interviewed doctors, teachers, nurses and police officers with responsibility for school-aged children, living in one of six communities along a 900-kilometre transect stretching from a thriving regional centre to a remote township in inland Queensland. As a comparative foil, we also interviewed parents of school-aged children working in the local councils of these townships in occupations that did not require professional credentials or registration. With the assistance of the Australian Medical Association's Queensland branch, the Queensland Nurses Union, the Queensland Teachers Union, the Queensland Police Service and the Local Government Association of Queensland, we interviewed four doctors, four nurses, ten teachers, nine police and five council workers along the same lines as the military families. These 32 families told of a total of 52 moves with children; 48 of these were within the same state, one was interstate and one was international.

As researchers we need to be alert to how a narrative is a re-telling inevitably fashioned to suit the occasion and sensitive to its audience. While the research interview can create expectations that impinge and constrain topics through a degree of 'formal narrative control' (Gubrium and Holstein 1998: 175), a narrative design allows the interviewee more control over its crafting:

> from the continuous and unstoppable flow of events a story must be constructed. The story-teller must seize hold of and verbalise just that sequence which serves her purposes.... The story has to be dissected out of life itself. Something must be transformed into a beginning ... something else into an end.... Personae and places must be inscribed by some means, however minimal ... all by means of a selective process which cuts away from the original experience all that the teller decides is irrelevant. ... There must be a stance towards the events.
>
> (Rosen 1988: 17)

Narrative interviewing allows the research participant to make the links, to choose what is relevant and what is peripheral (Riessman 1993), then to offer interpretations of significance, pass judgements and draw morals from the events, rather than the researcher imposing such interpretations.

Given our interest in capturing the intersubjective complexity involved in family mobility, we needed a way to both capture and manage that complexity. To this end, we built on the musical metaphor of 'harmonising' family projects identified in the literature to build a 'score' for each family. With the interviewer, each participant constructed a visual 'score' of how family members' work/family/education projects were 'orchestrated' over time and place. Each family member was represented as a horizontal line in the family's musical staff, reading chronologically left to right. The alignment of lines down the staff showed which other concurrent projects an individual member's projects had to 'harmonise' with (represented in the parallel congruence of lines). Vertical 'bar lines' or intersections were used to code major shared events such as the birth of a new sibling, divorce or household relocations. These scores helped to organise chronological details and visualise how the biographical projects of family members played out relationally. To explain the score to interviewees, the inter-viewer shared her own family 'score' showing cohabitation, births, promotions, relocations, child-care crises and changes of school. All participants quickly grasped the intent of the device and actively helped to construct their own, making active references and corrections to points on the score during their interviews.

As an example, Figure 3.1 offers a slice from one participant's family score, as constructed in the interview. It captures the beginning of the parents' relation-ship in Townsville, while both privates (entry enlisted level) in the ADF; their marriage in 1994; a move to Oakey in 1995 to continue their careers; the birth of a daughter in 1996, who went into informal child care so the mother's career could continue; the birth of a son in 1998, with both children placed in child care so the mother could return to full-time work; the family's relocation to Sydney in Christmas 1998, requiring new child-care placements; the father's promotion to lance corporal and absence on active service in Timor; and a child's illness that required another change in child-care arrangements.

This visual record summarises pages of interview transcript. It also served as a valuable prop to help participants recall, clarify and communicate details in their accounts of circumstances around family relocations: that is, to tell the incidental stories embedded within, and complicating, the larger narrative. The score meta-phor helped visualise a family's history of mobility with chronologically ordered coherence, but in practice the interviews often jumped back and forth in time, fol-lowing one family member's story then backtracking to overlay another's.

This 'score' representation complemented the narrative mode of interviewing. It helped to make evident the interweaving of projects, emerging complications and their resolutions in family units over time and space. The score also helped to capture the particularities of moments in family histories where competing priorities had to be explicitly weighed up and acted on in relocation decisions. This reflexive work to accommodate intersubjective claims is the relational stuff of families.

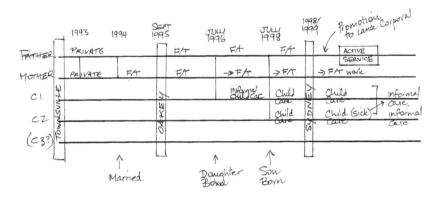

Figure 3.1 Example excerpt from a family orchestration score.

The next section presents a variety of family mobility narratives from both samples, demonstrating how a family mobility event can occupy a variety of positions in the narrative structure and accrue different meanings in family careers. Throughout the book, all names for participants are pseudonyms. Identifying details have been masked by glosses in square brackets. Occasionally, the researcher's voice plays a role. This is indicated by 'R'. Other times more than one parent voice contributes to the narrative. In these cases, the speakers are distinguished as 'P1' and 'P2'. Children's names are replaced by 'C1', 'C2' to indicate birth order, C1 being the eldest.

Mobility in the orientation

When participants started a story from the point of planning or desiring a move, there are a number of ways the story can play out – success in bringing about the move or failure to do so. The two stories presented illustrate these divergent plot lines.

Narrative 3.1 'We're not going to be here forever'

Kaitlyn: military family, two parents, three children

Orientation	With my boys, I tell them what's going to happen: 'We're not going to be here forever, we're going to move, you're only going to be here a short time.' Just get them used to the idea that it's not going to be constant.
Complication	We got about a week's notice that we were going to be moving there,
Evaluation	so I wasn't happy.
Complication	He's finished his training so that was his first official posting. We knew it was coming, we just didn't know where we were going.
Resolutions	So I prepared the boys and they helped pack up their clothes and things like that and I said we were either going to Brisbane or Darwin, that's all we knew. So I researched all the stuff in Darwin, all the stuff in Brisbane because I didn't know where we were going but I knew it was going to be one of those two.... So I went ahead and said I'm either going to go to one of these two places so I need to know about them. So I'm on the internet, talking to the DCO [Defence Community Organisation] here, talking to the DCO in Darwin. And I mean we had a week where we finally knew we were going to Brisbane so we had to go to [defence housing agency website], where you find a house.
Complication	It took two days to choose a house ... like we didn't even have two days before we had to leave so we had to choose the house straight away.
Evaluation	I was thinking there's no way I'm going to get somewhere close to my work because I'm working in the city so I had to organise transport into work, organise the house, packing.

Resolution	When we finally got our posting to Brisbane ... I sent out my resume before we even left, so my managers sent out my resumes to all the business managers in [her employer – a national agency] and they got picked up an hour later from when they sent them out and so they rang me and said, 'You've got a choice of three jobs, which one do you want?' They were all in the city so it didn't really matter to me, I'd always be learning something new ... I've got the house, I've got a sense of the area, I've got my job, [husband's] got his job, so it's all there ... I know whereabouts we're going to be, [husband's] work and everything. So I've picked four or five schools that I wanted to go and visit, made an appointment.
Coda	I'm very active in the sense that I want to be comfortable with where I'm sending my kids and I want to know that they're going to be well looked after.... It drives my husband completely mad but he loves that I do it.

This story was told by a young mother, whose partner had only recently joined the Australian Defence Forces. The orientation's premise, 'we're going to move', and the narrative more generally presents a highly motile family – poised and ready for the inevitable move, with skills, dispositions, support agencies and a sympathetic employer, which all contributed to effecting a successful outcome despite the short notice for the ADF member. The complications in this story are not that the family have to move, but first that they don't know where they will be moving to and second that such short notice was given. The work of finding housing, work placement for the female partner and schools was not the problem in this telling. The efficiency and intensity of efforts to reconstitute family life in a new location that the female partner describes mask the presumptuous demands of the ADF member's employer giving such limited notice to an employee with family responsibilities.

Another narrative that features mobility in the orientation came from an interview with a nurse with four children who was living in a remote town with one government high school. Many residents with the means chose to send their children as boarders into regional or metropolitan centres for their secondary schooling.

Narrative 3.2 'A money thing'

Lily: nurse's family, two parents, four children

Orientation	I've often wanted to send my kids away to school, because it's more education, better opportunities,
Complication	but it's always been a money thing.
Evaluation	I often look at [C2] who is so talented and I think perhaps it would have been so good for her ... even a scholarship will only pay a percentage of the tuition. You've still got to pay all the boarding.

continued

Narrative 3.2 continued

Lily: nurse's family, two parents, four children	
Resolution	There's never been the money to do it.
Coda	If your kids are Aboriginal and are good at sport, I don't think it costs you anything to send your kids to boarding school. Or if you live in those outlying towns. ... You'll get all the assistance, and if you can get a scholarship on top of that, it doesn't cost you anything. But if you live here ... there's nothing.

This narrative is a despondent story of failure to fund the desired mobility for some members of the family. Its orientation runs counter to the usual concern of maintaining stability for children's education, and serves to introduce the counter-narrative evident in many interviews undertaken with professional families in rural and remote communities, being the quest for more 'opportunities' and options to enrich children's education driving mobility.

Mobility as complication

Given a widespread preference to avoid moving children while they are attending school, the prospect of moving the household can loom as a complication to projects underway. Families told of a number of possible resolutions to mobility as complication – averting the move, delaying the move or limiting the move.

Narrative 3.3 'I'd like to stay'

Mary: military family, two parents, two children	
Abstract	My husband's actually asked ...
Orientation	well, we were here initially on a three-year posting and then because he got his commission he got another two-year posting.
Complication	[We were due to be posted]
Resolution	and when he had his interview he said, 'I'd like to stay in [town]' and because there are so many jobs in [town] it's not a problem and there are different posts he has to fulfil to get his career profile; to get to a major and you are able to do that in [town]
Evaluation	as long as you don't mind [town] which personally I don't
Resolution	so he's actually got another two years here.
Coda	So it means [son] will finish his primary school here ... it does actually annoy me when you see parents who move their children around and you know there are choices that they could make to actually keep their children more stable in their schooling.

This narrative came from a family that had migrated internationally in the hope of achieving more time together as a family while pursuing the father's military career. The implicit mobility event constituting the complication in this narrative is the imminent posting the couple were expecting given the 'back-to-back' postings in one location that the family had already enjoyed and highly valued for their children's schooling. Though the narrative foregrounds her husband's agency in asking to stay, the decision to grant this request still rested with the employer, not the family, and the positive outcome for the military career project in the resolution was enabled by the happenstance of multiple opportunities being available at an appropriate level, rather than by design. In her coda, she connects her husband's strategy in staying to achieving stability for her son's education, then offers her opinion of other military families that may not seek the same compromises. Her evaluation of other families' choices fails to acknowledge any role of the employer in demanding mobility or accommodating such requests. These institutional conditions and demands are taken for granted in this occupation.

Narrative 3.4 'I'll be the last to leave'

Julie: dual career military family, two parents, three children	
Abstract	When I say 'moving next year',
Orientation	where my husband works, the reason that we have to move – we really don't have a choice – is they're moving that whole area down south. They're moving it to Canberra
Complication	so therefore there's not going to be a job up here for him so we have to move. It could be within the next 12 months.
Resolution	He has put his hand up and said, 'I'll be the last to leave,'
Evaluation	purely because we've got one in Year 7 that's just started school we'd like him particularly to finish the year and not have to worry about that
Complication	because if he goes ... I'm not sure about Sydney and Canberra, but if we went back to South Australia, he'd go back into primary school because Year 7 in South Australia is still primary school.
Resolution	So that was like we want to finish the year
Coda	so this is optimistically thinking December.

While this is a similar situation to the previous narrative, the resolution here is to delay the complicating move, rather than circumvent it, for similar motives tied to the children's education. The projected move for this family implicated the confusion of border crossing between state educational jurisdictions, each with their own naturalised regimes, to which the families would be subject.

Mobility as resolution

At times, a mobility event offered or effected a solution to problems recounted in the family narratives.

Narrative 3.5 'A very traumatic time'

Ingrid: military family, two parents, two children	
Orientation	Then 12 months after that then [son] went off to child care ... a local child-care agency had started up a big business just up the road from us so [son] went off ... I went and had a couple of interviews. There were a couple of places at that point and, once again, it was only one day a week; it wasn't expensive and he would go off.
Evaluation	A very traumatic time
Complication	– he hated it with a passion –
Resolution	but it wasn't for very long because in 2003 we moved.

This family had moved four times with children, all of these interstate moves. They described well-polished routines to reconstitute life so the mother could pursue a nursing career around the demands of the father's Defence career. In this narrative, an unhappy child-care placement is 'solved' by a move and a fresh start in a new set of institutional settings. The following narrative from the same family tells about a later move and the emerging social and academic difficulties for the children. Two resolutions are posited – one involving moving again, the other involving not moving again.

Narrative 3.6 'Absolutely devastated'

Ingrid: military family, two parents, two children	
Orientation	My daughter wasn't so happy to be leaving her friends in Sydney.... It's definitely (an issue) as she gets older. My son was absolutely devastated. He left his very best friend behind and he was absolutely devastated.
Complication	It took him quite a while to make new friends at his new school.
Resolution	We put on what I call our 'making friends faces' and Mummy goes out and is embarrassingly shameful and says 'Hello' to absolutely everybody and we all make friends,
Evaluation	and that worked really well when they were little,
Complication	but now that my daughter's getting older she's not so interested in hanging out with Mum while she does this ... this could be what the issues are with [daughter] at the moment – she's not doing well at school.
Evaluation	She started off doing quite well in classes, sort of being towards the top of the class; we've just got her recent reports back and she's below national average in just about everything.
Complication	She's not coping and she's coming home and having issues at school every day and she's upset
Resolution 1?	and she's often said ... this is the first posting that she's said, 'I want to go back to [previous town], I want to go back to [previous town]; I don't want to stay here any more.'

Resolution 2?	We're near [the point of leaving the defence career] now.... It could be that we've got the house. It's also because I think [daughter]'s struggling and I'm becoming more aware that she's had no continuity.
Coda	She's in Year 5 and she's had five different schools in five different states. So is it any wonder that she's having trouble? No, not really.

In this telling, the mother reports her daughter's suggested resolution to her problems, being a move back to where they came from. In stark contrast, the mother suggests that the solution may lie in staying, which would entail resigning from the Defence career and its mobility demands. The daughter's projected resolution reinstates her social network, being her priority in the scheme of things. The mother's projected resolution achieves stability in schooling, being her priority at this stage, at the cost of the Defence career.

In the rural professional families sampled, mobility frequently emerged as a solution to complications emerging in the education of children. The following narrative from a female teacher who is the single parent of one child living in a remote town serves as an example.

Narrative 3.7 'A fairly major move'

Olivia: teacher family, one parent, one child	
Orientation	It was and that's I suppose where I get a little bit different now. I'm permanent – I can take leave without pay.
Complication	I suppose to preface that, at the end of last term, the arts teacher at the high school has gone ... The money to pay for an arts teacher has gone on other stuff so there's no money. So they currently don't actually have a dedicated arts teacher
Evaluation	and this is where I start going okay ... that's really important to her and also very important to me.... It's something that when I heard that, I was like oh, okay. I have to rethink this.... But yes, that's a serious consideration.
Resolution	The other consideration, I suppose, is at the end of Year 7 potentially taking leave without pay so that she does have access to a wider choice of subjects and so on. I don't know whether ... whether I go back to [regional centre], I go to [a southern state], I don't know.
A fairly major move, I think.

Mobility in the coda

When mobility events feature in the coda, they contribute to the moral of the story: that is, what learning is taken from the events narrated to inform future action, most obviously when contemplating future moves.

Narrative 3.8 'Moving is fun but ...'

Shirley: military family, two parents, three children

Orientation	[Husband] was meant to become a technician when we first got to Brisbane ... and when he was down in Year 2 he was going to go do the technician course and we were all meant to move.
Complication	But due to [son 1] coming out with his [special needs]
Evaluation	then I said to him, 'You've got careers aplenty in the army, [son 1] needs his education.'
Resolution	So we chose that then.
Coda	That's last year's course he's done so it all worked out in the end, he's still become what he wanted to become and everything like that but we chose [son 1's] education. So yes, if it came to a point where the kids' education and [son 1's] needs were more than career and moving around in the army, we would choose [son 1] ... kids with special needs and moving around it's just really like ... what do you do? So you work out your pros and cons, is it important for us to have 12 months' family time or is it important that we give him the education that he needs here? ... You get to see Australia, you get to meet heaps of lovely people and that was one of our goals, to look around Australia, to get out ... it was our dream to get out and have a good look around. Like moving is fun but ...

This narrative was told by a mother in a Defence family with three children, the eldest of whom had a behavioural disorder. The narrative tells of the family putting this child's needs first and refusing a posting, without too much eventual impact on the career opportunities for the Defence member. The coda reflects on how that will continue to be the family's priority, though moving around was one of the initial attractions of the Defence career.

The discussion above has provided a range of examples of how mobility is woven into family narratives and their complex of projects and concerns in different ways. Our parsing of the elements within these narratives has shown how moving can be the goal, can be the problem, can precipitate other problems or offer a solution. The examples demonstrated the tangle of intersubjective considerations vying for priority in family mobility decisions, and how they interact in messy ways that undermine neat mutually exclusive analytical categories of 'work', 'education' and 'family'. We would highlight how the reflexivity in codas makes evident the fact that family moves are not independent events, but part of a cumulative history that accrues its own causal force in shaping what happens next. These arguments will be further developed in the following chapters.

Re-placing family life

In narratives about mobility, places are necessarily constructed and contrasted in a 'progressive' (Massey 1993) relational sense: that is, through some juxtaposition of here with there ('should we move?') or of there with there ('where will we move?'). This juxtaposition applies on a number of spatial scales and combinations thereof: this nation or that nation; this state or that state; this town or that town; this suburb or that suburb; this school or that school; this house or that house. The construction of spatial options involves imagining, anticipating and assessing the affordances and prospects of locations, as the following narrative illustrates.

Narrative 3.9 'I didn't know where to go'

Peter: police family, two parents, five children	
Orientation	So I thought I wouldn't mind [western Queensland], because I'd applied for [remote town J] a couple of times but missed out and my boss at [north Queensland town] used to work on a property as a horse breaker and rigger on a property out here … I said I want to get a sergeant's job
Complication	but I don't know where to go, and that's the big thing, you live in Brisbane, if you had to go somewhere, where would you want to go? Do you know? I didn't know where to go. He said: Why don't you go out in that [western Queensland]? I said: where? He said: [rural town A], [remote town B], all that area.
Evaluation	So that got me thinking.
Resolution	So I started to jump on the net and look around, the police intranet, and have a look. Anyway, [remote town A] come on the horizon. It's got a convent school. It was a three-man station back at that stage, which had a bit of bearing on finances because that way you've got to man the station with overtime … so anyway, I put in for [remote town A], did the resume, it looks pretty good. I did the interview, aced the interview, yes preferred applicant.
Coda	April 2005 all the family tracks south from [north Queensland town].

Family mobility decisions will be underpinned by some degree and form of knowledge about 'there', be it authoritative knowledge from institutional websites and agencies or the 'hot' knowledge of friends, relatives and colleagues (Ball and Vincent 1998). In Chapter 1, we outlined Archer's (2007) notion of fallible readings being the operative truths and predictions that inform reflexive projects, for better or worse. In this section we profile the discursive work families undertake to build their 'fallible readings' of locations, and the resulting reputations that serve to channel mobility and contribute to the ongoing social production of places.

Narrative 3.1, 'We're not going to be here forever', described an intense research phase in preparation for an indeterminate posting:

So I went ahead and said I'm either going to go to one of these two places so I need to know about them. So I'm on the internet, talking to the DCO [Defence Community Organisation] here, talking to the DCO in Darwin.

All the military families described a period of intense research effort through formal and informal networks as a routine phase prior to any posting. This practice engendered a brisk trade in the reputations of schools, child-care options and suburbs within their networks:

> army families are particularly good at this so if you met somebody there would be certain questions that we would ask each other – 'Where do you shop, what's good, where do you eat out? What's good?
>
> (Peta and Bob, military family)

> A lot of people don't mind you ringing up after three or four years and saying 'Hey, it's me; we're moving, what's a good school for the kids?' that sort of thing. I think that's probably the most important thing – the networking.
>
> (Ruby, teacher family)

Local knowledge gleaned from contacts who had lived in the location, or attended the school in question, was highly prized and often favoured over official institutional information:

> Word of mouth is very useful. If you can find someone you can trust with a similar taste I would go by that first and then go onto the websites and then extend it from that.
>
> (Karen, teacher family)

Peers' on-the-ground reports could thus carry more weight than the sanitised official discourse of school websites and institutions.

The police families we interviewed similarly reported a practice of inheriting spatial solutions from their peers.

Narrative 3.10 'Where do all the police kids go?'

Chris: police family, two parents, three children	
Orientation	Yep, so we moved to [regional town] and once again we looked at schools.... Once again, we did a bit of research.
Complication	I rang the AOs [Administrative Officers] here and said, 'Where do all the kids go to school?' ... rang the station, 'Where do all the police kids go?'
Resolution	and they said they all go to [Catholic school]. So as soon as they said that, we automatically went there.
Evaluation	We didn't worry about the other schools, so we enrolled him in [Catholic school].

For the military families, the practice of seeking peers' local knowledge to inform decisions wore a path to certain suburbs and certain schools over time in towns with large Defence bases. This practice is partly explained by the dense supply of Defence housing in certain areas, but within these parameters the families were keen to exercise what choice they could. These desired suburbs and schools of choice in turn became associated with highly mobile military families by reputation, in a mutually reinforcing cycle, at the risk of deterring other groups in the community. In some locations the schools of choice had implemented strict zoning boundaries to manage enrolment pressure. Knowing where these boundaries fell became a crucial piece of local knowledge.

Narrative 3.11 'Weren't zoned for that area'

Ingrid: military family, two parents, two children	
Orientation	The same strategy again: looked at a house, looked at the surrounding schools which was a little bit of a shortfall on this move because the internet wasn't up to date so I'd researched all and we were all prepared to go off to school
Complication	only to rock up to school to be told we weren't zoned for that area and that our zoning school was in another area and because they had had a reshuffle
Resolution	and we had to then trot ourselves back off to this new school,
Evaluation	which was quite devastating.
Coda	Had I known we wouldn't get into that school then we may have chosen a different house in that area but ...

Knowledge of 'here', of 'this' state, town or school, is easily accrued, tested, nuanced and polished over time, while knowledge of 'there' is more conjectural and more relational: that is, understood through its contrast to 'here'. This in part explains the thirst for vicarious lived experience through the local knowledge of others. A juxtaposition of 'here' and 'there' can equally inform the choice to stay.

Narrative 3.12 'Better than what we had'

Yvonne: teacher family, two parents, three children at home	
Orientation	You know, getting close to the time when – yeah, by the time our three years had come up, we could move or stay another year, because the longer you stay, the more points you get. The more points you have, the more chance of getting to your preferred location.
Complication	The only problem is we didn't know where our preferred location was going to be and we wanted somewhere that had better than what we had.

continued

Narrative 3.12 continued

Yvonne: teacher family, two parents, three children at home	
Evaluation	Well, we had – everything was close for us, so we didn't have to drive a long way to get to work and those sorts of things. We had everything we needed at that point in time for the littlies, in that there was child care, if we needed it. There was play group that my husband would take the kids to. See, at that stage there, we weren't looking for lots of extracurricular activities. However, when we did need it, when the girls were growing up, they did ballet and jazz ballet. We could have joined soccer. We did join Little Athletics. [Rural town] had those things.
Resolution	So ... I stayed there until June 2007. .. I stayed at the one school ... I liked being with the littlies. So I just retrained in different things.

There are thus a number of possible plot lines when it comes to narratives about 'knowing' about spatial options, such as: one's prospective reading proves to be correct; one's prospective reading proves to be misleading; events that flow from not knowing enough; and events that flow from knowing too much. The narrative 'schools were very good here' offers an example of the first plot line – a purposeful move motivated by knowledge of the school market on offer, undertaken prior to starting a family and never regretted, to the point that the family would not consider another move until both children had finished their schooling.

Narrative 3.13 'Schools were very good here'

Anna: teacher family, two parents, two children	
Abstract	Yes, '94. We moved to [regional centre A]
Orientation	and we specifically moved because we wanted to raise a family, or start a family
Evaluation	and we believed that schools were very good here, we'd heard good things about them. We'd heard it was a great place to raise a family, it was safe. It was close to Brisbane,
Orientation	and I wanted access to educational opportunities in Brisbane, the museum, the art gallery and things like that,
Complication	but my husband didn't want to live in a city,
Evaluation	so we said as a compromise that we would move to [regional centre A] instead.
Resolution	We came down and we both started teaching and I worked for four years until I had my daughter in 1997.
Coda	Yes, well, we're both teachers, so that's a very high priority for us. So we made that decision that once we had children we would not move and would remain in the same place for the children's schooling.

In contrast, the narrative 'What have we done?' tells of a research phase as part of the first resolution, while the second complication makes evident that the knowledge or reading of 'there' the family had assembled prior to their move failed to adequately prepare them for their new location.

Narrative 3.14 'What have we done?'

Yvonne: teacher family, two parents, three children	
Orientation	I wanted to do country service. To do three years and then get back to the city. Get it over and done with.
Abstract	That was 15 years ago. Okay.... It was the beginning of the end. Yeah, the beginning of our out west stint.
Orientation	Now, I remember putting in for other places like [regional centre C]. Like, going out further west.
Complication	I had never heard of [rural town A].
Evaluation	Sounds all right.
Resolution	I'll just put it in there ... and got it, so had to find out something about it
Complication	and remember vividly, driving in that day, we all had the flu, the three of us, we had the goldfish and the nappies. We had the German shepherd in the back seat and the child and we rolled into this town and they didn't even have curbing and channelling in the main street.
Evaluation	I'm thinking, what have we done? What have we done?
Resolution	But never looked back
Coda	and so ... it was more to do your country service ... it says in black and white that you could be asked to serve anywhere in the state, so it made sense to us while our family was young, go and do it then and then get back.

The next narrative, 'Just arriving', gives an example of the 'not knowing enough' plot line, and the value of local knowledge as demonstrated by the consequences of its absence.

Narrative 3.15 'Just arriving'

Jamie: military family, two parents, one child still at home	
Abstract	That is an invaluable resource. If you know somebody that's been posted there.... If you can. If you're lucky enough.
Orientation	My experience was just arriving and then getting information
Complication	and once again, 'Too late, we're already in.' That was the problem here; you couldn't get out. Once you've been to that school, no other school will take you because you are labelled that you must have all the problems that go with that school.
Evaluation	And we were living on a navy base and we're air force so we didn't have that information, that foresight.
Resolution	They all knew and the trick was you go and get a house in the New South Wales side and get your child into a school ... and then you move onto the base and that's what people were doing but we didn't know that.

As an example of the 'knowing too much' plot line, the next narrative, 'Show this to your wife before you go', tells of a police family contemplating a possible move to pursue a promotional opportunity in a remote town with a tough reputation for racial tension and their response in terms of choices and attitudes.

Narrative 3.16 'Show this to your wife before you go'

Chris: police family, two parents, three children	
Orientation	Not only were we moving further away, we were moving to an isolated community, an Indigenous community[1].... Being [remote town A] we obviously did some research and they had a Catholic school there.
Complication	Because we're not Catholic, we rang and said, 'We've got a child but we want to send him to your school
Evaluation	because we really don't want to send him to the state school in [remote town A], because of problems there.'
Resolution	They said, 'Oh no, that's fine, you don't have to be Catholic. We'll accept any child.' And we knew that other police at the station had their kids at that school, so obviously ...
Complication	I'm not sure whether you've ever seen the movie [names movie which features this town unsympathetically]? ... So basically someone gave me that and said, 'Show this to your wife before you go.' I thought, 'Oh, I don't know if I should.' I told her. She said, 'No, I want to have a look at it.' So I showed her
Evaluation	and even after the movie she said, 'Oh, you know, they could have made that movie anywhere, you know.'
Resolution	So she went there with the right attitude and we moved there
Coda	and made the most of that for two and a half years.

Note
1 As educational researchers, our first instinct is to resile from casting Indigenous communities in a negative light, given the ongoing impact of colonisation on these communities' prospects and wellbeing. Our purpose here is to demonstrate how our participants constructed and invoked reputations through their own perspectives with the resources at hand.

Our broader purpose across this group of narratives is to demonstrate how the pre-emptive stage of collecting and sifting information to form opinions, assess alternatives and contemplate options is *an essential layer of reflexivity* in family mobility processes. Discursive constructions of towns, schools and suburbs and inherited reputations in circulation exert their own effects on places and family mobility decisions, whether or not there is substance in their claims. This effect puts pressure on possible destinations, both localities and institutions, to manage and cultivate the image they project from a distance. Received knowledge and first impressions need not be the end of the story, and families will start to build their own subjectively filtered local knowledge once re-placed in their new locality. However, the opportunity to reconsider and challenge such constructions does not arise if the reputation deters people from coming in the first place.

Circumstances and priorities within families are dynamic, and will shift over time, changing how a location and its prospects are read and assessed. As one participant explained, choices are subject to revision over time:

> I haven't found anywhere that I'd rather live. We're very happy here, but in saying that, I wouldn't say we'd never move, because things change.
>
> (Wendy, other occupation family)

The condition of 'happiness' that maintains the status quo helps to highlight the role of emotions in shaping mobility decisions.

Moving emotions

Narrative interviews as a mode of data collection invite, dignify and capture emotions as important ingredients in the making of family mobility decisions, where other methods might overlook them or construe them as mere effects, not as generating actions. Given the multiple projects inherent in family units, decisions about family relocations are more than the exercise of rational choice achieved through some 'objective' equation of costs and benefits. Rather, they invoke, process and reconcile a complex of hope, fear, aspiration, anxiety, excitement, doubt, worry, caution, desire, regret, dilemma, compromise, happiness, unhappiness, optimism and/or pessimism refracted across family members:

> The deliberative process involved has nothing in common with cost–benefit analysis. It is emotionally charged, rather than being a simple exercise in instrumental rationality, because it is maintained that our emotions (as distinct from moods) are commentaries on our concerns, which supply the 'shoving power' leading to action.
>
> (Archer 2007: 13)

Emotions will inevitably colour any reading of spatial options. As an example, the following narrative from a teacher in a remote town with two children approaching high school age is peppered with reports of emotions – both her own and those of others – which contributed to her thinking about future family mobility. She is pulled to considering whether she should move to a larger centre by her desire for more educational opportunities for her children, but her partner's reluctance to be part of this plan and her friends' reports of the emotional rigours of the 'solution' of living apart worry her. Her resolution to this emotional tension was to change her job, sacrificing one she loves in distance education to return to a more classroom-based role to better position herself for a future, still hypothetical, move.

Narrative 3.17 'Starting to get itchy feet'

Martha: teacher family, two parents, two children

Abstract	I'm starting to get itchy feet ... I think mainly because of the kids. I can see more opportunities for them in a bigger centre but I'm not prepared to move half of my family educationally until [partner] is ready to make that same commitment.... So discussion is underway ... work in ...
Orientation	I'd like better opportunities for my kids and
Evaluation	to get those better opportunities in that [boarding school] environment, that's a lot more financial burden for a family. That option of moving away is a good option
Complication	but I won't do it if [partner] won't even be prepared to come with us.
Evaluation	We see it [partners living apart for children's education] through school, through our families, our country families on the land. Probably in the last couple of years there's been a handful of families who have basically – Dad stays on the land, Mum moves to [regional centre] with the kids or moves to the town. That's happening a lot. I've got a very good girlfriend who lives on a big property out [small town] way, up that way and she's near [rural town]. She and the kids live in [rural town] during the week, the dad stays home and they travel home for the weekend. Yeah, it's happening a lot.... I've got probably, now that I'm thinking of it, probably five or six friends that have done the same thing. It depends – I've seen families who've continued to be separated and I don't think that it seems to be working, I think.
Resolution	That's why I've always said I would never do that if [partner] wasn't prepared to come with us
Evaluation	because I've seen my friend in that particular instance. She's moved down and she was hoping that her husband would follow but he hasn't. He just doesn't want to go and it is difficult for her. She's got two secondary students in [regional centre] and she finds it very hard to cope on her own. We've also got very good friends ... they had a special needs child and the schools here – the little one had been to both schools.... Anyway they just felt they needed to offer more as far as specialists, therapists. They couldn't continue to travel with this little one. So the mother decided that she was just going for the best of this little girl and move to [rural town].... He's come full circle within a year in that he didn't want to go in the beginning but now he just can't bear to be away from them. We've seen that first hand.... They wanted to do the best for this little girl and the way that they could do that was to see specialists frequently but they couldn't do it out here.
Resolution	Well, I've put in for a transfer actually back to the [local] school, only because

Coda	– not that I don't like where I work. I love where I work … I'm in distance education … But because I'm not face-to-face with kids, I don't want to lose my skills in that area purely for the reason that one day, if we do ever move away, that I don't want to be going straight from having no contact to trying find my feet in a schoolroom somewhere else.

In this case, she has collected the experiential narratives of friends regarding not a location or institution, but a mode of re-spatialised family arrangements, to inform her own mobility strategy. Narratives from peers who have been 'there' or done 'that' offer access to this more intimate, emotional register that official information sources can't match. This affordance may explain the preference for peer's local knowledge over official institutional information sources identified above.

Moving stories

This chapter has explored the unique strengths of the narrative genre, being its capacity to weave events, characters, emotions, times and places into consequential sequences to make sense of family careers and how work, family, and education projects articulate in mobility decisions on the participant's own terms. These textual affordances informed the design behind the parallel interview studies we conducted to explore family mobility – one with highly mobile Australian Defence Force families, the other with selectively mobile families of professionals in rural/remote Queensland. The device of a visual score of family projects and mobility helped to scaffold the interviews and elicit detailed, contextualised narratives of the considerations and complications that precipitated the chronology of events. This design helped to operationalise our theoretical lens on intersubjectivity and reflexivity.

Popular opinion would consider moving house to be one of life's great stressors, so why would families do it? The chapter used narrative structure as identified by Labov and Waletzky (1997) to unpack participants' narratives. While mobility events could constitute problematic complications in family careers, this analysis identified how they could also feature in orientations, resolutions, and codas. This perspective allows our understanding of family mobility to move beyond the everyday assumption that family mobility is necessarily problematic, and to distinguish between a mobility event, and any second-order complications that arise in the various institutions implicated in the re-placing of family life. The next chapter develops this line of argument.

We also identified the common step of families undertaking research to inform their mobility decisions, mustering information about spatial options from formal and informal sources. While this phase appears obvious in a common-sense way, we interpreted this effort through Archer's concept of reflexivity and its premise of fallible readings: 'Such deliberations are important since they form the basis upon which people determine their future courses of action – always fallibly and always under their own description' (Archer 2007: 4). This produced a number of possible plot lines which we could identify in the data set: when readings from a distance proved adequate; when readings from a distance proved inadequate; cases of knowing too little; and a case of knowing too much. Further, we identified a preference for the informal 'hot' knowledge of peers over official or institutional knowledge. This trade in experiential knowledge highlighted the circulation of reputations that inscribed places, and the relational comparisons between 'here' and 'there'. The logic in this discursive work accords with Massey's 'progressive sense of place': 'It is a sense of place, an understanding of "its character", which can only be constructed by linking that place to places beyond' (Massey 1993: 68). In addition, the chapter highlighted how narratives can account for emotions as both cause and effect in how family mobility unfolds, which may explain the added value and vicarious learning in peers' narratives of their own emotional trajectories.

From these grounds, Chapter 4 will look more closely and systematically at the narratives of the Defence families, who experience an extraordinary rate of mobility, and limited choice about the timing and placing of their moves. Chapter 5 looks more closely at the narratives from the professional families, who are more able to choose where and when they move. On the surface, these seem very different circumstances. Families that are free to choose where they live are in a position to optimise their placing. However, those with less control over postings still tell of exercising what choice they can on a smaller scale. This brings to the empirical surface the tricky work of progressing individual projects while harmonising the collective that families must increasingly undertake and absorb in the face of multiple institutions' individualisation.

Chapter 4

Seeking continuity in circumstances not of our choosing

> I love it … with moving there's always the new environment, new people you meet, just the learning experience because every state is so different.
>
> (Ruth, military family)

> I hate moving them because they're progressing really well … probably definitely by the end of 2011 we'll be posted again – not what we wanted, not what was planned and not what we were told.
>
> (Laura, military family)

> Where can I book? I can't book anywhere, I don't know where we'll be.
>
> (Jim, military family)

> [T]hey just need to keep everything in line, especially for us Defence families because coming in and out of states, it's really, really tricky.
>
> (Clare and Baz, military family)

Defence Force careers are often promoted in terms of the qualifications, travel and adventure they offer new recruits. There is, however, another more complicated and more vexed interface between education and mobility in the Defence Force career when young recruits mature into parents with family responsibilities. Frequent residential relocation is required of Australian Defence Force (ADF) members to achieve career advancement. Regular rotations also serve as a peacetime strategy to maintain skills in the forces:

> This policy is designed to provide personnel with the maximum exposure to operational and related Service environments, even if only in a training context, while ensuring that members are relieved before staleness or fatigue … ADF personnel should be aware that on joining the ADF they might be required to move frequently throughout their careers.
>
> (ADF Recruitment Centre, www.defencejobs.gov.au/recruitmentCentre/ supportAndDownloads/FAQs/Postings/ accessed 13 September 2013)

Current policy aims to achieve postings of a minimum of three years. At the time of data collection (2009), postings were typically of two to four years' duration. Such forced postings apply equally to members with family commitments, though consideration is given to members with children in their final two years of secondary schooling.

Meanwhile, schooling, as an institution, has historically been built around the sedentary assumption of 'permanently resident children attending the same school' (Kenny and Danaher 2009: 1). This institutional assumption is reinforced by the widespread preference to avoid any disruption to a child's schooling (Holdsworth 2013). Military families are typically denied this normative default, as are other populations with more mobile lifestyles such as seasonal workers (Henderson 2004, 2005), Aboriginal families in remote settings (Prout 2009) and travelling show communities (Danaher *et al.* 2007). As extreme cases of family mobility, the experiences of ADF families thus offer rich insights for mobility research. They pursue ordinary family lives in extraordinarily mobile circumstances, with limited control over when and where they are posted. Their frequent mobility events in turn expose the everyday work that families do to stay together over time and space. As such, their experiences help us better understand both mobility and the nature of families.

The ultimate decision of where and when the ADF family will be required to move rests with their employer, thus their relocations are circumstances largely beyond their control. These circumstances distinguish them from the selectively mobile professional family sample. The ADF narratives tell of efforts and strategies to exert what influence they can on the timing and placing of their posting, and also of exercising what limited choices they can in re-placing family life:

> Well, wherever we go obviously he's going to have work because the army put us there. Hopefully I'll have work wherever we go and the only thing we get a choice in is what the kids do. We don't really get to choose where we live, we don't get to choose how long for but at least we get to choose where the kids get to be.
>
> (Julie, military family)

This chapter explores narratives collected in interviews with 34 ADF families in 2009. It proceeds in five sections. First, research literature on military families is reviewed to distinguish the unique circumstances and challenges they face. Next we offer a brief summary of how Australian education systems are organised to demonstrate the significance and impact of the ADF families' high rate of interstate relocation. Then common story lines presented in the families' interviews are introduced. These include: managing space and time; acquiring motility strategies; education complications from institutional discontinuities; the accumulation of educational troubles over a sequence of moves; the viscosity of school practices; and their efforts to manufacture continuity. We then present narratives around the impact of ADF mobility on spouse employment. The analysis helps to distinguish between cases that report gaining motility over their sequence of moves and those that report an erosion of motility over their sequence of moves. The conclusion reflects on how the narratives of this hyper-mobile population point to a search for continuity as the mobile alternative to stability.

Military families research to date

Military families and their 'brats' (Ender 2002a), particularly in the US, have been the object of study from social work and psychological perspectives given their unique stresses associated with frequent relocations, parental absence on deployment, masculinities and normative constraints. To give a more balanced, less pathological view, authors have more recently sought to balance the stress of transitions and disruptions these families experience with the opportunities and advantages afforded by the military lifestyle (Ender 2002b; Tyler 2002). Rather than concentrate on problems as such, some research has concentrated more on these families' resilience, their positive identity and designs for proactive support services (Williams and Mariglia 2002). Other studies document the changes in military family demographics that reflect changes and more diverse family models in broader society (Kelley 2002).

In contrast, the US Army's recent review of research on military families (Booth *et al.* 2007) documents the changing nature of war, and thus military service, which has impacted negatively on family, in particular, the longer unaccompanied deployments of the soldier away from his/her family. The authors conclude that 'the major factor influencing the career decisions of married Soldiers who leave the Army is not salary or lack of opportunities for advancement but rather an inability to balance the demands of work and family' (p. 5). For those that continue, Booth *et al.* foreground the growing contradiction between the dated assumptions the army makes of the institution of family and its current realities: for example, 'the optimistic assumption that during a deployment, the civilian spouse who remains behind will be able to fulfil all responsibilities related to parenting' (p. 18). These institutional mindsets overlook if not actively deny women's growing participation in the workforce. Booth *et al.* also document the lower household income of military families given the damage done by mobility to the spouse's earning capacity. A later survey (Defense Manpower Data Center 2009) reported that 77 per cent of responding spouses wanted or needed work. Castaneda and Harrell (2008) documented that, compared to civilian counterparts, military spouses are more likely to live in metropolitan areas, have high school and some college education – all factors ostensibly enhancing employment opportunity. However, Harrell *et al.* (2005) reported that, when compared with civilians' spouses, military spouses have a lower rate of employment and are more likely to be looking for a job. In this vein, frequent relocations, considered necessary to maintain a highly skilled, responsive force, are associated with 'decreased satisfaction with military life. Spouses report that relocation negatively affects their ability to build a career ... and that moving frequently can create a lack of continuity in the educational and personal relationships of military children' (Booth *et al.* 2007: 25). According to Booth *et al.*, their research with US Army-raised adults described moving as 'the most stressful demand of military life' (p. 92).

The Australian Defence Forces face similar issues around more frequent and lengthy absences of the ADF member on deployment, frequent family relocations, and stress around the growing workforce aspirations of women. A recent study (Directorate of Strategic Personnel Policy Research 2009) conducted by the ADF noted that postings continue to have a reported negative impact on partners' employment and children's education. Of the 5826 ADF members responding, 68 per cent believed postings were negatively impacting on their partner's employment. In addition, 55 per cent of ADF members indicated that their children's education was being affected. These findings reflect an earlier study conducted for the ADF by the Australian Institute for Family Studies (Snider 1991) which reported that: 22 per cent of partners were not working because no work was available; one in eight partners were not working because employers wanted longer-term employees; and 11 per cent of surveyed children had attended five or more schools. Mobility also has an impact on the educational plans of spouses. Although distance learning has facilitated continuing education to some degree, the frequent additional burden of being the sole person maintaining home and family due to the partner's deployment often hinders rather than enhances study opportunity (Defense Manpower Data Center 2009; Directorate of Strategic Personnel Policy Research 2009).

This literature highlights first mobility as an institutionalised non-negotiable fact of the military lifestyle, but also a growing tension as past institutional solutions rub against new more varied family templates and more complex combinations of projects in family life. The Defence Forces demand that the family marches to its tune on terms which render the life projects of spouse and children temporary and interruptible. The high mobility in the military career thus has bifurcated impacts on family members – the ADF member's career builds in its continuity, enhanced by mobility, while the other family members absorb the externalities of this investment in the lack of continuity in their projects. The ADF family that is managing with these circumstances over time serves as an exemplar for how families absorb and resolve institutional contradictions in their day-to-day strategies.

Education systems and their institutional contradictions

The institution of schooling has traditionally been premised on local populations, where 'residentially-stable children are seen as the "norm"' (Henderson 2001: 125) and mobility, regardless of its motivation, has been considered a problem or risk. While some degree of mobility need not be a bad thing for a student and can nurture adaptability, it is typically an emotionally stressful time for the students (Commonwealth Department of Education Science and Training and Department of Defence 2002; Henderson 2002). In addition, factors such as its timing in the school year, the child's educational stage, the degree of change involved, the degree of mobility within school cohorts, and mobility beyond a certain rate have been reported to impact on school children's learning outcomes (Commonwealth Department of Education Science and Training and Department of Defence 2002).

The risks associated with changing schools have been exacerbated by Australia's eight different state and territory jurisdictions, each with its own educational system, nomenclature and history. These local orthodoxies and regimes can mean different ages for schooling, handwriting styles, curricular selections or sequences, and modes of assessment. Institutional boundaries are drawn at slightly different cut-off points, and the devil is in the detail for mobile families. These matters could be understood as institutional contradictions within the broader education sector itself. It is the student moving interstate that encounters and must negotiate these institutional misalignments.

The details of each system are well known within its own territory, often taken for granted, considered normal, right and common-sensical by those with local knowledge. However, the mobile ADF family will need to piece these details and their implications together at short notice. Mobile families will have their own histories and may subscribe to the arrangements in the state they are most familiar with. Any other state's arrangements they encounter will be marked by the difference which disrupts what they have come to expect of schooling. Schooling in the new locale will thus be viewed not only on its own terms (what it is), but also through its relational contrast to the previous or familiar state's arrangements (what it is not). This situation can make the mobile family a more informed and potentially more critical customer, given their experience and comfort with alternative frames.

Australia's recent move to a national curriculum, which is in the process of being rolled out over school phases and subjects, promises more continuity across state borders. As such, the national curriculum constitutes a major investment in lowering institutional viscosity for mobile families. Population mobility was part of the argument legitimating this federal government intervention in what has historically been a state government matter (Garrett 2010). Not surprisingly, the ADF's Defence Community Organisation has been a strong voice lobbying for this development. However, issues of assessment and aligning other state particularities are yet to be addressed, so interstate moves remain problematic for families with school-aged children.

The authors of a large Australian focus group and survey study found that 'mobility acts as a multiplier, compounding learning difficulties' (Commonwealth Department of Education Science and Training and Department of Defence 2002: 29). Parents expressed particular concern around the lack of consistency or articulation of services for students with disabilities. These ADF families, although well supported in their moves, were vocal in their complaints and concerns around moving school-aged children. This assertiveness suggests that their strong advocacy should alert services and systems to similar issues for more marginalised, less vocal mobile families. Henderson's (2001, 2004, 2005) research with seasonal farm work communities in north Queensland, and MacArthur and Higgins's (2007) research in a small high-transience school in New Zealand argue for less 'deficit' judgements of student mobility, less hostile communities and more responsive schooling sectors that are willing to understand the circumstances of mobile families and work with them. This work, though limited in scope, serves to validate parents' typical concerns about moving school-aged children.

Risk factors will be mediated somewhat by the family's socio-economic position and resources. McLachlan's (2007) interview study with both parents and children in 45 'global nomad' families enrolled at a private international school in the UK reported a high degree of 'parental guilt' (p. 235) around giving priority to career opportunity over geographic stability. Though this could build a more cohesive and self-sufficient 'family bubble' (p. 236), 'the majority of IM (internationally mobile) mothers in the study put their careers aside and reverted back to traditional roles of mothering ... in the frequent absence of their partners' (p. 243). Another strategy for managing transience in these families was parents' explicit and active coaching of the children in social strategies to ease their transitions, such that McLachlan concluded that these relatively privileged families 'not only survived, but thrived' (p. 246).

In a review of research on mobility in learning, Leander et al. (2010) argue that the dominant discourse of 'classroom-as-container' is so powerful that much research as well as schooling itself fails to account for the flow of people through places of learning. They argue for new perspectives on learning to address this systemic blind spot, including a focus on 'learning trajectories – understanding how people create pathways through and across localities, so each site is better understood as a nexus-like intersection' (p. 336). Their concerns mirror the critique by the new mobilities paradigm of 'a-mobile' theory that 'treats as normal stability, meaning, and place, and treats as abnormal distance, change, and placelessness' (Sheller and Urry 2006: 208). Both frames make mobility visible and seek to account for movement as a normal, necessary and constitutive part of social processes. Leander et al.'s (2010) frame offers a potentially different resource to the other literature reviewed, because it does not start from the assumption that mobility is problematic. Rather, to borrow a phrase, mobility happens. Whether it becomes problematic will stem not from the fact of moving, but rather from its treatment in the contexts through which families and students move.

For the purposes of this study, the available literature investigating mobile populations in schools has highlighted first how the institution of schooling has not been well equipped to deal with mobile families, and second how the institution of the family serves as a safety net, absorbing some of the stresses associated with re-placing a family's multiple life projects. In this regard some families are better positioned than others to do so, but on balance, 'greedy' institutions (Coser cited in Segal 1986: 9) such as the military are heavily subsidised by the intersubjective give-and-take within families. The next sections exemplify common plot lines that emerged in interviewees' narratives about ADF family relocations. These plot lines include: managing space and time; juggling housing and school choices; discontinuities across state boundaries accumulating troubles across children's learning trajectories; strategising for the future; the complication of sedentary institutional practices; and accommodating spouse career aspirations.

Managing space and time

Of the 34 ADF families, all but one had primary school-aged children (aged approximately five to 12 years) at the time of interviewing. Seven families also had preschool-aged children, while five also had high school-aged children. Such age spreads meant that these families were often simultaneously negotiating child care, preschool, primary or secondary schooling placements as well as adult workplaces, having to reconcile these different choices into manageable routines and daily transport routes. When it came to re-placing all members' projects, space in its rawest form of commuting distance and time could not be ignored. The following narrative came from an ADF mother with two children, who was committed to pursuing her nursing career despite four interstate relocations for her partner's ADF career. She described a well-worn strategy of mapping the spatial possibilities for school and house choice in terms of commuting time to enable both adult workers to get to work on time.

Narrative 4.1 'I do the corridor thing'

Ingrid: military family, two parents, two children

Abstract	So then we moved to Canberra and once again I do the corridor thing ... once again I looked at the location of the house, the hospital, my husband's work, the children's school ... [drawing a] mud map of where we're going – child-care centres and what was available. I looked at it all.
Orientation	I don't know if you know Canberra very well but because it's over the border, you can either go to an ACT school or you can go to New South Wales in Queanbeyan.
Resolution	Now we chose a house a Queanbeyan and the children went to a Queanbeyan school.
Complication	Part of the choice was because, once again, for me to get to work and for him to get to work,

continued

Narrative 4.1 continued

Ingrid: military family, two parents, two children	
Resolution	it was the only school that provided us a location within that area that was close that we could do that route and still get to school on time and get to work on time so even if my husband had to get to work by 7.30 in the morning, if we lived in Queanbeyan, he could drop the children off at before-school care
Complication	which didn't open until 7.00 o'clock I think,
Resolution	he could still have enough time to drop them off and get to work.
Evaluation	If we had've chosen a location anywhere else, it wouldn't have been possible; he would have had to have a late start and because most families rely on a partner working 9.00 till 5.00 which I don't do, it's a big factor.
Coda	So we need to be in such a location that we can drop the kids off at before-school care and my husband still gets to work before 7.30.

Institutional conditions such as child-care opening hours and shift times produced the non-negotiable complications that their choices had to work around. By this account, the family was able to find a location, services and placements that worked for them and the constraints within which they had to work. The following counter-narrative of a less satisfactory outcome from another family demonstrates how many details must align across school services, care places, service hours and commuting time to fully re-place all members' projects.

Narrative 4.2 'It was just not possible'

Lisette: blended military family, two parents, two children	
Abstract	We got lucky with this house but our house in Sydney was ... yeah. No, couldn't find child care at all. I got offered the most amazing job in the world – awesome wage, great house; couldn't find child care – had to turn the job down.
Orientation	Yeah, I went to everything
Complication	and a couple of places it was the cost – there was no family day-care[1] places at all, unless I wanted to drive for two hours through Sydney traffic ... nothing. And the school had no before-school programme or after-school care programme, so I had to find someone that could have preferably both my kids and would do a school pick-up run and drop-off run, or I had to find two places that were close enough that I could leave work and still get to both kids before they shut
Evaluation	and it just couldn't happen – it just was not possible,
Resolution	so I didn't work for the year we were in Sydney.

Note
1 Family day care is a child-care scheme where registered caregivers provide care in their own homes. This is less costly than care in child-care centres.

This narrative bears witness to the difficulty and lack of recourse for mobile families when services are booked out well ahead. Another family's narrative about the search for a Kindergarten place makes this difficulty evident.

Narrative 4.3 'You can go on the waiting list'

Pat and John: military family, two parents, two children

Orientation	We'd never been posted to [town] before so I didn't really understand geographically where things were or how far things were and so I started closest working out ... and this was October, I was ringing around ...
Complication	'Oh no, we're fully booked, you can go on the waiting list.' 'Oh, okay, how long is the waiting list?' 'Oh, it's about forty at the moment.' So I rang the first four or five ... the last two were prepared to send me an application form. By the time I was ringing the last few I was starting to work out a few sort of [tactics] ... and the one that she eventually got into, but I didn't know this at the time, backs on to the [suburb] barracks. So I happened to drop the old, 'We're a Defence family'.... 'That makes no difference, we make no preference for Defence families!'
Resolution	But she did offer to send me an application and I filled the application out, sent a deposit back and within ten days, she'd been accepted.
Coda	I don't think we'd have a lot of scope to do much differently.... We're pretty lucky in a number of aspects, yeah.

The coda reflects on being 'lucky' in the absence of any alternatives in the educational market they arrived in. Reducing mobile parents to a reliance on 'luck' to find early childhood placements seems to be an abrogation of responsibility by this marketised sector to acknowledge population mobility and cater for it.

Institutions such as child-care services and schools operationalise a model of the family in the hours they operate and presume residential stability or predictability in their booking systems. However, these models may not coincide with the model of the mobile or shift worker that large employing institutions such as the ADF and hospitals demand. Such institutional contradictions impinge on all families, but the work these mobile families must undertake to reconstitute family life in a new location at short notice renders them visible.

House or school first? Acquiring motility strategies

Among these calculations of permutations of daily routes, much attention was paid to the social attributes of place. Places were associated foremost with the reputation of schools, rather than with a choice of housing. As discussed in

Chapter 1, where the local school used to serve as the default, decades of neoliberal policy have encouraged schools to differentiate themselves in the market. Such policy has also taught parents to shop around and choose a school according to particular needs and preferences (Campbell *et al.* 2009). Ironically, under such 'choice' policy, popular schools, preschools and child-care centres often resort to practices such as zoning their catchments, waiting lists and booking fees to manage the enrolment pressure from their popularity. Thus, when and where one lives can become important determinants of whether families can enrol their children in their school of choice. Such considerations rely on local knowledge to which mobile families may not have access, or residential longevity that ADF families cannot presume. These marketisation practices of zoning, waiting lists and booking fees could be considered 'immobility systems'. That is, they are viscous institutional practices that penalise mobility, reward immobility and add more complexity to relocation decisions.

ADF families that nevertheless had to move told of learning over time how to manage these conditions by undertaking an intense research phase, then making astute choices of housing within their desired school's catchment. This learning became part of their motility tool kit, part of their 'coping' strategies for frequent relocations. The following narrative was told by an ADF partner with three young children. She described her 'luck' in an early move, and made fun of her naivety in accepting the allocated house and its nearby school on face value.

Narrative 4.4 'Very lucky for someone who had no idea'

Justine: military family, two parents, three children	
Orientation	Mid-year (interstate) posting.... The house –
Complication	there were no houses available, I think, when we were moving so that was quite stressful
Resolution	but [ADF Housing] really sort of just went, 'No, we'll put you up a bracket and we'll get you a house because we need to get you into a house.'
Evaluation	It's just by chance that we went to [school]. I hadn't heard anything about it. I didn't know – I'm all new to this so I didn't know how to research, I did do the whole map thing and worked out that I was only a couple of ks from the school, which was good – walking if I wanted to.... It was just all very foreign – the whole scenario.
Coda	And I'm not taking anything – I'm just going to do as I say from now on.
Evaluation	So we moved – we got a great house, really lovely location so we were very lucky for someone who had no idea.

Though the move delivered a good outcome on this occasion, her coda attested to the learning and assertiveness acquired over their subsequent series of moves when she declares, 'I'm just going to do as I say from now on.' This accrued wariness and determination to exercise choice replaced her earlier trust and reliance on 'luck' in the system.

Families that included a child with special needs were typically very concerned about school choice and eager to ensure an optimal placement for their child. The ADF's Defence Community Organisation offers extra funding to these families to allow them to visit possible schools in person with their child before making a decision. The next narrative is from an ADF family with three children, one of whom is autistic. They had undertaken six moves with children, three of these being international moves.

Narrative 4.5 'You play the game very early'

Karen: military family, two parents, three children	
Orientation	Well, we knew we were working within the sort of autistic spectrum and so we wanted to find a school that had a good special needs [unit].
Complication	We knew that he's a mainstream child and if and when he needed that extra help he needed to have the teachers that are understanding, sympathetic to that with the support at school … and the facilities … a proper-sized place for him. So that's what we looked for
Resolution	and we found this at [school]. We got in touch with them and I had a conversation with them and decided, yes, that would be the school, and then we looked for the house.
Coda	Now this move up to [town] was very interesting. I've learnt a lot about the army system … you play the game very early … the army system and the whole moving thing … that as soon as you find out you're deployed you get the balls rolling, you get everything going as quickly as you can. Try and beat everybody else, that's the way.

Again, the coda highlights the learning of strategy that allows these families to maintain their motility despite extra challenges. Such a honed strategy will not be foolproof. The next narrative was told by the experienced mover profiled in Narrative 4.1, 'I do the corridor thing'. In this second narrative she tells how her best-laid plans and the execution of her usual research strategy backfired through no fault of her own.

Narrative 4.6 'Only to be told'

Ingrid: military family, two parents, two children	
Abstract	When we moved back to Sydney, she went to a public school again and started Year 2.
Orientation	The same strategy again; looked at a house, looked at the surrounding schools,

continued

Narrative 4.6 continued

Ingrid: military family, two parents, two children	
Complication	which was a little bit of a shortfall on this move because the internet wasn't up to date so I'd researched all and we were all prepared to go off to school only to rock up to school to be told we weren't zoned for that area and that our zoning school was in another area and because they had had a reshuffle
Resolution	and we had to then trot ourselves back off to this new school,
Evaluation	which was quite devastating ... we hadn't [bought uniforms]; we hadn't got that far
Coda	but I look at the schools so this was the school where I wanted my children to go to school. Had I known we wouldn't get into that school then we may have chosen a different house in that area but ...

Her coda reinforces the pattern of high priority given to school choice in ADF family mobility. The 'devastating' evaluation of being denied one's choice in this narrative, and the acquired dispositions in the previous narrative speak to how the marketisation of schooling has coloured the relationship between schooling as an institution and the parent/consumer, now 'the risk managers of [their] own lives' (Pusey 2003: 1).

A similar narrative came from the family presented in Narrative 4.2 'It was just not possible'. Again, by this account, children's special needs heightened the family's anxieties and investment in school choice.

Narrative 4.7 'The housing is irrelevant'

Lisette: blended military family, two parents, two children	
Orientation	[C1] at that point was having some speech therapy and she had a really bad lisp ... and we were told when we went there we were going to be there for at least two years and [C2] has asthma and a few other medical issues
Complication	and we wanted a school that was set up for the kids that had special needs
Evaluation	and we did some research through the Defence special needs group and the lady said to us, 'Definitely go to [name] Primary – they're awesome, they've got some fantastic programmes and they really look after those kids that have special needs.'
Resolution	When we were looking for a house we specified we had to get to the school.
Coda	Yeah, for us the housing is irrelevant; it's everything else that's important. We don't care ...

This narrative first serves as another example of how many families solved the chicken-and-egg dilemma of school and house choices by baldly prioritising school choice. Her coda outlines a generalised principle ('housing is irrelevant'), which these serial movers could apply repeatedly. Second, it highlights the trade in school reputations and their role in family mobility decisions, whether or not the reputations are deserved or reliable over time. These discursive truths circulate and exert their own force as socially constructed attributes of places. Schools are in their own way vulnerable under this trade, but equally contribute through their own marketing efforts and impression management.

The educational complications of institutional discontinuities

Following the work of making school/housing choices, families moved into the work of settling their children into the new locality's various settings. At this point, the interstate discontinuities and misalignments emerged as common complications in family mobility narratives. Initial year placements in schools were particularly problematic for many families, given arbitrary but non-negotiable age requirements. Table 4.1 offers a summary of the age requirements operating in early childhood schooling across Australian states at the time of data collection. These strict cut-offs travel with the cohorts as they age and continue to govern entrance to higher grades.

In this way, a few days' difference between states' requirements could be amplified into a year-long detour or jump in a child's educational trajectory.

Narrative 4.8 'This is the problem'

Robin and Rob: blended military family, two parents, four children	
Orientation	April 2006 we were moved to Darwin.
Complication	This is the problem – the school systems are different in every state. What they call it's different, what ages were different; it's more unified now but back then – even just a couple of years back, like where in the school year they were born affected whether they could start or not. The cut-off is 30 June –
Evaluation	[C1] is born 5 July
Resolution	so he had to wait an extra year.

Given the frequency with which these ADF families moved, they could experience a number of such disjunctures in a child's education, adding complexity which they and their children found hard to understand or legitimate.

Narrative 4.9 'Just completely stuffed up'

Justine: military family, two parents, three children	
Orientation	She's in Grade –
Complication	well, see, that's the thing because we've moved so much it doesn't work like that, because she's gone from Grade 1 to Grade 3 to Grade ... you know, it's just we've gone from Tassie to Queensland to Victoria, back to Queensland again
Resolution	so the years are just completely stuffed up.
Coda	That's why it's so hard.

Table 4.1 Early years schooling nomenclature and starting ages by Australian state as at 2010

State	Two years before schooling	One year before schooling	First year of schooling
QLD	No compulsory pre-prep	'Prep' Aged 5 by 30 June	'Year 1' Aged 6 by 30 June
NSW	'Preschool' Aged 4 by 31 July	'Kindergarten' (compulsory) Aged 5 by 31 July	'Year 1' Aged 6 by 31 July
VIC	'Kindergarten' Aged 4 by 30 April	'Prep' Aged 5 by 30 April	'Year 1' Aged 6 by 30 April
TAS	'Kindergarten' Aged 4 by 1 January	'Prep' (Compulsory) Aged 5 by 1 January	'Year 1' Aged 6 on or before 1 January
ACT	'Preschool' Aged 4 by 30 April	'Kindergarten' Aged 5 by 30 April	'Year 1' Aged 6 by 30 April
SA	'Preschool' At least aged 4. Intake each term	'Reception' At least aged 5. Intake each term	'Year 1' Child completes 11–14 terms across Reception, Year 1 and Year 2. Generally, those starting in first term have 12 terms, those starting in second term have 11 terms, those starting in third term have 14 terms, those starting in fourth term have 13 terms.

WA	'Kindergarten' Aged 4 by 30 June	'Pre-primary' Aged 5 by 30 June	'Year 1' Aged 6 by 30 June
NT	'Preschool' Aged 4 on or before 30 June (those turning 4 after 30 June may start after their birthday provided they attend preschool longer than 12 months)	'Transition' Aged 5 on or before 30 June.	'Year 1' Aged 6 by 30 June

Sources: this information was compiled from the various state and territory education departments websites, accessed October 2010:
ACT: www.det.act.gov.au/school_education/starting_school.
SA: www.decs.sa.gov.au/portal/community.asp?group=matters&id=startingschool.
QLD: http://education.qld.gov.au/studentservices/inclusive/prep/docs/prep_info_sheet.pdf.
NSW: www.schools.nsw.edu.au/gotoschool/primary/startingschool.php.
VIC: www.education.vic.gov.au/aboutschool/preschool/default.htm; NT: www.det.nt.gov.au/parents-community/schooling/stages-of-schooling.
WA: www.det.wa.edu.au/education/ece/enrolments.html#cal.
TAS: www.education.tas.gov.au/school/parents/starting/starting-and-leaving-a.

As a counter-narrative, the same parent described a family tactic of playing down the importance of labels, to reduce anxieties associated with year placements across state borders:

> Yeah, so it's always been the same level of education so it just was called differently and that's how I tried to explain it to my kids. They know now … and I always try to make it fun, it was an adventure; it was exciting so it was never anything scary.
>
> (Justine, military family, two parents, three children)

For the non-mobile family, the local rules can be taken for granted, and family life is lived and planned accordingly. For the mobile family, however, the details of these arbitrary cut-offs emerge suddenly on news of their posting, upsetting family plans and contradicting taken-for-granted knowledge established elsewhere. The following set of narratives give some sense of how such institutional discontinuities played out, and how individual children fared in such transitions.

Parents approached year placement negotiations with different dispositions, some more assertive than others in promoting what they considered to be the best placement. The negotiations produced considerable stress and emotion on top of other relocation demands. In the first narrative a mother tells of a child who, though entitled and planning to start schooling in his former state, had to 'drop back' to a preschool programme in the next state. The mother describes her compliance with an inflexible reception, some degree of annoyance, but ultimately a good outcome for the child. Her coda maps the programme in the new state against her default, or naturalised, schema and nomenclature ('Kinder') for schooling drawn from the previous state. This effort to translate understandings across the different states' not-quite-congruent templates is the relational work at which mobile families become expert.

Narrative 4.10 'Different states have different age cut-offs'

Rose: military family, two parents, two children

Orientation	[Daughter] actually went into Year 3 because when we went up to Queensland they actually brought her up. So she was in Grade 3 and Grade 4 there
Complication	and then when we got there [son's] age actually came into play as well because different states have different age cut-offs for when you're supposed to start.
Resolution	So [son] actually started going to the preschool that was on the school campus and I just went in … and was just lucky that there were a couple of places becoming available within the two weeks of getting there.
Evaluation	I was probably more on the annoyed side of the factor as well because I thought, 'He's actually been at school, how come I have to drop him back down again?'
Orientation	We had our interview with the principal first and they were talking about the dates for the cut-offs

Complication	and I said, 'Well, how does it go there because he's actually supposed to be at school and now I have to drop him back down again?' and he said, 'Well, it's just because of our state's school laws.'
Evaluation	He was very nice about it but I came out of it feeling disgruntled and annoyed and just thinking, 'Well, now he's just going to go back to where he was.'
Coda	But it worked out good because the preschool actually gave him nearly as good as what say a Kinder[1] or something … not quite a Grade 1 class, but like a Kinder class because they would actually sit down and do specific tasks and it wasn't like a day-care centre where they just play all day, they actually had structured learning. But in a way it sort of helped him because he ended up being more advanced when he actually did start school.

Note
1 'Kinder' is a term used in the state of Victoria to name the Kindergarten programme available for 4–5-year-olds.

By this telling, 'luck' features again in achieving the resolution, rather than any systemic process that predicts and caters for mobile families arriving in the locality.

In the next narrative, the parents, as a couple, told of a similar concern about year placement for a child starting schooling in a new state, but with the opposite goal in mind (holding their child back to ensure foundational learning was in place) and with a more assertive stance.

Narrative 4.11 'Coming in and out of states, it's really, really tricky'

Clare and Baz: military family, two parents, two children

Abstract	P1: we just fell upon it [school] literally … and thought we'll have a bit of a look around and it looked beautiful, the principal was lovely and the teachers were lovely, and the only hiccup we had with that school was when we enrolled [son 1].
Orientation	Because we got there November, I think it was, he was due to start the following year,
Complication	they wanted to put [son 1] in Grade 1 but he only did preschool so he would have missed the kindergarten … and they wanted to put him straight into Grade 1 because of his age and we've gone 'Hang on a minute, he can't go into Grade 1 because he hasn't got the fundamentals,'
Evaluation	he could write his name and a few letters, but that was the only hiccup we had there and we were very, very happy there.
Resolution	P2: Oh yes, we demanded it. We just said, 'Well, he cannot go into Grade 1.' … Well, they were okay. The principal he was very, very good and

continued

Narrative 4.11 continued

Clare and Baz: military family, two parents, two children

Complication	he said, 'Well, I really think because of his age and because he was such a big boy ...'
Resolution	Well, they didn't really have a choice. We said, 'This is what we want and this is where we think they should be,' and they were accommodating.

Despite the different tactics, fears and concerns, it was the same discontinuities and misalignments across the state education systems that created the complications. In this second narrative, however, the school was reportedly more pliable.

In the next extended narrative about year placement issues on arrival in a new state, the parents tell of advocating for an accelerated placement on the basis of the child's demonstrated academic capacity and concern about the misalignment between states' differently paced curricula for the same age group. In contrast to the forceful advocacy in the previous narrative, these parents gave a more ambivalent sense of misgivings and fortitude in the face of a formidable bureaucratic process.

Narrative 4.12 'We hit our first snag'

Pat and John: military family, two parents, two children

Abstract	P2: Okay, so at the end of 2007 we moved to Queensland.
	P1: Well, we hit our first snag,
Orientation	the difference between New South Wales and Queensland was that effectively New South Wales was a year in advance, I suppose, in terms of the curriculum.
	P2: Basically [son] learned to read and write in kindergarten in Sydney and
Complication	we came in at an awkward time because it was just when they were introducing Prep and plus they'd changed the age.[1] So according to his age he was supposed to go into Grade 1.
Orientation	There's a support person called a REDLO.[2]
Evaluation	So four to six weeks out from our move in Sydney ... I wanted to get this resolved before the new year started, and so it was sort of this horrible tense time trying to work out what was happening.
Resolution	So when I talked to [ADF support person] she said, 'Push for him to go into Grade 2 because he's a bright little button.' And she said if he was just doing the exact same as what he was doing in Sydney, he would go crazy. So I rang the school.
Complication	They were insistent that he should go into Grade 1.
Evaluation	P1: Well, I'm not sure if that's accurate, I think an individual was [of that opinion] but there were others within the same school organisation that were fairly open to the level of education and where the most appropriate place he should land.

Resolution	P2: Basically we had to follow a formal pathway to get to where we … to an outcome, and the person that we had to deal with was the guidance officer and the guidance officer works within several schools. I got onto her … I also got her talking to the principal of [son's] current school in Sydney who was quite happy to support my choices in putting [son] up. So there was this communication and
Evaluation	I was also very active in chasing up the decision-making because it was very slack as to what was coming back to me and I needed … for my sake I needed to be able to tell [son] something very concrete before we moved and for [son's] sake too, I think.
Complication	So there was a bit of to-ing and fro-ing about what was going to happen and then I got this phone call saying that it had to go to the Special Needs Committee and apparently it was brought up at this meeting and what was going to be decided and … and she felt that [son] was going to be very, very young compared to his peers and that she would encourage him to go into Grade 1 but it was going to go to the Special Needs Committee.
Resolution	Anyway, the outcome of the Special Needs Committee was that [son] could go up into Grade 2, but would we be happy for him to go into a 1/2 composite³ and, if he struggled, that he could go back into Grade 1 and I was agreeable to that … we were agreeable to that … as long as he was doing the Grade 2 work … as it turned out … by the time he had enrolled in the next year, they had so many Grade 2s that there was no composite grade. And so he went into Grade 2.
Coda	P1: I mean apart from all that noise and distraction I guess the two issues were that … the noise and distraction of having to step through all of that because, you know, if you're an outsider looking in you would have thought we were the only army family ever moving between states. P2: I was made to feel that we were being difficult … I was made to feel that I was being a pushy parent rather than a parent trying to do the right thing for their child. And then after all that sort of carry-on we then had to front up at the start of the year with me thinking, 'Oh God, are they going to go, "Here's Mrs [name]"?' … So that was also difficult because then you felt like you'd created a perception of who you were before you actually arrived.… He's happy and he's settled in really well. And the thing was when it came down to it … just one example … when they sat down their readers were sorted out, the majority of the kids in his class were on reader 12 and [son] started the year on level 25 … it was good for me because that sort of validated that I had actually made the right … well, pushed for the right thing … I guess what worries me in moving is, if we go back down south, it's going to be just a reverse … I don't know, I'm hoping it's not going to be as difficult but …

Notes
1 'Prep' is the name given to a formal preparatory year that was introduced in Queensland schools in 2007. The age for school commencement was also adjusted at the same time, to bring Queensland's age of commencement into closer alignment with other states (see Table 4.1 in Chapter 4).
2 The term REDLO refers to Regional Education Liaison Officer, a position staffed by the Defence Community Organisation in each state.
3 A composite class is one that caters for more than one grade level.

The evaluation moments through the narrative give a sense of the personal cost of their efforts – in emotion (a 'horrible tense time') and energy ('I was very active'). The coda's reflection on being made to feel 'a pushy parent' captures how heat can be produced by the friction between the mobile family and the viscosity of an intransigent institution. From this narrative, we would highlight the imbalance of power in how the mobile family, though members of a highly predictable flow of similar families, is thrown onto its own resources to negotiate with the institution as individual cases, rather than a collective. P1's droll observation, 'You would have thought we were the only army family ever moving between states', suggests that, in their opinion, this school had failed to build productive attitudes and practices that acknowledged and normalised interstate transfers. We would also highlight P2's closing comment and the concerns expressed about anticipating the next move. Though they achieved the desired outcome in this current school, she reported taking away a sense of trepidation rather than any buoyant sense of confidence and efficacy. In this way, we argue that a viscous institutional setting can erode or damage a family unit's motility.

The next narrative outlines another family's more muted strategy in similar circumstances of a capable child facing a less challenging curriculum.

Narrative 4.13 'Better for them to just see it for themselves'

Jen: military family, two parents, three children	
Orientation	She went into Grade 1
Complication	but she's basically repeating the same thing … which is what she probably needed to be for her maturity level but academically she's just floundering for 12 months.
Evaluation	Her teacher's being really good and extending her but I just think it's always going to happen because she picks up things so quickly.
Resolution	I went and saw the principal before school started and I took along her box of things that she was doing at the time and just spoke to her about it, but she said it was probably best to just keep her with her age peers.
Evaluation	I've always thought it was better for them to just see it for themselves,
Orientation	like in child care she was put with the toddler group
Complication	and I knew she was above that
Resolution	but I let them see it for themselves and within the month they had put her up.
Coda	Well, I'm thinking now that in the future it's going to get harder and I'm hoping at the end of this year I'm going to be a bit more forceful than now and say she needs to be in a 2/3 so she can do some of the 3 stuff,
Evaluation	because at the beginning of the year it was a bit of an issue because she would dumb herself down and pretend she couldn't do things … and her reading level has only moved a couple of spaces … she's definitely improved but I think it could have been improved even more.

As in many other ADF narratives, the school allocated year placement according to the state's age cut-offs with the child slotted into local systemic defaults. This ADF mother described her original strategy, allowing the school 'to just see it for themselves' and not push her desire for an advanced placement. This strategy was based on her learning and confidence from an earlier experience that she narrates. However, in her coda, she revises this strategy, given how negative consequences have played out in her child's efforts to fit in with peers. By this account, the rub between institutional misalignments can manifest as private trouble in the child's education.

Another short narrative also serves to illustrate this conversion of the public issue of institutional discontinuities to a private problem, borne by the mobile family and individual child.

Narrative 4.14 'Huge dramas'

Elizabeth and Tim: military family, two parents, three children	
Orientation	[C1] was doing Kindergarten in Darwin
Complication	but then when we got down to Adelaide they didn't have it for her age
Resolution	so she had to stay at home again
Evaluation	so she wasn't happy because she was used to going ... Was not happy at all. Had huge dramas because she was already used to going to the kindergarten in Darwin ... we had huge dramas because she couldn't go and she had to stay home
Coda	but that again comes down to the moving state, ages of things that they do and they don't do.

The coda here succinctly attributes the young child's distress to the underlying institutional discontinuities.

Accumulating troubles in learning trajectories across space

The institutional contradictions between state education systems also produced differences in curricular knowledge, discourse and pacing for the same age groups. While the immobile child unproblematically progresses through cohesive, coherent, dovetailed curriculum sequences, the mobile child can experience disruptions and unevenness in the learning trajectory. Many narratives told how such trouble could accumulate and scar the academic career of the individual child. The following narrative tells of a family's marked decision to pursue an additional change of school to allow a child to repeat an early year with more success.

Narrative 4.15 'So confused with the change'

Ingrid: military family, two parents, two children

Abstract	She repeated Year 2 because she was so confused with the change in terminology from Victoria to New South Wales – that's what we worked out was the issue in the end.
Complication	She didn't understand
Orientation	because she was in a composite class of Grade 1 and 2
Complication	and she didn't understand what the teacher was saying so, rather than ask, she just pretended to be working very studiously and not get anything done.
Evaluation	It was very sad.
Resolution	So at the end of the year we decided that we would move to a new school and she would redo Year 2 again
Coda	which will hopefully give her the opportunity to get a grasp on what was New South Wales education.

For a mobile student this solution contains two significant risks: the additional disruption of another change in school for a student already likely to experience multiple school changes, something which the immobile family would avoid; and repeating an early grade when year placement across state boundaries could produce more such complications in the future. However, the family's strategy also speaks to their motility: that is, their disposition towards moving as a possible solution, not necessarily a problem.

Another family found it hard to distinguish between their child's academic troubles and the educational fallout of serial interstate moves across incommensurate curricula.

Narrative 4.16 'If we can get over the current hurdle'

Cath and Trev: military family, two parents, one child

Orientation	P2: He was going to school in Queensland and then we got posted here,
Complication	because the school system is different from Queensland to here ... so – P1: He did one term of ... P2: one term there
Resolution	and pretty much had to get put back a year because Queensland was so far behind.
Coda	P1: If we can get over the current hurdle.
Evaluation	There are concerns that he may be dyslexic so we're just trying to determine whether that is the case or not. The transition from Queensland to here might have had some effect on it. P2: I don't think so because his maths is really good, his main thing is just writing down on paper. So everything else is going really well.... And his mathematics are really good. It's just when he writes. So I don't know where it breaks down there. If he can read it, why can't he write it?

The family here is struggling to construct some sense of causality that might enable them to design and pursue a project as a future resolution to their son's troubles. Another father expressed his own distress over the learning gap his young child experienced moving from a play-based curriculum to one based on more formal, structured pedagogy.

Narrative 4.17 'Gutted, absolutely gutted'

Carmen and Mark: military family, two parents, two children	
Orientation	R: How did the Prep to Year 1 transition [Brisbane to Darwin] go? How did you find that?
Abstract	Gutted, absolutely gutted,
Complication	because in Brisbane all she learnt in Prep was how to stick glitter on a piece of paper and make toilet bloody roll binoculars, which is crap! She gets up to Grade 1, she's expected to be able to read and write.
Evaluation	So for the first two months I was massively stressed because my daughter didn't know how to read because she never got taught how to read. Now she was able to read a little bit.
Resolution	It's only through the work put in by us and her teachers after school that she's really good at it now.
Evaluation	So for the first two, three months when we got here I was really stressed having to get tutors and that sort of thing.

While the complication in this narrative is of the institution's making, the work of resolving it comes from parties beyond the institutional setting – in this case, the parents, teachers out of hours, and hired tutors. For our purposes, we would highlight that it is not that one or the other curriculum is better or worse – they are both valid, viable designs in their own contexts. The problem for the mobile child stems from the discontinuity between states' curricula and associated pedagogies.

Low viscosity settings

Beyond the contradictions between state systems, the particular school itself can make a difference for the mobile family in terms of its institutional viscosity: that is, the degree of resistance or enablement school practices, roles and routines offer to transitions into and out of the school community. To illustrate the capacity of schools to make a difference, we present accounts of experiences in low viscosity schools.

In response to a final question about what advice they would give schools regarding mobile ADF families, one participant offered the following effusive evaluation of her children's school.

Narrative 4.18 'This school has got it right'

Justine: military family, two parents, three children	
Abstract	This school has got it right. [School] have got it right.
Orientation	They've got people there to look after kids, to help them readjust to a new school. I don't think there's anything really.
Complication	I've come across a few bad teachers; maybe need just a little bit more of an understanding that these kids have ... their whole lives have been uprooted – maybe that's it.
Resolution	But this school has it right.
Evaluation	This school is a good school,
Coda	and if I could keep my kids in there – if they'd bloody open up a high school I'd be stoked. They're just a good school, you know?
Resolution	And they've got two great education liaison officers there and they're just beautiful people who also have lived the army life so they know.

In this account, a seasoned ADF parent celebrates the way a school has built an understanding of the mobile children's situation, and its proactive practices in facilitating a successful transition. The liaison officers alluded to are Defence School Transition Aides (DSTAs), support staff employed by the ADF to work in schools with a high proportion and turnover of ADF families. Her mention that they 'have lived the army life' suggests that the hypermobility of ADF families will be familiar, appreciated and normalised by these staff members, and, with their support, by the school more generally.

Another interviewee similarly told of another school that endorsed mobility as a positive experience for children, and had strategies to facilitate the children's eventual arrival and integration, and acknowledged the presence of mobile families in the community with consideration in their booking processes.

Narrative 4.19 'I just love that school'

Simone and Warren: military family, two parents, four children	
Orientation	The interesting thing about that year – he got sent to [active service] again in December.... So I took the kids over to [another nation] which is where my family is because I didn't think I would be coping very well for three months over school holidays with four and having just moved and yeah,
Complication	so we went over for the whole three months which meant that they actually missed the first five weeks of school of that year.
Resolution	But we were living in [suburb of school] before we all left. We went to see the principal
Evaluation	and I just love that school, I really do.

Resolution	Their deputy principal was very supportive, saying, 'Oh look, the kids are going to be getting life experience and they're so young; you don't need to worry about them missing that much school.' We had email contact with their teachers at the start of the school year – we sent a photo of the kids to their classroom and their teachers printed them out and put them up on the wall so everyone could get used to seeing them … so it was not a problem that they had missed the first five weeks of school then. It did take a little bit of adjusting when they got there because everyone had already been settled in.
Evaluation	The thing that I like – even just with the Kindy level – they keep places open for people who are recently posted into the area and that's the biggest complaint I hear from my friends is if they move somewhere and they want to get their children into a private school, most parents have had their kids on wait lists for ten years – as soon as they're born, they put them on the wait list and there's a real disadvantage to moving around.... It would be a big relief to a lot of parents, I'm sure, to know that they can move and get on the list.

By these reports, these could be considered low viscosity schools that have developed the culture and practices that support and enable mobile families to make their way through their community. These reports contrast with the 'deficit' framing of mobile populations that Henderson (2001, 2004, 2005) and MacArthur and Higgins (2007) described, and the frustrations that other ADF families narrated in their dealings with less flexible or accommodating schools.

Protecting the future by manufacturing continuity

For an ADF family, any location is potentially a temporary transit stop along a chain of stops and not necessarily a final destination. They were mindful of a next move and keen to protect, promote or manufacture what continuity they could for their child's trajectory into the next place. In this way, it was not just a matter of fitting in 'here', but also eventually fitting in 'there'. Losing a grade or slipping in academic achievement constituted an immediate problem now, but could also snowball into a larger problem later, into the next setting. A school that considered itself a destination point, rather than a transit point, focused its efforts on absorbing the new student on local terms. It was left to the family to factor in, and protect, the child's learning trajectory on exit. In the following narrative, an experienced ADF mother told of anticipating and avoiding the predictable pattern of stress around adjusting young children's handwriting styles, by making it clear to teachers that they were passing through, not stopping. In this way, she sought to stop 'little things' escalating into 'big issues'.

Narrative 4.20 'Just little things like that'

Louisa: military family, two parents, three children

Abstract	One other problem that we do actually find going interstate is the terminology for the kids that they struggle with.
Orientation	The simple things ... even school terminology for words like 'adding' or 'multiplying', they use different words
Complication	and the kids get so confused and they ... like [daughter] was getting upset because she didn't understand it
Resolution	and we explained in the way they'd learned it in the past and they go, 'Oh!'
Evaluation	Just little things like that,
Complication	and also the handwriting is a big issue because the three different states are completely different and at each different school they try and teach them that state's way of the handwriting.
Resolution	They do work on it and I've found probably this year, I've said, 'Don't try and change it because we're not going to be here for that time. Focus more on other things.'

Another narrative from an ADF mother offers a more extreme case of protecting continuity for the next move.

Narrative 4.21 'I do a lot of work with them at home'

Josephine: military family, two parents, two children

Orientation	And after comparing NT's results to every other state in Australia
Complication	it is a big concern that next posting we may be back in Victoria which will put her in a different education style ... I tried to get them to look at it, I tried to get them to look at it this year and they told me no, she's exactly where she needs to be and they weren't prepared to change anything ... I got told that I could not change schools because of the zoning. I tried to change her to [school], [school] was told by the education department ... that they must take children from their own area, they may not take any other children and we can't afford to send her to Catholic school. I would have actually sent her to the Lutheran school if I had the money because it's $5000 to send the children for a year.
Resolution	We're basically just tolerating it and I do a lot of work with them at home. I buy them books to keep them up to Victorian standard and they also work on the computer programs so that way they work through at their own pace,
Coda	that's all I care about.

This parent made a vigilant reading of the context and assessed the local standards as below that of other states. Whether or not this reading was valid, it informed her design of a strenuous project for herself and her daughters. She told of 'a lot of work' supplementing her children's academic programme to ensure a successful transition back into other settings. By her account, these concerns were not dignified by the school and she was unable to negotiate or afford a change of school. Her resolution of the perceived complication drew on resources outside the educational institution. Her 'home work' project in this regard sought to manufacture continuity and proactively protect her children's future.

This work of anticipating future postings and doing what could be done to manage potential risks was evident in many interview narratives, particularly with regard to the high-stakes years of upper secondary schooling. The following narrative was typical in its intent to privilege stability for those years of schooling, even if it meant the family unit had to temporarily separate.

Narrative 4.22 'Come the crunch'

Ruth: dual military career family, two parents, three children

Abstract	R: So that's interesting – so your husband is actually making career decisions for the sake of the children's education? P: Oh, absolutely, yeah. But at the same time looking at where it can benefit him for promotion and things like that.
Orientation	He actually laid a plan out last year of the years that he's got left, so to speak, and what years the kids would be in
Complication	and working out that when the eldest gets to, say, Year 10, he wants to be in an area where he can finish 10, 11, 12 all together
Evaluation	because they're sort of your crucial last three years
Resolution	so he's worked out, 'Right, I want to be in one place for that period of time.'
Evaluation	After that we … I mean we do what we can. At the end of the day he just talks to the people that move us around. We can only put our story forward and if they listen then that's a bonus.
Complication	I mean, we've discussed also that, come the crunch of 10, 11 and 12, if we're in a situation where we're living somewhere where we're not happy with the schooling or we can't find anything that's going to provide for his needs and wants and things like that,
Resolution	then I will go back to [home town] with the kids and he will continue on,
Coda	so having said that, that's probably plan C, D, down the track a bit.

Given the ADF member cannot choose the next posting, these plans are conjecture and hope at best, with contingency plans explored and worst case scenarios anticipated. These narratives use future tense, so any resolution is necessarily hypothetical, or yet to be revealed, as in the next example.

Narrative 4.23 'Our absolute nightmare'

Peta and Bob: military family, two parents, two children	
Abstract	This [high schooling choice] has just been our absolute nightmare at the moment.
Orientation	We, at the moment, depending on what day you ask us, we might start living apart so that I can get the children into one high school, a good one we know in Adelaide ... which friends of ours have got their children at. It has a really good reputation.
Complication	We don't want to live apart and that's the problem and a really hard decision of 'what's right for the children and what's right for us as a family', because we came over here to live together and now ...
Evaluation	P2: This is something that in the UK they deal with a lot better ... they use boarding schools because they know that we move around so much, they allow for stability of education by putting them into boarding schools. It's not ideal because then you don't have the family unit you would like – going to a local school, but in terms of stability of education really then it's subsidised by the services so a good package to have. Over here they don't have that and boarding schools aren't the norm anyway and there's not a lot of them.
Resolution	
Coda	P1: We just don't know. I wish somebody would tell me what to do. If I could just ... I to and fro and we don't ... but then you know we're going to do perhaps one year in Canberra and then move to wherever the staff college is and we'll do two years there and then we don't know where we're posted to after that.

While ADF families consistently constructed the same future complication around final years of high schooling with stability accorded a high priority, they projected a variety of possible resolutions to get the family through that phase. The narrative above is still in the process of juggling possibilities and sorting priorities between 'what's right for the children and what's right for us as a family'. The worst case scenario this particular family was considering was the possibility of the family temporarily living apart. For other families, the likely resolution lay in leaving the ADF career for something more family friendly.

Narrative 4.24 'Done and dusted with the army by then'

Jen: military family, two parents, three children	
Abstract	R: How do you think about high schooling? P: That's my horror.
Orientation	We're hoping to be done and dusted with the army by then. My husband's only doing a few years. I think it's got a lot to do with he's had enough as well. Because he's been in it a while.

Complication	I would hate to have to move high schools, really. And I've never had to do it so I do actually feel sorry for the kids. Likwhen we left [town], my daughter was just distraught because she had to leave all her friends and she still talks about them all.
Evaluation	She's made great new friends and it's been great for her socially because she's not much of a social person so it's been really good for her, but I think when she got older it would be a lot harder for her.
Resolution	I'm actually hoping that next time, when I go back to work, my husband can get some long service, maybe go back for re-training.... We're hoping because he's a sergeant now he might be able to get into [state] police because of his rank.

The family's solution to the high emotion ('horror', 'hate', 'distraught', 'had enough') arising from their circumstances is an attenuated chain of 'hopes' – to re-train, to enter a new career, and to be 'done and dusted' with the military career and its mobility demands.

A third family's narrative rules out both options of living apart or leaving the ADF, and resolutely plans to 'keep moving' in the interests of maintaining the family unit.

Narrative 4.25 'Work at keeping everyone together'

	Karen: military family, two parents, three children
Orientation	I think one thing that we have discussed is that our family life and our marriage is very important
Complication	and we're not prepared to sacrifice that and many people get to a stage where the kids get to high school and they don't want to move them so the mother stays with the children and the husband moves on to the next posting.
Resolution	That's something that's not on my radar and it's something we've discussed and we will keep moving and the children will move
Coda	and they will just have to find a positive ... they will have to look for the positives. And it will be tough, but life is hard, but we feel that the family ... because we are pulled apart for these courses and deployments we have to work at keeping everyone together. So we know that's ahead, most likely ahead.

By their account, this family do not dispute the challenge of the complication, but express a more determined, resilient motility that aims to accommodate the multiple demands of the ADF career. Another participant refused to construct mobility at this phase as a complication, citing her own mobile history as evidence.

Narrative 4.26 'Oh, come on'

Simone and Warren: military family, two parents, four children

Orientation	For me, in the US high schools, just Years 9 through 12 –
Complication	I went to three high schools
Resolution	and I actually graduated top of my class
Evaluation	and I think having moved so many times actually helped me just to get that more well-rounded life experience and knowing how to cope with change and setting my own timetables and goals, you know.
Coda	So to me, when people say, 'We don't want to move because they're in high school,' I think, 'Oh, come on, surely you can go somewhere and they'll be educated.'

The previous set of narratives construct 'we'/'our'/'us' accounts of couples' joint positions and shared thinking around the future. The next candid narrative disrupts this amicable pattern by pitting 'him' and 'I' against each other.

Narrative 4.27 'Moving time at our house is extremely stressful'

Ingrid: military family, two parents, two children

Abstract	And moving time at our house is extremely stressful
Complication	because we start the arguments – he says, 'Well, you know it's my career,' and I go, 'Yes, it may be your career, but you know I have a career too and the army isn't the be-all and end-all of everything and we both have to work and they need to understand that you have a family and as such, they need to be supportive of the fact that you have a family.'
Resolution?	He says, 'Well, I can get out,'
Complication	and I went, 'Yeah, and what are you going to do?' but anyway . . .
Evaluation	We're near it [the point of leaving the ADF] now.
Complication	It could be that we've got the house. It's also because I think [C]'s struggling and I'm becoming more aware that she's had no continuity. She's in Year 5 and she's had five different schools in five different states. So is it any wonder that she's having trouble? No, not really.
Resolution?	Well, he comes out with the old argument that 'you knew that it was my career when we got married',
Evaluation	but I honestly don't know because he won't discuss it. It's not an option.
Coda	For him, more so lately, he keeps saying that he could get out.... So I don't know – he keeps talking about getting out ... at some point the issues are going to become too large and he probably will just get out.

In this narrative, proffered solutions are rejected, complications mount up and tensions remain unresolved. The narrative describes a habitual cycle with arguments flaring up with each posting. Given the mounting complications, 'getting out' emerges as a possible but unpalatable option reluctantly tabled, but increasingly likely in her opinion. By this account, the family's intersubjective give-and-take is in the process of unsettling its former agreement. The mother is increasingly reluctant to watch the child accumulate more educational trouble or her own career suffer. In the next section we consider the non-ADF spouse's participation in paid employment as another major project that needs to be considered in family mobility.

Accommodating spouse career aspirations

Existing literature has clearly identified the negative impact of frequent military relocations on non-military spouses' employment, their challenge in building any continuity towards a cogent career path, and the opportunity cost over time in terms of their earning capacity. Given the gender bias in the military workforce, the issue of spouse employment will also inevitably be gendered, hence entangled with the unpaid work/care demands still deeply embedded in female gender roles. This conjuncture produces a difficult double jeopardy, whereby some (women) are held more intersubjectively constrained and accountable than others (Doherty and Lassig 2013). Notwithstanding the challenges, women are increasingly seeking meaning, identity, community and income through the labour market. In this section, we present narratives from mobile ADF families that address spouse employment, to understand the reflexive processes and intersubjective conditions invoked around re-placing the female partner's paid work. The family relocation inherently protects and progresses the ADF career, typically for the male partner. How do non-ADF female spouses protect and progress their careers in circumstances not of their choosing?

Two interviewees had employment in large national organisations – one in a government department, the other with a large retailer. Both of these women reported successful transfers achieving continuity in their employment status. The sample also included women who identified as homemakers and sought no involvement in the workforce, either permanently or for a period of time. However, such relatively unproblematic narratives were the exception. For the majority of interviewees, a common complication in their family mobility narratives was the combination of uncertainty and hope of finding new work for the non-ADF spouse on arrival. There were various resolutions to this complication as exemplified with the following selected narratives.

In the following narrative, a participant describes her efforts to repeatedly reinvent her career by winning available positions with each posting.

Narrative 4.28 'I had to take a demotion'

Carmen and Mark: military family, two parents, two children

Orientation	When we met I was a full-time public servant in Canberra, I was a Level 6.
Complication	And then I had to take a demotion to a 4 to go to Geelong.
Resolution	And then I got back up to the 6
Complication	and then I took a demotion to the 4 to go to Darwin.
Coda	I was finding jobs, I had to apply for jobs, they weren't just handed to me, unfortunately.

The resilience evident in this narrative contrasts with the following narrative from another non-ADF spouse, in which the frequency of posting discourages investing in the effort to locate work.

Narrative 4.29 'There's no point because we're moving again'

Pat and John: military family, two parents, two children

Orientation	It was an 18-month posting and he was born four months before we left.
Complication	About halfway through that year we found we were getting posted at the end of that year anyway.
Resolution	So by that stage I thought there was no point because there's no point in even looking for work because we're moving again.

In these two narratives it is the singular 'I', the non-ADF spouse, who serves as the agent of the resolution, making the necessary adjustments and swallowing the disappointment. To make these family units work, the female spouse's aspirations were allowed to slide in priority among other family projects, thus reproducing traditional gender roles. In the next narrative, it is the male ADF member who pursues possible resolutions to the complication that mobility posed to his wife's career investment in further study, and who offers to absorb the adjustment by delaying promotion and later taking an unaccompanied posting.

Narrative 4.30 'In the end I said no'

Clare and Baz: military family, two parents, two children

Orientation	P2: I'm there for a year and then I do all my promotion courses
Complication	and then get offered a posting and it was all over the place. Like Australia-wide; it had Tasmania, Western Australia …
Evaluation	these were the options they gave me and I just went over and over it

Resolution	and in the end I said no.
Complication	[Wife] was at the time doing her study to become a teacher's aide and they wouldn't accept some of the cognates [subjects] ... I think we were looking at going to Tasmania and we rang the TAFE[1] and they said, 'No, she'll have to start all over again.'
Resolution	And we just said no. So I put my foot down. I just said, 'Look, I'm not going to take the promotion.'
Evaluation	P1: Huge decision ... the kids had just got settled. Like, we'd just come back and they had just set up their network of friends and school was lovely and everyone was happy, everyone was settled and it was a happy home.
Resolution	P2: Well, this is ... delaying a promotion ... I said these are the reasons why and they said fine,
Complication	and about two weeks later, I get a phone call and they say, 'Would you like to go to Cairns?'
Resolution	And I've come home and we've talked about it and I end up doing it unaccompanied. So I did two years up in Cairns while [wife] and the kids were located in Townsville.
Evaluation	P2: Well, I think it was quite easy because I'd always wanted the promotion but then the options that they gave us I just thought, well, no ... [wife] and the kids had kind of sacrificed a lot for me and I thought no, I can't do that again, especially a year and while [wife] was doing her studies so yeah, we came to the decision that I would just ... I'd take the promotion and move to Cairns for two years, and I think the decision was made a little bit easier due to the fact that it was only a four-hour drive, it wasn't that far.... Like I'd come home for weekends, I'd drive home on a Friday night and I'd have to go on a Sunday afternoon but I got to see the kids.

Note
1 Technical and Further Education.

By this account, the complication stemmed from one state TAFE system refusing to recognise or credit subjects completed in another state's system. The male partner reflects on the 'sacrifice' his wife and children have made in their previous accommodation of his career's mobility demands. This narrative marks a shift in family ballast and priorities. We would highlight that this tipping point comes after a sequence of moves. In this way, motility should be understood to be a variable, not a fixed attribute, and one that will continue to be shaped, augmented or eroded over a history of moves.

The final narrative comes from a dual career ADF family: that is, both parents employed full-time as ADF members. The narrator is the female partner. She reflects on the challenges ahead for the family if they are to achieve career progression for both partners in the same, if not the current, location.

Narrative 4.31 'We're in a hard position'

Laura: dual military career family, two parents, three children

Abstract	We're in a hard position
Orientation	because we both go next year for the next promotion.
Complication	For next rank we probably won't clear because there are, for me, six positions and fifty others fighting for them so more than likely not going to clear so they've offered me a third year in [regional city]. [Husband] – I don't know what they're doing with him because he won't want to stay in his unit for a third year but hopefully they'll offer him a position in [regional city] as well.
Resolution	They have told us that if we want to get promoted to [next level] we have to leave so probably definitely by the end of 2011 we'll be posted again
Evaluation	– not what we wanted, not what was planned and not what we were told.
Coda	It's all hypothetical but you sort of hope that they're going to stick to the plan, but no, it hasn't quite worked out that way.

She is despondent and resigned about their chances of seeing their preferences come to fruition. The resolution depicts a forceful, uncompromising employer, with the family told what to do, when and where to go. In other words, they must accept circumstances not of their choosing if they are to achieve their promotions.

The range of positions evident in the examples above suggests that the family project around the female partner's employment is a more unpredictable dimension in these families. Women are making different choices about how they might engage with the world of work, when and on what terms. These ADF families will be situated along the same continuum of possibilities evident in broader contemporary society. However, the stringent mobility requirements of the ADF as employer, evident in the dual career narrative above (Narrative 4.31), mean that the intersubjective give-and-take that allows family units to reconcile and harmonise a variety of projects becomes very one-sided, with one partner's diminished prospects heavily subsidising the other's. Narrative 4.27, 'Moving time at our house is extremely stressful', gives us a window into the strains that such imbalanced bargaining can place on family units. Narrative 4.30, 'In the end I said no', makes evident how such a settlement might come to be redressed over time. While our discussion in this chapter has addressed issues of school choice and spouse employment separately, these two projects will inevitably be lived in the same conglomerate mix and swirl of hopes and anxieties surrounding a family relocation, and come to impinge on each other.

Waxing and waning motility

ADF families learn about moving across their sequence of moves. This learning either enhances or diminishes their motility, in terms of resources, strategies, dispositions and supports that make mobility more or less thinkable and doable. In this section, we present narratives to demonstrate how a family can either grow or diminish in motility across their sequence of moves.

In the first narrative, a mother outlines her strategy in purposefully choosing the school on the ADF base, with its high turnover of families, to reinforce a motile disposition in her child.

Narrative 4.32 'We're going to move'

Kaitlyn: military family, two parents, two children	
Orientation	Yeah, he was in [ADF base school] and that was the start of primary school and I wanted him to go there for the teachers
Complication	as well as being surrounded by the army children
Resolution	so he has a concept of we're not staying there forever,
Coda	and with my boys, I tell them what's going to happen: 'We're not going to be here forever, we're going to move, you're only going to be here a short time.' Just get them used to the idea that it's not going to be constant.

Her coda describes a conscious and habitual coaching in a motile mindset to support the mobility anticipated for the family. In the next unresolved narrative, another mother shares her misgivings about allowing her child to grow roots into a community, knowing that there are more moves in the future. This strategy is an intriguing reversal of other parents' more typical search for extracurricular activities to build new social networks for their children. Here the mother alerts to potential distress in later 'pulling' her out to start again elsewhere. By avoiding growing roots into the community now, the mother seeks to protect and promote her child's motility for future moves.

Narrative 4.33 'If we're here for one year or two'

Louisa: military family, two parents, three children	
Abstract	But it's also hard.
Orientation	[Daughter 1] has just come home,
Complication	she wants to join the Scouts here,
Evaluation	and I'm kind of thinking, do I really want her to join if we're here for one year or two? Like, do I really want her to get involved in that and then pull her out of that and start again?

In a similar vein, another mother described the life skills she hopes her children will take from their mobility.

Narrative 4.34 'If we weren't going, they would be'

Liz: dual military career family, two parents, four children	
Abstract	I think it makes the children resilient
Complication	because they're pretty shy kids,
Resolution	they'll get used to making friends in different areas
Evaluation	and growing up near the air force base myself, I had friends coming and going ... it's good to toughen them up a bit I think [laughs] ... a wide group of friends.
Coda	Yeah, they've had friends come and go. So if we weren't going, they would be.

The sense of 'tough love' behind this narrative is balanced by the parent's own childhood experience of transient friendships as evidence of a tried and true strategy. There were other narratives that similarly described a parent's military childhood as preparing them for their current mobility:

> my father was in the British Royal Air Force so he moved around every two to three years.... Good for two years anywhere and that's my lot ... I'm already mentally packing and we've got another year here to do.
>
> (Bob and Peta, military family)

As a counterweight to these narratives of waxing motility, the next extended narrative profiles a family for whom an interstate posting is not working. This narrative touches on many of the plot lines identified previously – educational troubles from system discontinuities, lack of spouse career opportunities, and doubts about the ADF career – but not as separate issues. Rather, here they are bundled into an incoherent, unresolvable crisis with complete erosion of motility to sustain this or future moves.

Narrative 4.35 'Go back in a heartbeat'

Chloe: military family, two parents, two children	
Abstract	To be very honest I was not happy. I hated it, I wanted to go back to Melbourne straight away.
Orientation	My eldest came into Grade 3 and Grade 3 here he had done in Grade 1 in Melbourne.
Complication	So he was not happy. I had him coming home in tears nearly every day, saying that he hated it and didn't understand why he had to keep doing it all when he'd already done it all and then getting told by the teacher that he was just a disobedient child and things like that ... I came down to the school and I had a meeting with the principal and everything in regards to it and I think I got to my worst when his teacher in Grade 3 actually told me that she thought that he was stupid.

Resolution	So, you know, I brought – because I keep everything that my kids do – and so I brought all of his work in that he had done at the previous school in Melbourne and that's when I had the meeting with the principal and showed her everything that he had done and he was like the top of his class all through school and it wasn't until Grade 4 when he got another teacher that they realised that he was extremely smart. So then they started giving him ... because they couldn't put him up because of his age, he was doing the year above work in that year.
Evaluation	That was the year that nearly broke me here ... I have not built up anything here for the whole time I've been here. I find it very, very hard up here.
Complication	My husband and I are actually in the process now of talking about going back to Melbourne because I can't stay here. I don't like it at all ... he's just got his posting order again now and he's in the same unit that he was in this year for the next two years. So it's different like on my husband's side, he's posted here for the next two years but on my side I'm actually finding it very hard to get a job up here and I've told my husband that I don't know how much longer I'll be here.
Evaluation	I know that if I went to my boys now and said, 'Mummy's booked a flight to Melbourne,' they would just walk out. They would go back in a heartbeat ... we've got no family or anything up here so I think that in itself is hard. And we were very, very close to our families.... No, I have not had one good experience. I found it extremely hard. I think if the education was the same level as Melbourne it would be different because then I wouldn't have to worry so much. I worry a lot that my kids are being held back ... see, I'm stuck in the middle because I worry so much about my kids and that's why they reckon that I probably got so sick last year because I worry so much about my kids, but then I worry so much about my husband and I don't want to leave my husband to make my kids happy, but I don't want to wreck my kids' education to make my husband happy.
Resolution?	But then that's what my husband said when he got his posting saying he was here for another two years and he could tell that I was not happy. Because I've been mucked around so much he said that he would get out.
Evaluation	R: And how did you feel about that? P: Worried again because of the economy at the moment, it's just not good. Because that's what I said, you don't want to be stupid. I rang my mum and I was chatting to my mum and my mum said you would be stupid to tell him to get out and I said I didn't. That, yeah, it probably would be a lot harder, but the way I see it we would be back in Melbourne.

The narrative weaves layers of complications in educational troubles, stress about future trajectories, attempts to map one state's curriculum against another state's curriculum, trouble finding work, distance from family networks and poor health. The mother negotiates some resolution to the educational issues, but takes no comfort from the arrangements and continues to worry about institutional discontinuities, whether imagined or real. The prospect of another two years in their location is not celebrated as stability that might resolve educational issues, as it is in many other families' narratives. Rather, it merely extends her purgatory, 'stuck in the middle' between her reading of her children's and her husband's interests. In her final evaluation, her husband's offer to 'get out' of the ADF is rationally rejected on one hand while desired on the other hand. With this move being so stressful, she is only entertaining a move 'back' to her home town. What motility this family had at their disposal prior to this posting has evaporated.

This section has briefly considered how a family's motility might wax and wane over time. A move for these families is best understood not as a singular independent event but rather as part of a sequence that makes the family more or less likely to entertain future moves. In this way, the kind of treatments family members receive in their various institutional interfaces can impact on the motility of the larger unit.

Conclusion

The 'new mobilities' paradigm (Sheller and Urry 2006) seeks to account for 'issues of movement, of too little movement or too much' (p. 208). This chapter has analysed family mobility narratives offered by hypermobile military families. Given their high frequency of interstate moves at short notice in circumstances not of their choosing, these families serve as extreme cases of how families experience and manage 'too much' mobility. Their experiences in re-placing all aspects of family life have highlighted how the variety of institutional conditions members pass through contributes to the success or otherwise of mobility events, which in turn sets up the prospects for a next move. Despite being members of a predictable and sizeable population flow, their narratives typically cast them as individuals facing inflexible institutions and bureaucratic processes.

Through an analysis of their narrative constructions of events and reflections, this chapter revealed the internal work these families undertook to reconcile the mobility demands of the military career postings with other ongoing and equally compelling family projects, in particular their children's education, and the non-ADF spouse's participation in the workforce. These families could not presume the stability that most other families take for granted. In its place they sought to maximise continuity across settings. However, by these accounts, the necessary institutional transitions involved in re-placing life projects often produced complications lived as private troubles.

They told of being caught by the detail of discontinuities between states and institutions that created issues around year placement, gaps or wrinkles of repetition in children's progress from one system to another. Similarly, the non-military spouse's capacity to participate in the workforce often suffered from lack of continuity. As serial movers, they accumulated experience and learnt strategies over time. These acquired skills and dispositions became part of their motility tool kit.

Families' motility could wax and wane according to how their suite of projects played out across their sequence of moves. A bad outcome for one member impacted on all. The variability in educational institutions' capacity to enable, constrain, complicate or simplify the mobility of these families was conceptualised through the concept of institutional viscosity. Relocating families with school-aged children has become onerous and complex work in the current policy context that encourages school differentiation and marketisation. Parents have learnt to distrust the simple default solution of arriving and enrolling at the local school. Though proximity is still an important consideration, these mobile families are as committed as others to their children's education and keen to exercise choice to promote their children's interests. Viscous marketisation practices such as booking systems and waiting lists, premised on predictable residency, made it difficult for ADF families to exercise what choice they hoped to. Nevertheless, the families described acquiring active strategies around achieving enrolments in their school of choice.

These narratives of accumulated troubles worn as private stresses within the family unit serve to balance economic literature celebrating or advocating worker mobility. Relocating a worker will implicate their family members, who will absorb much of the associated stresses through their intersubjective subsidy. Only a small number of narratives described schools with a culture, routines and roles that normalised and facilitated their mobility. We would argue that all families stand to benefit from low viscosity practices that facilitate continuity and help make mobility more thinkable and doable. Australia's investment in a national curriculum may go some way to reducing the viscosity of school systems and the common associated fear of moving school-aged children, but there is further alignment necessary around year placement and local particularities such as handwriting. On a systemic scale, these may appear 'small issues', but these 'small issues' can scar the learning trajectory for individual children and dampen the family's motility. These ADF families had secure work and were well supported in a number of ways. Other more vulnerable mobile families, such as seasonal workers, or families seeking work opportunities will not have these systemic supports behind them and will be more reliant on the institutions they engage with to build some continuity. The strong preference for stability in the later years of schooling shows that the institution of family enters its own low motility phase, where it resists mobility, and prioritises children's projects. Continuity is not enough, given the biographic stakes of these high school years.

We are mindful that the narratives present just the parents' side of the story and their representation of both the schools' intentions, and their children's needs and aptitudes. However, the power of narrative data is that it allows us some empirical access to how social actors made sense of the events and reflexively folded that meaning and learning into their future actions and strategies. As Margaret Archer reminds us, an actor's reading of context exerts its own effects: 'the perception (or anticipation) of constraints or enablements can serve as a deterrent or an encouragement ... this effect is a result of our (fallible) reflexive judgements' (2007: 9).

To understand issues of 'too little' mobility, the next chapter turns to narratives from the professional families sample. We are interested in the motivations and considerations behind their restricted and selective mobility that produces the public problem of poorly serviced communities. We apply a similar analysis of how they construct complications and resolutions in their narratives, to understand what is similar and what is different about this population's narratives and those of the ADF families.

Chapter 5

Optimising location in circumstances of our choosing

This chapter explores family mobility narratives from professional families who manage education strategy and career projects across time and space within a surplus of potential career locations. Like the ADF families profiled in Chapter 4, these were families with school-aged children, so any relocation similarly implicated multiple institutional fronts. However, families of professionals differ in that they live with multiple options for career relocation by dint of their valuable credentials. In Chapter 2 we conceptualised credentialism as a mobility system: that is, social infrastructure that makes expertise and occupational status portable, thus facilitating geographic movement. Such professional credentials license the holder to work in restricted occupations needed to staff the human services required in all communities. However, not all communities can produce their own supply of certified professionals, so there is a necessary social reliance on the mobility of such credentialed professionals. Given the widespread demand for their expertise, the professional family can enjoy a far greater degree of spatial autonomy than the ADF family, and can thereby move under a different logic. Our analysis in this chapter shows how the professional family is typically able to optimise their location, such that neither careers of adults nor educational projects of children need subsidise the other in an either–or bargain, as was often the case for ADF families.

We borrow the concept of *spatial autonomy* from Weiss's (2005) work on inequalities in transnational space to show how private choices by the spatially autonomous can produce public problems. For Weiss, spatial autonomy, being the freedom to choose one's location, is an advantage in itself: 'If spatial autonomy is compromised, the quality of the spaces to which an actor is limited or gains access is an important factor shaping positions of social inequality' (p. 714). Weiss further argues that spatial autonomy need not indicate high mobility. Rather, 'the ability to remain in a suitable place can be seen as a privilege. It is the option to move to better places or to exploit differences between locations' (p. 714). Autonomy thus lies in having options at one's disposal, and the capacity to make choices to move or to stay. This concept of spatial autonomy articulates with Massey's idea of 'a politics of mobility' (Massey 1993: 63) and progressive sense of place outlined in Chapter 2, in that the im/mobility choices of the spatially autonomous will impact on the quality of life and space for less spatially autonomous populations who are on the 'receiving end' (Massey 1993: 63) of their selective mobility.

Our interest in the professional middle-class family and their selective mobility stems first from the fact that Australia suffers from a chronic maldistribution of its professional workforce and ongoing difficulty staffing human services in rural and remote localities (Haslam McKenzie 2007; Miles *et al.* 2006). A similar politics of mobility is equally evident in other countries in terms of rural shortages of professionals, and in terms of a 'brain drain' of professionals from 'third world' countries to 'first world' labour markets (Kingma 2001; Marchal and Kegels 2003; Voigt-Graf 2003; Mulkeen and Chen 2008; Mulkeen 2010). These dynamics in concert have reinscribed rural and remote Australia as increasingly transnational space as state governments look overseas to fill professional vacancies.

Government departments responsible for delivering human services across Australia's vast space and low population density have developed institutional solutions for 'gamekeeping' (Urry 2000a: 5) a professional workforce in rural and remote localities with a combination of 'carrot' and 'stick' levers that encourage them to come, and then to stay longer. For example, the Queensland Police Service offers housing, but requires personnel to serve three years in one position before being eligible to apply for another. Teachers in the Queensland public sector are expected to fulfil an obligation of country service and, by doing so, are rewarded with 'transfer points' that promote their chances of achieving a desired location later. Doctors and nurses are offered locality allowances and additional benefits, in proportion to the remoteness of the community and their time served. Medical staff recruited from overseas are currently required to serve a probationary period in rural and remote areas of need prior to achieving full registration. Medical students are offered rural scholarships that require them to serve a stipulated number of years in rural localities on graduation. Nevertheless, the maldistribution of human capital continues, hence our claim that these families enjoy a surplus of possible locations.

Second, the middle-class professional family is of particular interest given its marked investment in educational markets and strategies to protect and promote the educational accomplishments of children. This fraction of the middle class has positioned itself in the social order by garnering academic success and credentials that underpin their relative advantage. As parents, they are eager to ensure their children have the same prospects. As a result, this group have embraced the neoliberal policy environment encouraging school choice and marketisation of the education sector. Where the provision of public schools and registered teachers was once sufficient to attract middle-class professionals to less populated areas (Wells *et al.* 2005), the context has changed significantly. Since the 1980s, the ascendancy of neoliberal metapolicy (Rizvi and Lingard 2010) has encouraged the exercise of consumer choice and marketisation as mechanisms to improve public sector efficiency in Australia and elsewhere

(Wells and Crain 2000; Connell 2002; Pusey 2003; King and Kendall 2004). King and Kendall (2004: 209–210) highlight the 'increased burden of responsibility for self-actualization, self-fulfilment and self-securitization'. We interpret that as raising the stakes and intensity of reflexivity around children's educational projects within family agendas.

The close affinity between the middle class (particularly the professional fraction) and the educational market is well documented. Ball's (2003) work in the UK described the strategies of closure and exclusion practised by anxious middle-class parents in their effort to reproduce their educational distinction for their children. He describes their 'vigilance' (p. 169), their 'prudentialism' (p. 179) and their 'efficacy' (p. 3) in mobilising as both individuals and a classed group with shared interests to sequester educational advantage. Power *et al.* (2003) were more particularly interested in the professional fraction of the middle class, and their historic reliance on private schooling to achieve a different socialisation steeped in cultural capital. In the US, Lareau's ethnographic study (2003; 2011) describes deep class differences in the 'cultural logic' (2011: 3) of childhood. She contrasts the conscientious 'concerted cultivation' of the middle-class children she observed with the commitment to the 'accomplishment of natural growth' (p. 3) in her working-class sample. By her description, middle-class children are primed for success, raised with a sense of entitlement and an appreciation of how the game is played, while working-class children are raised to have a different, more wary and constraining relationship with institutions. Her work particularly highlights the 'hectic' (p. 38) programme of after-school, or extra-curricular, activities that middle-class parents coordinate for their children, devoted to 'the individual development of each child' (p. 39). In Australia, Connell *et al.* (1982) described the segregated nature of the secondary schooling market organised by choices between public and private schooling, and reinforced by the spatial segregation of classes: 'Social inequality was hardly a problem: it was built into the system from the start' (p. 15). Campbell *et al.*'s (2009) more recent study tracks the impact of neoliberal marketisation policy in Australia that has escalated middle-class aspiration, anxiety and strategic planning, when such parents use school choice as an 'insurance exercise' (p. 11): 'Finding the "best" schools, the "best" universities, the most suitable peer groups within which to lodge their children, is an increasingly common set of strategies observable in middle class families' (p. 23).

We suggest that this policy zeitgeist will exacerbate the problem of professional workforce shortages in rural and remote areas. First, middle-class professionals are likely to be closely engaged in educational markets as anxious parent-choosers at some stage. Second, educational markets (both schools and extra-curricular offerings) in smaller communities will offer more limited choice, which may not satisfy the escalating aspirations of middle-class parents (Doherty *et al.* 2013). In a nutshell, these professionals may provide the public solution for such localities but these same localities can present private problems for professionals with family responsibilities, being middle-class parents subject to the same aspirations and anxieties as others, with a heightened disposition to exercise choice.

Our sample was designed to capture a graduated cline of professional status and credential investment. It included four doctors, ten teachers, four nurses and nine police, sampled within a transect of six communities along an internal highway, from a large regional centre to a remote town servicing cattle stations 900 kilometres to the west. The regional centre, with a population of over 100,000, boasted 14 secondary schools and 29 primary schools spread across public, independent and Catholic systems, all within daily commuting reach. At the other end of the scale, the remote town, with a population around 600, hosted two primary schools, one public sector and the other Catholic, and a high school that stopped at Year 10. We were interested in how the families came to live in these localities, and under what conditions they were prepared to stay or to move. While their cline of occupational differences would be reflected in status and remuneration, we were also interested in whether there were differences across the cline in the approach to children's schooling. As a comparative foil, we also conducted interviews with five locally recruited workers employed by the local councils along the same transect, to see how they reconciled career with educational strategy, and whether their strategies and decisions were different from those of the professional families.

The ADF families presented in Chapter 4 were largely not in control of when and where they moved. By contrast, the professional families were much more able to choose the timing and placing of their relocations. For this reason the analysis here will focus on *the projected or accomplished route over a sequence of family moves* to identify the circumstances and considerations that precipitated mobility events. We first present the most common story line of a mobility circuit into rural/ remote areas to achieve a professional start, followed by increasingly family-conscious moves to targeted destinations to optimise the combination of emerging family projects. Then we present some variations on this theme, where such a game plan was changed or challenged when new circumstances arose. Next we present a set of counter-narratives. These include cases whose routes continued to exploit career opportunities across rural/remote locations, and cases of less mobile professionals and other workers who were rural at heart. Finally we illustrate the professionals' responses to institutional gamekeeping solutions that seek to address rural workforce shortages. Our conclusion reflects on how the relative spatial autonomy of the professional families and their selective mobility under circumstances of their own choosing differs from that of the ADF families.

The optimising circuit

There was a strong pattern in the professional families' mobility histories whereby early household moves served initially as resolutions to the complication of achieving a start in their chosen professions. New concerns (particularly educational ones) emerged later that would precipitate household moves, with a gravitation back to larger centres with deeper educational markets. We term this strategy the 'optimising circuit' because it optimises first the career, then the children's education through relocations. A set of narratives in this vein came from a female teacher married to another teacher, with two primary school-aged children, that we interviewed in the large regional centre. She and her partner had taught in three remote settings before using their accrued transfer points to request positions in the regional centre.

Narrative 5.1 'We did so much time'

Anna: teacher family, two parents, two children	
Orientation	Yes, there is a system of transfers. Usually people who haven't been outside a major city are usually offered a transfer,
Complication	but because we did so much time in isolated schools on [remote island] and in [remote town C] and [coastal town], we had a lot of points when we came to [regional centre].
Resolution	So it's considered we've done our isolated duty.

By her account, the early mobile career phase also fulfilled her employer's expectation of country service, thus facilitating the future stability they valued for the education of their (yet to be born) children, as explained in the next narrative.

Narrative 5.2 'We believed that schools were very good here'

Anna: teacher family, two parents, two children	
Abstract	Yes, '94. We moved to [regional centre]
Orientation	and we specifically moved because we wanted to raise a family, or start a family and we believed that schools were very good here, we'd heard good things about them. We'd heard it was a great place to raise a family, it was safe.
Evaluation	It was close to Brisbane, and I wanted access to educational opportunities in Brisbane, the museum, the art gallery and things like that.
Complication	But my husband didn't want to live in a city,
Resolution	so we said as a compromise that we would move to [regional centre] instead. We came down and we both started teaching and I worked for four years until I had my daughter in 1997.
Coda	Yes, well, we're both teachers, so that's a very high priority for us. So we made that decision that once we had children we would not move and would remain in the same place for the children's schooling.

Their move to the regional centre was staged prior to starting a family, yet was firmly premised on the reputation of the town's educational market. Her evaluation points to the 'educational opportunities' available in the capital city, but the 'compromise' resolution is to settle in the nearby regional centre.

In terms of future plans, she is considering moving, but not until her children have finished schooling, by which time 'there will not be anything here for us'.

Narrative 5.3 'There will not be anything here for us'

Anna: teacher family, two parents, two children	
Orientation	Just recently we've been talking about moving out of [regional centre]. R: So that'll be about 2019, will it? Yes, I would like to move from [regional centre]
Complication	but we haven't quite nutted out where we'd like to move, somewhere maybe on the coast. But once my children have finished their schooling, there will not be anything here for us.
Resolution	Yes, I'm keen to move.
Coda	I do definitely want to get them through their schooling to Year 12.

This sequence demonstrates first the strategic capacity and reflexive intention of this family to plan the timing and placing of their relocations, and second how intimately their decisions are related to optimising the educational projects of their children, in terms of both schooling choice and extra-curricular enrichment. Although subject to their employer's expectation of country service, they successfully managed this requirement to further their plans.

The next set of narratives comes from a young female doctor with two children, married to a partner whose work role could continue remotely online, thus allowing the family considerably more flexibility around mobility. At the time of interview, she was fulfilling her scholarship bond conditions in a second rural placement. Establishing her career was at this stage the deciding priority for the family. She described the 'lottery' process that produced her first appointment.

Narrative 5.4 'It was a lottery'

Carol: doctor family, two parents, three children, pregnant	
Abstract	Well, I took a scholarship at the start of med school, a rural health scholarship.
Orientation	So when it came time for the intern jobs – so that was at the end of 2004 – you nominated where you want to go. And there were several positions allocated for scholarship holders.
Complication	You put in your nominations and then if the places were oversubscribed they actually had a bingo ball wheel and you were assigned a number, like a ball. They spun the wheel and they'd pull the balls out. If you got pulled out then you missed out on a spot there.
Resolution	So I got pulled out [laughs]. Well, I put in for [regional centre] but I ended up going to [coastal town].
Evaluation	[Partner]'s work is based at [city] ... he would have been able to stay in [city] to continue to work.
Coda	It would have been ideal if he could have stayed there at the office but that wasn't the way it worked out.... It was a lottery.

The resolution of 'ending up' in a town that not only wasn't her second choice, but also wasn't ideal for her partner, still offered a solution to the problem of gaining a 'spot' or initial foothold on her career path. In her narrative of the family's next move, her career is again the priority, given the motility of her partner's work, but this time she is more proactive in the decision.

Narrative 5.5 'I had to move on'

Carol: doctor family, two parents, three children, pregnant

Orientation	Well, I had to move on. I needed to move on but it was my choice as to – I organised it. I got rung up by one of the SMOs who worked here and who knew that I'd be looking for a job ... people were leaving so they were keen to have somebody else to come and work [laughs].
Complication	I actually tried to get a job in [country town C] first.
Evaluation	I came to [rural town B] as a medical student and I also went to [country town C] as a medical student and I just – I think I probably preferred [country town C]. The medical centre down there is well known to be fairly proactive and supportive. I'd heard that there'd been problems here ... Well, the location's good too but they're both the same sort of distance from family in Brisbane.
Complication	But the [country town C] job that was going ... the job involved going to a rural town further west – working one week in four out there. I can't do that with small children.
Resolution	But I didn't end up taking that job, I came to [rural town B] instead ... he [Partner] just moved his job again.
Evaluation	What he does is very transportable. So as long as he's got a computer and a high-speed internet connection he's pretty right. ... So he was happy enough to come down here.
Coda	Yeah, it works well.

The intersubjectivity of her family circumstances, however, constrains the choice, ruling out the job at her location of choice given its complication of travel. In her evaluation, she also invokes a criterion of how far each location is from their extended family. Accessibility to extended family is a common consideration in the professional families' narratives, and frequently an explicit part of the 'optimising' equation they apply to assess options (further discussed in Chapter 8). In contrast, the ADF families could not hope to take this factor into account, and rarely mentioned it, except in terms of its absence. The next narrative offers another contrast to the ADF families and their narratives of their frustrated encounters with waiting lists on arrival in a new locality.

Narrative 5.6 'But I won't be able to start until ...'

Carol: doctor family, two parents, three children, pregnant	
Orientation	I came down beforehand to suss it [child care] out. I just came down for a weekend or for a few days.
Complication	There're three child-care centres in town
Resolution I	and I went and had a look at all three of them and, again, picked what I thought was the best one.
Evaluation	I think it makes a difference when the centre director actually knows the name of the children. Where there's not food dribbled down the front of the adults who are looking after the children [laughs]. I went to [child-care centre], which is where my kids go.
	There's [another child-care centre] ... which, to me, seemed to have some really funny philosophies. 'Do they do art work?' 'Oh no, we don't do art work here'.... Then the other choice was [third child-care centre] and the kids are crying and the woman that's looking after them had stuff all down her front, obviously her lunch. The director didn't know what the names of the kids were and it was just like, 'I'm not leaving the dog there!'
Resolution 2	So it was a fairly clear-cut decision
Complication	and then I just had to use a bit of emotional blackmail to get ... I went to put this baby on the waiting list and it's locked. 'You can't book them.... You can't, it's closed' – so anyway, how did I get them in?
Resolution 3	I know I went and saw them on a fairly regular basis [laughs]. I said, 'I'm a new doctor up at the hospital and I'll be starting – but I won't be able to start until I've got baby-sitting for my child, blah, blah, blah.' I think there's some nurses who work there and I suspect they had a word [laughs]. 'There's a new doctor starting and she needs some day care.'
Coda	I think a lady doctor at the hospital is a good thing for the women.... There's two lady doctors up there. I mean there's quite a few lady GPs around and that's great. But I think when people come up to the hospital and particularly up to the obstetrics side of things often they like to see a woman.

As a new doctor in a small town, this young professional had the status of her profession and the advocacy of other professionals to bolster her 'emotional blackmail' campaign, which allowed her to circumvent the waiting list in her chosen centre and resolve her child-care needs. Her evaluation of the different centres applies the middle-class criterion of cultural enrichment, while her agency in negotiating a resolution demonstrates the middle-class professional's comfort in dealing with institutions and 'playing the market' as an active, assertive chooser.

When questioned about the adequacy of the medical facilities available for her family in this rural town, she provided the following account.

Narrative 5.7 'It would be education which we would leave for'

Carol: doctor family, two parents, three children, pregnant	
Abstract	[Re local medical services]
Orientation	You shouldn't treat yourself. You shouldn't treat your own family.
Complication	Certainly if my kids become unwell,
Resolution	I just book them into one of the hospital doctors. I have a good friend who I work with and I'll get her to quickly cast her eye over them.
Evaluation	But they're not particularly sickly children. [C2]'s got a bit of asthma but they're pretty reasonable.
Coda	It would be education which we would leave for.

Her coda is telling. It projects, in a matter-of-fact way, the future expectation that the family will inevitably move on to optimise the children's education. This expectation renders the rural town as only ever a temporary residence. She further explained that they had made bookings, well into the future and at considerable cost, at three high status independent schools for their children.

Narrative 5.8 'But I think it's good to have that option'

Carol: doctor family, two parents, three children, pregnant	
Orientation	The timing is that [C1]'s booked into [school in regional centre]. Well, he's got a selection of schools on the off-chance we will end up in Brisbane or we may end up in [regional centre A]. But that's for Year 7 and that will be maybe 2019 … [school 1 in Brisbane], [school 2 in Brisbane].
Complication	I guess it costs you a couple of hundred, maybe it costs you $1000 to book them into the three schools.
Resolution	But I think it's good to have that option, to have a choice and be able to choose the school which suits them the best … [regional centre] or back to Brisbane, probably [regional centre A].

The set of bookings map and schedule the family's eventual route back from the rural setting into a larger centre with a deeper educational market. The family's contingency planning allows for two possible locations at that stage, and a choice of schools within one of these. There is both risk management and educational strategy in this family's plans that will ensure that the children have access to 'top of the range' schooling.

The next two narratives come from a policeman and his partner living in a remote township with four young children. They plot a similar 'optimising circuit', using rural/remote placements for early career advancement, but undertaken with the intention of returning to an urban centre with a high priority on optimising children's schooling. This family has less material resources than the doctor's family presented above; however, within their means, the strategy to optimise location for school choice is the same.

Narrative 5.9 'They were speaking about rural service'

Martha and Chris: police family, two parents, four children	
Orientation	P1: They have a peer select preferences. So peer preferences,
Complication	but then after that if they want to send you somewhere, that's where you'll be going.
Evaluation	[Coastal town C] was one of the options and it was only about a 20-minute drive for me. After driving about an hour and a half every day, 20 minutes was great. So obviously because we had the house, we wanted somewhere close on the north side and the majority of my intake were from the south side so it worked well.
Resolution	So I applied for [coastal town C] and I got [coastal town C]. That was my first year. First-year constable,
Abstract	in 2009 we moved out here.
Complication	I always wanted to give country service a try. During your first year, you still have to keep going back to the academy and getting more training. I went back one day and they were speaking about rural service and all the coppers were saying, 'It's great, it's great, come out here and get this' ... You get posted for a year and then you have three-year tenure, which is what I'm currently doing. They said, 'Yeah, it's great.' I always wanted to try it. They said we get a house to live in. We can live next door to the station, all these great things.
Resolution	So I went home and spoke to [partner] about it and we decided because the kids were small, it was a good time for us to move.
Evaluation	They're not in high school or anything ... cheap house which was always good. P2: Yeah. We felt we'd been there long enough and we do like to give it a go.... We felt we were a little stuck. We wanted to do something a bit different. P1: We were sort of, like, let's do it. So we ... P2: We thought it was good for his career too – be able to move up the levels pretty quick and experience stuff that he wouldn't in the city.

This narrative describes how the male partner achieved a first career placement close to the city, but later sought a 'country service' location as a way to get ahead financially and for his career progression. The next narrative tells how, halfway through the required three-year tenure in the remote location, they are actively planning a return to the city, and their choice of location will be attuned to school quality and zoning.

Narrative 5.10 'If there's a good one'

	Ross and Martha: police family, two parents, four children
Orientation	P1: If the kids want to work and learn, they will regardless of what school they're in. What were you going to say?
Complication	P2: No, I was going to say I think when we're looking at moving back to Brisbane in another year and a half or whatever, we're definitely looking at the different areas and what schools fall in those catchments. But that's important, but it's not maybe too [like] economic – I don't want to be too judgmental but ... P2: We want it to be a good school. P1: Some state schools do differ from others regarding what area they fall in.
Resolution	So we do have preferences on what area but state school to private school ... P2: I guess if there was a good state school and a good private school, we would go to private school – public school, sorry. P1: Public school.
Complication	Maybe it is because we're at a stage where we can't afford to send all four kids to a private school. Like, we send our kids to the private school out here and we do like it, don't we?
Resolution	If there's a good one [public school]. If not, we probably would consider a semi-private high school like my brothers used to go to, like a Christian college kind of thing, so it's not as expensive but you still have a little bit of a [unclear] I guess to what they ...

The male parent's orientation first downplays the typical fetish of school choice. However, when his partner tries to find some palatable way to describe what they are looking for, he is more direct, 'We want it to be a good school.' With four children on one income, this family cannot rely on expensive booking fees and high-fee exclusivity. Rather, they are mindful of the typical spatial segregation of classes in different suburbs, and how the 'good school' they seek will be a public school of choice in a zoned catchment, or a low-fee religious school. The distinguishing factor they seek, but struggle to articulate given its possible political incorrectness, is understood to be the middle-class peer group their choice would engineer for their children.

The three professional families profiled in this section shared the same strategy of an optimising circuit to reconcile career prospects with educational strategy for their children. This patterning in private decisions means that the rural/remote location plays the role of 'professional nursery' (Miles *et al.* 2006: 137), and that these populations come to be largely serviced by a churn of relatively inexperienced professionals. An experienced teacher-as-parent in a remote town tells her version of the pattern and its demand of the local schools.

Narrative 5.11 'And you start from scratch again'

Nancy: teacher family, two parents, two children

Orientation	They've got a couple of boomerang teachers at the moment. That's what they call them. Those ones there are our boomerang ones because they're told by their school – I don't know who tells them – 'Oh, can you just go out to [rural town] for two years and you're assured of getting your job back when you come back. We just want you to go for two years.' ... They're guaranteed of getting their current position but they have to come out here and do their service.
Complication	Those schools struggle. All of those schools in [remote town] struggle absolutely dreadfully because our turnover is so rapid. We don't keep the experience, and the experience that we do keep isn't enough. The schools really, really, really struggle.... They're usually filled but generally with first years who are fresh out and you start from scratch again.
Evaluation	But you know – nothing against new teachers. They're great. I love them because they're fresh and they're excited
Resolution	– but you've got to teach them how to run records. You've got to teach them how to do all the basics and it's hard work.
Coda	They're great. They've got a lot of energy and a lot of enthusiasm, which they need, but I quite often see them burning out very quickly.

Next we present some variations on this theme – narratives that start out with this strategy but meet with constraints or opportunities that were not part of the original plan.

Variations on a theme

The first variation on the optimising circuit theme is exemplified by another police family, with four children and both parents working in the police force, living in the large regional centre. This family had undertaken earlier regional moves to advance both partners' careers. Their present location with its deep educational market suited their children's needs and had offered them a choice to change schools for their son at one point. However, the same location did not offer appropriate promotion opportunities.

Narrative 5.12 'He's happy with that decision'

Joanne: teacher family, two parents, four children

Abstract	R: So in terms of looking into the future, you're going to be located at [regional centre]? Probably until at least my son has finished school.
Orientation	The girls are more adaptable. [My son] had such a difficult time from the other school and his behaviour changed, and because it's been such a positive experience and he's really achieving well for the first time in his schooling life, he's happy. We won't move him.

Complication	Well, my husband, they recently did a round of promotion which he was expected to put in for.... It's sort of like a train that you can't get off. Once you go down that promotional path there's an expectation that you'll continue,
Resolution	but he didn't because we don't want to move.
Evaluation	The hierarchy is not necessarily happy with that decision. He's happy with that decision.
Coda	All of them [my children], I would say, are priorities, definitely the children, not work.

This narrative resonates more with those of the ADF families, in terms of forcing a choice between either pursuing career opportunities or prioritising children's education, where the optimising circuit strategy would aspire to progressing both through selective mobility. The emergence of educational troubles tips the balance for this family, and establishes the premises of their orientation, 'We won't move him.'

In a similar vein, a male teacher with a partner and three children told how 'On my application, I ticked that I'd go anywhere' in order to achieve a foothold on a career change. As the family later approached three years' tenure in a rural town fully expecting to move on, on reflection they found themselves reluctant to do so, as he explains in the next narrative.

Narrative 5.13 'It's better for her to be here'

Alex: teacher family, two parents, three children

Abstract	R: Now how long do you think you'll be in [rural town]? A long time I think.... Let's say, there are three years before you can apply for a transfer ... and I've actually started the process and when it comes down to it ... I don't really want to go but with this tiny little house we've got to –
Orientation	we'd built a brand new house ... [in previous locality, regional centre] it was 2006, brand new, four bedroom, twice the size of this. Beautiful house which we had to leave and then the fourth year was this little shoe box. So that was a big motivation for going back because we still own that house. Because the market's dropped out ... it's rented out. So that was probably one of the big motivations for heading back there.
Complication	With my wife, she's on her way – once you do three years' continuous work, they put you on permanent. We don't think there would be the opportunities for her back in [regional centre] that there are here so she'd be starting from scratch there.
Resolution	So for her, it's better for her to be here.

continued

Narrative 5.13 continued

Alex: teacher family, two parents, three children

Evaluation	We're really pleased – like I said, the second child, but first child also, through here – Grade 4 and 5 she used to go for learning support. Grade 5, I think she was learning support student of the year. Grade 6 she sort of struggled, 7, now in Grade 8, she got an academic award for 50 per cent As on her report card, so in those three years she's had a massive turnaround.
Coda	We think we don't really want to upset her in moving now because she's cruising on very nicely. R: How about your opportunities for promotion here? That doesn't interest me. No desire to move up, not at all. . . . Most people seem to be motivated to get back where they've come from. That would be the big motivation.

This narrative offers another case of the professional career stepping back to protect the progress of other family members' projects, despite the added attractions of going 'back' to the family home. Here, the spatially autonomous professional can choose to stay longer while circumstances suit the family.

Where the previous variation involves some degree of trade-off in terms of sacrificing promotion opportunities for other priorities, a second variation on the optimising circuit theme requires no such trade-off – the circuit is broken because every family member thrives in the rural/remote locality. The next such narrative came from a teacher married to another teacher. They had three children and were living in a rural town.

Narrative 5.14 'Seventeen years later we're still here'

Gabrielle: teacher family, two parents, three children

Orientation	We kept saying, 'Transfer us anywhere. We'll go anywhere.' Every year at transfer time we would put in a letter saying, 'We don't care, we'll go anywhere in the state, as long as you send us together.'
Complication	But they didn't, until we got married in 1995 and that was when they decided. So in January 1995 we got married and bought our first home, on the Gold Coast, and in October 1995 we got transferred out here to [rural town]. So for five years we'd been saying, 'Do it, do it, do it!' We're just renting. Then all of a sudden, as soon as we got married and bought a home, that was when they transferred us. I did not even know where [rural town] was. I had to get a map and check where [rural town] was.
Evaluation	So I was shocked, to say the least, and devastated because family were in Brisbane and the Gold Coast and

Resolution	so we did the whole 'We'll do our two years of country service and then we'll come back', so we rented our house out down the Coast because obviously we'd just bought it and were halfway through doing it up, and didn't really want to sell it, and wanted to come back there.
Coda	Seventeen years later we're still here in [rural town]
Evaluation	because we absolutely loved it ... Seventeen years and everyone laughs. All our family and friends laugh, because they know how devastated I was when I rang everyone and went, 'We have a transfer.... Oh my God, how are we ...' – you know, and now they all laugh and say we're still there. So we're still here because we came in 1996. Within that first year we just went, 'This is a lovely town. This is really nice. It's a great school. They're great kids, really nice teachers.' Everything we wanted, like all the sports that we both play, was all here. We didn't have to travel anywhere for anything. We went 'Wow!' We could see ourselves starting our family here because we were at that stage of thinking of starting a family ... so we did.... Yeah, and after we'd had [C1], I said we were not leaving [rural town] until we'd finished having our babies because it was such a wonderful experience
Coda	and we're still here.

Her orientation reveals the common professional strategy of satisfying country service expectations in an early career phase. Her resolution invokes the optimising circuit strategy, considering the rural transfer as merely temporary before going 'back'. The mobility narrative thus unfolds as a typical professional family mobility story. However, the variation from this theme comes in the evaluation and coda. The temporary location becomes a permanent and active choice, with no 'going back', no further complications and no regrets. There were no further moves in their sequence.

A third variation to the optimising circuit plays out in a gendered pattern: single professional woman takes the rural/remote job opportunity to get a foothold in her profession, then finds a partner in that local community. This turn of events interrupts their projected circuit and extends their stay in the rural/remote location, with a variety of outcomes.

Narrative 5.15 'Much to my mother's horror'

Wendy: other occupation family, two parents, four children	
Abstract	Posted straight to [remote town] ... Much to my mother's horror ... I thought it was a bit of an adventure. Yeah, I'll go out and have a look, see what it's like.... It didn't bother me.
Orientation	Well, we were in [coastal town] when my letter came through and Mum said, 'Do you want me to open it?' 'Yes, please.'

continued

Narrative 5.15 continued

Wendy: other occupation family, two parents, four children

Complication	'Ohhhhh – [remote town]!' she said. I said, '[remote town], [remote town], where's that?' 'It's west, you know.'
Evaluation	At college, the big joke was always you get [remote town B].... It was always a bit of a joke.
Orientation	So I was ringing Mum from a call phone and so we went back to the place where we were staying and I was saying, 'I've got [remote town].'
Complication	'Where's [remote town]?' 'Yeah, all right. Let's get a map out.' Okay, so we looked up the map of Queensland and it said, like, G10 or something and we go, G, 10 [mimes plotting co-ordinates on map] and Mum's going, 'Of course, you're not going out there!'
Resolution	I said, 'Well, of course I am going out there. I've got a job!' So I did. I came out.
Coda	I had a wonderful time. Met my husband.

Of the four professional women whose stories followed this variation, all their partners were less credentialed than themselves, therefore less motile. This difference impacted on the family's capacity to later contemplate moving to optimise family projects or resolve emerging complications. A nurse working in a remote town and married to a local man explained the conundrum this created for her family in progressing their children's educational prospects.

Narrative 5.16 'If we lived down there'

Lily: nurse family, two parents, four children

Orientation	Yeah, and so what's happened with [C1] is that in Grade 10 she got this scholarship through the school to [Brisbane university]. It was this family ... they started a scholarship for kids in country areas. It's been amazing. She has got $1000 in Grade 11, $1000 in Grade 12, and then when she goes to university at [Brisbane university], she'll get $4000 for each year.... It'll help for accommodation.
Complication	But we've just come to a huge thing with [C1], because I went off to Centrelink[1] to try and get Youth Allowance, and we can't get it because we earn too much money ... we're earning too much money and we can't get Youth Allowance, or Living Away From Home Allowance, or anything for [C1].
Evaluation	So yeah, and [C1] – she's so keen to go to university. I've seen kids that stay back and do a gap year,[2] and it can be fantastic for them, but sometimes it actually stops them going to university altogether ... I don't know. And it's because she wants to do it, I can't say, 'Well, no, you've got to do a gap year so you can get Youth Allowance,' because I can't do that to her ... I mean, all that's fine and she's talked about these shared houses, and I don't know how much they would cost. But it's a huge thing.

Resolution?   If we lived down there, she would live at home and go to university, and there wouldn't be that living expense.

Complication   Now there's suddenly this living expense that we have to try and find, and we can't get absolutely no Living Away From Home Allowance or anything, unless we earn less money. If we earn less money, I keep thinking, well, then, how do we pay for everything? ... So I don't know what to do. It's a big thing at the moment.... Well, I've said to [partner], we could move down there, but he said, 'Because I'm not qualified,' he said, 'I wouldn't get a job with the [government department] down there' ... he just doesn't have any tertiary qualifications. So he's nearly 50 and he doesn't want to try and find a job in the city, and I can understand that.

Resolution?   Now he's talking about maybe, 'If I go out and work on the mines – see if I can get a job in the mines'

Complication   – and then he's away from home and I don't know.... Well, it wouldn't be good for [C3]. [C3]'s the only boy in the family and he's going, [C3]'s struggling a bit now too. I would love to be able to send [C3] away to a boarding school, because he's the only boy in the family. His football has completely finished because he's now in the under-14s and there's no footballers this year. Cricket's going to completely finish for him because – he needs something.... The other issue is we wouldn't be able to sell our house here in [remote town]. There's houses everywhere in town for sale at the moment. Nothing is really selling and we would definitely not get what our house is worth. If we sold our house below value, we wouldn't have enough money then to buy a house in [regional centre].... So I feel that ... I don't know.

Resolution   We actually don't know what to do at the moment.

Notes
1 Centrelink is the Australian government agency that handles welfare entitlements.
2 A 'gap year' is a year taken between schooling and further study for recreational or employment purposes. Here, the narrator is referring to the potential in a gap year to earn sufficient income to meet eligibility requirements and be considered an independent of parents for the purposes of Youth Allowance.

By this narrative, family life in the remote town has arrived at a crucial but unresolved juncture where children's educational prospects and the partner's work prospects can no longer be reconciled. As a nurse, she is confident of finding work if they were to move to an urban or regional centre, but her partner is much less confident. A very similar conundrum is described by a teacher in the same remote town, who works through possible solutions to her desire for 'more opportunities' for her children in upper secondary schooling.

Narrative 5.17 'That's happening a lot'

Nancy: teacher family, two parents, two children

Orientation	I just don't think I could send my kids away in Year 7. No. I think that we'll give the high school a go but there's probably a fairly big option for boarding school for 10, 11 and 12 ... I would say that probably 90 per cent of teachers send their children to boarding school.
Complication	Just that they miss their children dreadfully and the kids do as well. I often see kids don't necessarily want to stay away and a lot of times come home.
Evaluation	I wouldn't say probably all – probably less than 90 per cent, now that I think about it. There's not a lot of teachers that still have kids here and are making that decision. So it's probably only really for less than 10 ... that I can think of. A lot more families are sending their children away to boarding school, now more than ever ... is harder financially unless your child can get a scholarship.
Complication	That's why I think that it's important that the 10, 11 12 – my kids have that choice and they're not limited to limited choices that we have here ... I'm starting to get itchy feet. I could see – I think mainly because of the kids – I can see more opportunities for them in a bigger centre but I'm not prepared to move half of my family educationally until [partner] is ready to make that same commitment.... So discussion under ... work in progress that way ... I'd like better opportunities for my kids and to get those better opportunities in that environment, that's a lot more financial for a family.
Resolution?	That option of moving away is a good option
Complication	but I won't do it if [partner] won't even be prepared to come with us.
Evaluation	We see it [living apart for children's education] through school, through our families, our country families on the land. Probably in the last couple of years there's been a handful of families who have basically – Dad stays on the land, Mum moves to [regional centre] with the kids or moves to the town. That's happening a lot. I've got a very good girlfriend who lives on a big property out [small town] way, up that way and she's near [rural town]. She and the kids live in [rural town] during the week, the dad stays home and they travel home for the weekend. Yeah, it's happening a lot ... I've got probably, now that I'm thinking of it, probably five or six friends that have done the same thing. Depends – I've seen families who've continued to be separated and I don't think that it seems to be working, I think.
Resolution	That's why I've always said I would never do that if [partner] wasn't prepared to come with us
Evaluation	because I've seen my friend in that particular instance. She's moved down and she was hoping that her husband would follow but he hasn't. He just doesn't want to go and it is difficult for her. She's got two secondary students in [regional centre] and she finds it very hard to cope on her own.

Boarding school is raised as a likely option, but reluctantly so given its emotional and financial toll. This professional tells of 'itchy feet' and her consideration of living apart from her locally embedded partner during the week, a solution other families in the district have used with more or less success. The low motility of the partner renders moving problematic and her pursuit of educational opportunities for her children renders staying problematic. The necessary condition for mobility that she outlines in her resolution decides their circumstances for the moment, but her 'itchy feet' suggest this is a temporary solution.

These cases show how this gendered variation on the optimising circuit can delay, but does not erase, the gravitational pull back to larger educational markets. However, it produces other forces that make it difficult. The tension between the male partner's work role and children's education in some ways resonates with the ADF families' circumstances. However, moving offers a resolution to educational complications for these professional families, where it was immobility that offered a resolution to educational complications for the ADF families.

A further permutation on this variation was how marital breakdown could precipitate a move away from the remote home, thus reconstituting a circuit but under a different logic and urgency. We interviewed a female teacher who was a single parent of three children living in the regional centre. She had met and married a local farmer in her career's fourth rural placement, then established a family home on his isolated station, while planning distance or bush schooling for her children:

> Then I walked out February 2001 … I walked out with all the babies, yes …
> I left [exP] with that house that we built. Yes, I left him set up and I walked
> back into here, and lived with my mum and dad … with the children. Yes
> all three.
>
> (Suzanna, teacher family)

Her narrative of a sudden relocation mirrors aspects of the ADF families' narratives, with a similar learning curve around waiting lists and school zoning. However, her choice of where to move took her to the supportive base of her extended family, from which she could rebuild her professional career.

A final variation on the optimising circuit is where achieving the route back into the larger urban/regional centre becomes more problematic than anticipated. In the following narrative, a police officer in a rural town tells of the institutional conditions that he feels are making it harder for police families to achieve that final leg of their planned circuit. His coda reflects on the number of contingencies that must align to make a move 'back' possible for his dual police career family.

Narrative 5.18 'But to go back is so very hard'

Ian: police family, two parents, two children

Orientation	In the last ten years, the amount of females that have been introduced to the police service has increased. We're trying to move. The police service is trying to get that 50/50 balance.
Complication	But now that they've introduced more females, naturally there's been a progression towards police couples. Now, what the police service is experiencing is that because police couples are at different stages of their profession, one will take a promotion there, then they'll drag the other one in, and then this one will get a promotion there, and they'll drag them. They're getting a surplus of ranks, because to accommodate when the wife goes over here, they don't have to hand his rank back, but they've got a glut of sergeants, so to speak, over here.
Resolution	So now they're saying, 'In the private sector, if you want to apply for a job, you have to consider your family before you go. If your family doesn't fit in, then you don't go.' Do you know what I mean? Now they're trying to introduce that to the police,
Evaluation	and there's a bit of a resistance from the police, because we may go out here, but to go back is so very hard.
Coda	Now when [partner] and I want to leave here, we have to find two jobs, not one job. Plus we then have to – we'll make a decision about kids and schooling, but then we have to find, if we want to go to a particular area, we have to find the school plus the two spots. That restricts us.

The following extended narrative comes from another police officer in a rural town who, in anticipation of a promotion, was undertaking a pre-emptive process of working through exactly such contingencies to achieve a family move 'back' to the urban seaboard. He tells of the difficulty in placing his three children in the schooling sectors of choice, and the family's high priority on minimising school transitions.

Narrative 5.19 'If, if, if – if I get promoted, if we move, if you go to this school'

Chris: police family, two parents, three children

Orientation	R: How about your partner? Yeah, she'd be happy to move to the Gold Coast.... She said she'd rather go to the Gold Coast because it's more long term there. If we get there this year, we can have a look at the schooling, so what we've done already is we've gone down to the Gold Coast and saw what changes will impact on our decision-making process on what we're going to do. Last school holidays we went to the Gold Coast, kind of looked at it, okay, we've got to start thinking.

Complication   Now if I do get offered a spot, it's going to be August, September. Most schools would have already finished their enrolments for the next year, so we went to a Catholic school down there. We thought because our kids were in the Catholic system already that it would be the same process and we've realised it's a lot different on the Gold Coast. [Remote town A] and [regional town B] accept almost anyone because the enrolment figures aren't up to what they can get to, so they'll take anyone. Went to a school on the Gold Coast. [Partner] went and spoke to them, said, 'We want to enrol our kids next year which is Years 7, 4 and 1.'
They said, 'Yeah, no worries. We'll put you on the waiting list with the other fifty people we've got on our waiting list. We can't guarantee you a spot.' And [partner] said, 'We're already in the Catholic system.' She said, 'Have you been baptised?' 'No.' 'You've got no hope – you have to get baptised, then you have to go on a waiting list.' If we get one of our kids in the school you then go to the top of the list because they look after the siblings in the school.... Went to another Catholic school. They said exactly the same thing – 'Not baptised, waiting list, no guarantee.'

Evaluation   My way of thinking, well, we're moving, I'm not going to put our kids into one school for six months and then wait for them to say, 'We can put you in,' and have to move again. That's why we've got to make a decision now. If we can't get our kids in a school, we don't know what we're going to do.

Resolution   So we went to another school. We went to [independent school] on the Gold Coast.

Complication   They said, well, Grade 7 at their school is high school and 'Your son', the way that their schooling's worked, 'will be a year behind the level of what we're doing.' ... Yeah, so we went to another school and they said, 'Okay, we can get your daughter in Grade 3 probably, no worries. Once she's in the other two go to the top of the list ... except your boy won't get in because that's high school' ... that's their big intake.

Resolution   And they suggested, well, if he goes to that school, he does Grade 6 again ... the way we're looking at it and explaining it to [C1], he's not repeating as such. He's going to be the top year of primary school, so next year here he'd be ... top year in Grade 7. Here he'd be a top year at primary in Grade 6 and then he goes to high school. He'll be the oldest in his class because they have a cut-off of June, so he's born on 22 June, so if he goes there he'll be the youngest in Grade 7 and he'll be behind because that school in particular ... it's a different type of school.

Evaluation   Anyway, he likes it.... He wants to be the oldest kid in his class, instead of being the youngest. We said to him, if you go to this school – and what we're saying to him is if, if, if – if I get promoted, if we move, if you go to this school, you know, this is what happens ... I'm not going to find out anything till September. If we then start ringing around it's going to be too late,

continued

Narrative 5.19 continued

Chris: police family, two parents, three children

Resolution   so we've already paid deposits on schools without even knowing that I'm going there, to try and secure ... because what we've looked at, with my promotion too, I've put Gold Coast/ Brisbane, so we're hedging our bets. If I get Brisbane, so we are trying to look at somewhere halfway.... What we're doing is we're picking our school first, okay, because what's most important to us is getting the kids' education, so we're picking the school first. If I get Gold Coast, we'll move to Gold Coast then they'll just go to school. If I get Brisbane, we'll live at [school suburb] somewhere [around the Gold Coast hinterland] and I'll commute every day.... So we're picking their school first,

Complication but we're finding it very hard to find a school so we've made an application, we've sent all the principals' reports and teachers' letters to them, put the application in. There's still no guarantee that we're going to get all three kids in there because they've said, well, there'll be probably ... we can probably get that one, [C2] in and if [C1] does Grade 6 we can probably get him in, but once again Grade 1 for next year is very hard ... Yeah, and they've said that, basically, we'll be able to accept those two. We said, 'Well, what do we do with the other one?' They said, 'Well, you're going to have to put her in another school' until they ring up, and they say a lot of people don't get all their kids, they just pull out. They said, 'Look, generally, nine times out of ten we might say no, no, no and no. Day one, two kids mightn't turn up.... It could take one day. It could take a week. It could take three months.'

Evaluation   Like if they said to us, 'No chance, you have to put him in another school and the year after we'll get him in', I would say no because I'm not going to move [C1] from here to another school to another school.... Once, if it happens, we will stay there in that. They'll stay at that school for the rest of their schooling.

Coda   Oh yes, so basically I always try and get promoted, but there's more opportunity in Brisbane and Gold Coast; it's a bigger area and there's more positions available if we can just get down there ... so we're trying to plan as much as we can for the future.

By this telling, the family's first preference for schooling in the religious sector is not based on religious affiliation, but rather inherited from their school of choice in the limited rural market of their current location. Despite considerable difficulties placing their children in this sector and in the independent sector, this professional family do not contemplate the public sector as an option. They are prepared to pay booking deposits at multiple schools 'without even knowing that I'm going there'. Resolution lies in, first, agreeing to an extra year's schooling for the eldest and, second, 'hedging our bets' with arrangements for two possible eventualities. From the coda, we can appreciate that the degree of strategy, planning and prudential insurance invested towards optimising children's education is equally optimising the career trajectory, but the efforts described demonstrate what is considered non-negotiable. They are prepared to move their children, but only once, to a school of choice. This combination of conditions becomes exacting and fraught when faced with schools' booking practices.

This section has exemplified four variations on the optimising circuit whereby unfolding events impacted on the projected circuit. These included: the emergence of family complications that claimed priority over optimising the career; finding that the rural/remote location fulfilled family projects; the (typically female) professional marrying into a rural locality; and difficulty in accomplishing the final move 'back'. Nevertheless, the professional family could exercise spatial autonomy in deciding to leave or to stay, as conditions changed.

Counter-narratives

Next we present a set of counter-narratives that do not construct an optimising circuit. These include the mobile career movers being cases whose routes continued to exploit career opportunities across rural/remote locations, and the less mobile who are invested in rural settings. These counter-narratives also produce their own rubbing points, whereby intersubjective concerns within the family can disrupt plans.

The following narrative came from a teacher interviewed in a remote town. She had three children, one of whom was doing senior secondary school in a regional boarding school, and a new partner whose own career had temporarily taken a back seat to allow her to pursue a promotional career path while her star was rising. She was waiting on notification of promotional vacancies across the state, but had to filter these according to opportunities for her second child.

Narrative 5.20 'If an opportunity arises, the door opens, I'm going to walk through and off I go'

Yvonne: teacher family, two parents, three children

Abstract | R: What are you going to do with daughter 2 next year?
I don't know. I do not know.

Orientation | I've been told that I have capability for the next banding, okay? So in that, it's a primary school, so the type of school that I'd be at would be a bigger centre. So somewhere like [coastal town] or – you know, that sort of area that will have a number of different primary schools. So I'm hoping that a place will come up that will have a high school that she could fit into nicely.... It's all up in the air ... The preferences come out tomorrow, so I have to then say where I'd like to go.

continued

Narrative 5.20 continued

Yvonne: teacher family, two parents, three children

Complication	So there may not be one at my band, so I may not be going anywhere, so then, what does she do next year?
Evaluation	I mean, she would dearly love to stay with us, but there's not going to be any girls here ... yeah, how do I reconcile these? ... Because of what I know about education, I'm not panicking at this stage. I know that she'll get what she needs here, in terms of academic life. In terms of social and even the sporting will decrease, because once again, up into high school years, she – it probably wouldn't worry her too much.... It's just that she hasn't got the competition here to egg her along that bit more. So academically, not worried. I could sit here for the next two years and not be fazed at all, because she will do well and my youngest son will do very well ... I'm not worried about that at all. Like, if we move, will the other schools match up?
Complication	My husband would love to go back to the [coast], though I'd rather eat rocks.... Life goes on. He just keeps telling me that 'Wherever you want to go, wherever you're happy' ... and I'm – well, you know, 'Decisions need to come from both ways. You need to have your input. Whatever you want to do,'
Evaluation	but see with his job as a [occupation], if he goes back to the coast, there's no work there anywhere ... so I sort of rub my hands together and go, 'Goodie for me!' I would like to go up north.... Lifestyle. I love the warmth. I don't like the cold at all. Because it's a part of Queensland I haven't lived in, as well. Just something different. I'm that sort of person. If an opportunity arises, the door opens, I'm going to walk through and off I go ... I don't care whether I'm promoted, demoted or go back into the classroom.
Resolution	I've already said to my boss, 'If I don't get anything,' and I don't know whether it's just me talking or whether I'd really do it, 'I'll go back into the classroom next year'.... Then they say, 'Well, where do you want to go to?' I don't know.... Just wait and see what happens. I suppose
Coda	– that's how I sort of live my life, in that what will be, will be. Yes, I do a little bit of planning. See, when [C1] was born, I had her enrolled at a school before she was – well, before she was born, sort of thing, okay? ... In [regional centre]. Yeah, she was enrolled in a school there for when she went to Year 1. I used to be very much like that, but now I'm 'What will be, will be' and when the door opens, that's when I'm meant to walk through.

This narrative's coda describes a very different, highly motile disposition towards family mobility, with its relish in new unexplored opportunities. The only condition stipulated for relocation is whether the next location offers comparable schooling. This parent's own professional knowledge ('what I know about education') is mobilised to monitor her children's progress and prospects, and to allay the typical middle-class anxieties ('I'm not panicking at this stage'). Her evaluation of their remote town is alert to the diminishing extra-curricular opportunities for her children, but this is balanced by this confidence in their academic progress. In this way, she can reconcile pursuing promotion in rural/ regional settings with educational strategy for her children. Her assessment of her partner's prospects in the second evaluation mitigates consideration of his preferences, thus reversing the typical gendered bargain around whose career to privilege.

By this telling, this career mover had thus far been able to make things work. Another narrative from a male teacher interviewed in the regional centre describes how his similarly motile disposition and interest in career-focused mobility is curtailed by the family complication of a child born with high medical needs.

Narrative 5.21 'We changed our tune'

Michael: teacher family, two parents, four children

Orientation   When she fell pregnant we decided we would move back to southeast Queensland

Complication   and at that point we were in two frames of mind. We weren't sure if we wanted to be at the [coast] or come back locally to [regional centre] where my family and her family were.

Resolution   We ultimately decided that we wanted to come back this way.

Evaluation   Well, here's the thing. Yes and no there was [promotion opportunities]. At that point I think we wanted to come back this way with our [transfer] points ... and if anything my intention was to at some point to travel, go back out west. We had seen you can live anywhere

Resolution   but we decided we would come back this way and just see how we handled having a child.

Complication   It was when my second-born, my son was born, with the health problems we changed our tune. I was on ... District Principal's Relief and I did some work as Acting Principal ... I'd come back this way, we had moved back to [regional centre] in 2004 ... 2006 brought the birth of my son [C2] in January. Now at that point my wife was going to take leave that year anyway knowing that we were going to have a child.

Resolution   From that point on she never returned to work ... I pull off the Acting Principal Relief and I went back on class teaching.... Yes, back in the classroom.

Evaluation   I just can't really commit to being in, like, any management or promotion positions because, and it had been said to me from management, perhaps it would be a good idea not for me to do that because of family commitments. Ultimately, when it came to things like that, I tended to put family first.

continued

Narrative 5.21 continued

Michael: teacher family, two parents, four children

Coda	I still contemplate taking a job out west to seek a promotion, to be honest, I do.... Like, deep down, that's what I would have liked to have done. I still contemplate it. Logistically I don't, my wife has said to me, 'That's fine, you can do that but I'm not coming with you.' I still feel long term, like when I look at retirement age, I will be working for another 35 years. I think in that time there is still a lot of opportunity to follow that trail.

While he had originally planned to continue rural/remote positions to work up the promotional ladder ('we had seen you can live anywhere'), family circumstances changed, radically altering the motility of the family unit. By his coda, the promotional 'trail' remains unfinished business for this professional.

The narratives of these highly motile career movers contrast with those of more settled families we encountered in rural and remote settings, for whom their location was a lifestyle choice, not a temporary stepping stone. It was in this category that we encountered some professionals who themselves were raised in a rural setting. For example, we interviewed a female doctor with a young family living in the rural town in which she grew up. Her partner was a teacher who took prime responsibility for family duties. She told of her preference for rural settings, and her time as a bonded rural scholarship holder.

Narrative 5.22 'They owned me'

Beth: doctor family, two parents, three children

Abstract	R: What were the conditions of the bond at that stage?
Orientation	That [the health department] owned me so they could send me wherever they liked.... Well I did three years and – you're bonded for three years.... Then I moved to [rural town].
Complication	Basically I was told.
Evaluation	I didn't mind at all. I requested [rural town].
Resolution	Well, [partner] came in January and I came in July.
Coda	So you ask where you want to go, you apply. So being female and Australian-trained, you go wherever you want ... I was always planning to go rural. So really he moved here because I was planning to move here.

By this telling, the conditions of the bonded scholarship suited her and her partner, and she achieved exactly the location she hoped for. Her coda mentions being female and being 'Australian-trained', which distinguishes her from doctors recruited from overseas, who are subject to more stringent requirements to fulfil registration. By her experience, these attributes make her a rare and valuable commodity, enhancing her spatial autonomy. Being a middle-class professional, she is predictably mindful of the limited educational market available in her rural locality. In the next narrative she outlines her thinking around educational strategy for secondary schooling.

Narrative 5.23 'I don't know yet really'

Beth: doctor family, two parents, three children

Abstract	I don't know yet. It depends what the girls are into and what they're up to, really. When they get towards the end of primary school. I'm not sure. I probably think at the moment we're leaning towards boarding school.
Orientation	Probably boarding school or we're relocating for a few years.
Complication	But it depends what the girls are like.
Evaluation	Because, yeah, [C1]'s a bit of a softy. So she may want to stay in [regional town B] I would have thought till Grade 10 maybe. I think [C2] will be trying to talk us into letting her go in Grade 7.
Resolution	We'll just see. 'I don't know' is the answer.
Evaluation	But it doesn't – it honestly doesn't faze me. I think there's positives and negatives on both sides. I went to boarding school and I don't feel too scarred.
Complication	Well, I was a little bit stressed [about bookings] for a while because all my friends in Brisbane have their children booked in on the way home from hospital into high schools.
Evaluation	I've spoken to lots of people around this area and it's actually not that big a deal.
Coda	I mean, boarding schools are too expensive and still out of the reach of a lot of people. But if you do want boarding school, they're pretty easy, you can go wherever you like.

Her response does not consider local schooling in the final years, only the options of boarding school or family relocation for this stage. As a rural child herself, she is comfortable with boarding school and the solution it offers the rural/remote professional family. In her coda, she also points out that this option remains open to those with the material resources and will not rely on booking places well in advance. With this card up her sleeve, she can afford to be more relaxed about this phase than her urban counterparts. With all these dimensions of spatial autonomy at her disposal, she chooses to stay in this rural town.

Across our transect, boarding school became more attractive and imaginable as an educational strategy for settled rural/remote professional families, but at considerable cost which government subsidies do not cover. These costs became the educational complication in narratives of extended rural service. In this vein, a police officer described the prospect of mounting financial pressure from educating his six children in Catholic boarding schools. He has worked for seven years in a remote town where schooling is not offered beyond Year 10. Over time, as he explains, groups within the community who favour the religious or independent sector of the educational market have established the norm that boys in particular leave for boarding school for Year 7, rather than wait for Year 8, which would attract some government subsidy.

Narrative 5.24 'We've got to find 20-odd grand'

Peter: police family, two parents, six children, pregnant

Orientation	But there was a proportion of boys here that went down to [all-boys Catholic school] so we went down. You look on the net and you can compare prices and that.
Complication	Because, bear in mind in Grade 7, he's a full fee-paying student; there's no assistance in Grade 7. Once he hits Grade 8 you get a bit of government assistance, which makes it a lot easier, but not Year 7.
Evaluation	We thought he was going to stay here till Year 7.
Complication	It's probably a bit of a boy thing, too, they get a bit of testosteroned up and all of a sudden … I think they outgrow the school.
Resolution	So we made the decision to send him in mid to late Grade 6, 'Right-o, he's going in Grade 7, he needs to go.'
Evaluation	He'll drive the school mad, and I think that's another reason why a lot of boys go, because at that stage, as I said, they just outgrow the school and they need more, more than what the school can give them.
Complication	He's going there for Grade 7, so we've got to find 20-odd grand that we hadn't budgeted for, of course, to send him away;
Resolution	but that's the decision we made and it was probably the best thing … even now with government assistance I probably still fork out probably about $12,000 a year.
Evaluation	This is one term at [all-boys Catholic school], $3900, that's one term … that's after the government subsidy. Every year, because it goes up, he's in middle school now, so it'll get a bit more; then when he goes to senior it will get a little bit more too.
Complication	R: So that bill's coming in every quarter … but then in a couple of years you'll have two of them there? Yes, and that's when you've got to decide is [remote town] the place for us? Can I afford to educate my children and live in [remote town]? That's what I've got to decide, yes.
Evaluation	Two is going to struggle, three, unless you're on – you get paid, I get paid X amount of dollars, X amount of dollars goes X far and how much money are you willing to spend on education or children? While you don't want to look at it in a purely economical point of view, as I said, my boy [C1], I don't know how much – that's one term – I'll spend on his education over the course of his secondary career. He's no Fulbright scholar. He won't go to university and I have no problems with that.… So we'll have subsidised kid at boarding school, and an unsubsidised one, so that year we'll probably have to find a spare 30 to 35 thousand.

| Complication | Well, wherever I go from here I'm going to earn less money unless something happens, and when you're at my age and you've got kids all coming through, finance is probably – your career isn't a big thing, it's where you can get the money. |
| Complication | Yes, and that's when you've got to decide is [remote town] the place for us? Can I afford to educate my children and live in [remote town]? That's what I've got to decide, yes. |

In this unresolved narrative, the first resolution to an educational complication produces the ensuing financial complications. In the later complications, he points out his conundrum in how, given the incentives associated with their current remote location, he has already maximised the family income, but this location in turn entails this excessive expenditure to fulfil educational aspirations that are not overly ambitious. This raises the possibility of moving as a solution to help balance the family equation.

A contrasting example of a settled rural professional juggling financial constraints and school choice comes from a nurse who returned to her rural home town with two young children to seek the support of her extended family after her partner's death. These were much more circumscribed economic circumstances than those of either the rural doctor or the police officer above, and in this case the local public high school was the only tenable option.

Narrative 5.25 'Once again, monetary reasons'

Ellen: nurse family, one parent, two children (blended family)	
Complication	R: So the high school choice?
Resolution	[Local rural high school], the same one I went to.
Orientation	We only had one other alternative
Complication	and I certainly couldn't afford to send him to [regional centre], to any of the schools there.
Resolution	Once again, monetary reasons – there was no way I could afford to.

She rules out alternatives that would incur fees. Such a locally contained and financially constrained resolution was more typical of the five non-professional parents we interviewed. For example, one such mother described a life moving around remote towns for her work opportunities as a council administrator, then settling in the same remote town as the police offered profiled above, on the strength of its small public high school: 'another reason to just come here – because they've got high school ... they go to Year 10 at the school and it's a small school and he loves small schools' (Tania, other occupation family with two parents and one child).

What do these contrasts between the strategies of settled rural families tell us about family mobility? First it makes evident that these families as much as other ones are mindful of educational opportunities, and work to achieve a work/life/education balance. Each family identified with a particular educational sector, thus moved on different planes within the educational market. The financial theme running through this set of narratives highlights how relative wealth allows some to transcend the limited choices of the geographically local educational market through boarding school choice. This choice allows these families to spatially separate career and lifestyle opportunities in rural/remote localities on one hand and educational strategy on the other. However, in the case of the remote police officer, this strategy was becoming untenable and at risk of precipitating a family move. Other less wealthy families moved on the public sector plane. The council worker, however, describes a schooling choice within this sector as a motivation behind a family move. Hence the educational market can be understood to exert its influence through family mobility decisions on the different planes.

Professionals and institutional solutions to their selective mobility

In this chapter's introduction, we outlined how the government departments responsible for ensuring human services in rural and remote communities have developed gamekeeping solutions using both 'carrot' and 'stick' approaches to attract and retain professionals. We interpret these as tactical adjustments to viscosity to create firstly a flow of mobility into these regions, then some 'stickiness' to delay their outward mobility. Given the spatial autonomy of these professionals through their surplus of possible locations, some of our interviewees told of how such institutional solutions could be sidestepped when other family projects warranted it. As an example, in the next narrative a female teacher with four children and a partner living in a rural town outlines her family's plan to move to southeast Queensland to further the eldest child's transition to the workforce, regardless of whether the employing department transfers her position.

Narrative 5.26 'Where to, I don't know'

Helen: teacher family, two parents, four children	
Orientation	We'll be transferring at the end of this year.
Complication	Even if I don't get a transfer,
Resolution	we're probably going to go anyhow. We'll just work it out.
Complication	Also, [C1] just went for interviews with government departments last week.
Resolution	Yes, there's a definite move … there's a definite move there.
Complication	Where to, I don't know.
Resolution	It'll just be closer to Brisbane.
Evaluation	I've said within two hours-ish of Brisbane. I don't necessarily want to move all the way back to Mum and Dad, but I want to get that closer so that I can.

Complication	And [CI] – they're going to be searching for a traineeship for her in the [government department], so she needs to probably be back.
Resolution	We will move – it costs a lot of money to move from here, so basically we would just move to wherever we could afford the rent … I would just take leave. I would just take leave for a year and do relief[1] work for a year. Do relief and contract, and then apply for the transfer again and say, 'I already live here.'
Coda	Basically when you do that, you're guaranteed of the transfer – when you already live there – because they go, 'Well, we need to fit you in.' They can fit you in generally to that area. I mean, I'm pretty open.

Note
1 'Relief' work is working on call to cover teacher absences at short notice. This is also termed 'supply' teaching.

The narrative's final resolution outlines a fallback strategy of 'just taking leave for a year', working on temporary and short-term contracts, and then approaching her employer as a resident in the new location. This strategy would require the family to pay removal costs, but the family's immediate priority rests on helping the eldest child to take up a work opportunity. Her coda provides her reading of how employment policies play out, a reading that may be fallible but nevertheless informs this strategy.

In the next narrative, another female teacher, a single parent of one child living in a remote town, reflects on her spatial options to optimise her child's education after having achieved permanency.

Narrative 5.27 'I have to rethink this'

Olivia: teacher family, one parent, one child	
Orientation	I suppose this is where I get a little bit different now. I'm permanent – I can take leave without pay.
Complication	I suppose to preface that, at the end of last term, the arts teacher at the high school has gone … The money to pay for an arts teacher has gone on other stuff so there's no money. So they currently don't actually have a dedicated arts teacher
Evaluation	and this is where I start going, 'Okay…. That's really important to her and also very important to me'…. It's something that when I heard that, I was like, 'Oh, okay. I have to rethink this.'
Resolution	The other consideration, I suppose, is at the end of Year 7 potentially taking leave without pay so that she does have access to a wider choice of subjects and so on. I don't know whether … whether I go back to [regional centre], I go to [a southern state], I don't know. A fairly major move, I think.

Her professional status and permanent tenure give her the capacity to 'take leave without pay' to relocate temporarily in the interests of her child's education, without the risks that other families would face. In this way, her permanency ironically temporarily frees her from the institutional solutions around fulfilling country service.

In the next narrative, an experienced police officer who had served in four rural settings before moving to the regional centre with his family tells how other officers have learnt to sidestep institutional solutions put in place to address rural/remote workforce shortages.

Narrative 5.28 'Pandering too much to too many people'

Brian: police family, two parents, two children

Abstract	R: Tell me, does the police force ever forcibly transfer people? It can do.... Look, it can happen but it doesn't ... the police has allowed itself get into a bit of a rut. I think that they can be the master of their own demise in some respects.
Complication	On the one hand, we have corporate governance here, which is the driver; on the next hand, we have crime over here. It's managed a lot of times like the CEO would manage BHP, yet it's a service and we can't pre-empt the next murder and these things. They're clashing in the middle and that seems to be the problem. Then, when you have all that, then we have all those laws ... which every employer is subject to which is your workplace health and safety ... discrimination, equity, diversity, all these different policies but they can sometimes clash with policing and its core roles. Does that make sense?
Evaluation	I mean, it has to be there, I understand, but ... I suppose there was a time – when I was [working in another occupation], for instance, if my managers had asked me to go to [rural town], 'We're going to transfer you out there', I wouldn't be game to say no. It'd be, 'okay, good!' and you'd go off because it was sold to you that when you joined, that's the way you – and the police force said that you could be transferred anywhere in the world but, pretty much, there's plenty of loopholes that you can create a position for yourself wherever you want.... The service is not hard enough on some of these things.
Orientation	I'll give you example. This is a loophole ... a new police officer, he has done his training. Once you finish training pretty much that's the only time that I see that the service really has that power to move you to another spot.
Complication	Now, that police officer got sent to a remote spot, didn't want to go there, kicked and screamed a lot, went there under duress,
Resolution	then resigned and then reapplied and then went through a programme for rejoiners which is designed for interstate police who come from Queensland or police who have got out and come back.... With that programme, to attract interstate police with experience you choose where you go. He resigned, reapplied, got accepted and said, 'I want to go to here,' and found that loophole and that's the way it worked.

Evaluation	The police, they haven't lost the plot; I understand that, but.... It's a delicate balance ... put it this way ... it's driven on a hierarchical structure, okay? I mean, it's drummed into you from day one. If it doesn't work that way, the whole structure falls down. I think, coming from my last job, I find that the hierarchy structure in the private sector was stronger and more rigid than it is here because there's so many courses of redress. If I'm not happy about a decision which is made ... in the police, I can argue the point or I can put in a grievance or I can review this person. In the private sector, if you didn't like what the boss said, 'Go and find another job!' and that's the way it was.
Coda	I'm actually speaking as I'm thinking but if I had more time to sit down and formulate a response, I think the police are losing track a little bit in respect to that ... I think we're over-accommodating. Does that make sense? ... We're actually pandering too much to too many people.

In the first complication, he grapples with the systemic contradiction between operating a public service that ought to be in place where it is needed and the various employment policies that protect the interests and rights of individual employees. He then offers an embedded narrative of a particular officer who exploited a 'loophole' to avoid serving in a remote location, to illustrate his sense that 'we're over-accommodating'.

Where the first two examples demonstrated the capacity of the professional to exercise spatial autonomy in the interests of family projects, this last account gives another, more critical, side to the story of how professionals can sidestep institutional solutions. In Chapter 8, we further explore the tension this police officer has identified between the public service ethic of the professions and their private interests.

Conclusion

This chapter has considered narratives of family im/mobility from a range of professionals with school-aged children living along a 900-kilometre transect through regional, rural and remote townships in Queensland, to understand the conditions under which they are prepared to live in these locations. Smaller localities cannot produce their own professionals, and hence have to rely on their mobility to attract such valuable, credentialed and registered expertise to staff essential human services. We have argued that this widespread demand ensures such professionals a heightened degree of spatial autonomy, being the capacity to choose whether, when and where to relocate. It also encourages employers of these professionals to adopt gamekeeping strategies and viscosity tactics to attract, then retain, staff in these localities. Our introduction outlined the con-founding issue associated with this same group of middle-class professionals, being their well-documented anxieties and investments in the educational market to protect their children's prospects. The narratives bore out our prediction that educational strategy would be accorded high priority in these families' mobility decisions.

We identified the 'optimising circuit' as the dominant pattern in the sequence of moves these families undertake, or plan to. Under this strategy, the professional is prepared to take an early rural/remote position to launch their career, then over time purposefully returns 'back' through promotional opportunities to larger population centres with deep, variegated educational markets, thus optimising both career and educational projects. For some families, this circuit was interrupted: when educational troubles emerged that deterred further movement; when a rural setting proved to be the optimal location; or when a local partner eventuated in the rural/remote location. For other families, moving 'back' was a complex negotiation of re-entering an educational market governed by waiting lists and booking fees.

We also presented narratives that did not operate under the logic of an optimising circuit. These included the more opportunistic career mover whose 'trail' aimed to exploit vacancies across rural and remote opportunities, while their children's education could accommodate such mobility; and the settled rural family that managed aspirations for their children's education according to their means. Each pattern was shown to produce its own complications that could precipitate a family decision to move or to stay as the solution. Where institutional constraints were in place to deter or defer such mobility, there was evidence of professionals being able and willing to undermine these in the interests of other family projects.

This capacity to choose the timing and placing of family mobility is an obvious point of contrast from the ADF families, who had very limited capacity to decide the circumstances of their moves. Most professional families could settle on a destination, while the ADF family experienced a sequence of transit stops. The professional families we interviewed at no point entertained the idea of the interstate moves that had proved so problematic for ADF families. The ADF family's sequence of moves privileged and protected the career, while children's education and spouse employment were left to absorb a disproportionate amount of stress from transitions and discontinuities. Beyond the initial move to gain a professional foothold, the professional families' move could progress both career and education projects – it was not an intersubjective either/or bargain, rather a both/and solution. In the same way, proximity to extended family for social support emerged as something that could be achieved when needed by professional families, while it couldn't be hoped for by the ADF families. Through their greater capacity for choice, the professional families could thus impose more conditions on moving or staying.

We would also point to similarities at a deeper level between ADF and professional families' narratives. In neither group was career untrammelled by family considerations. The dense, generative intersubjectivity of families at the child-rearing phase was evident in both narrative sets. Children's education as a project rose in priority over time to become pivotal in mobility decisions. This project created a time schedule for family careers – for making it 'back' on the circuit, for school fee budgeting, for getting out of the armed forces or for staying put.

We suggest that the interdependence between work projects and education projects within the same family unit means that professional workforce shortages in rural/remote areas will not be amenable to policy interventions that only address employment conditions and incentives. The shortage is essentially a public issue that manifests in one domain, born of patterned private choices involving more characters and their projects in other domains. It is a complication for communities stemming from resolutions devised within family units. As a social phenomenon it folds back recursively on itself in the way human services such as schools in remote towns are deemed to be of insufficient quality to attract and retain the professionals needed to staff them. In this way gamekeeping such professionals to work in rural and remote localities amounts to a 'wicked' problem (Head 2008), by its complexity, from being symptomatic of other problems, in an open system that defies simplistic solutions that can be delivered within one government portfolio.

Chapter 6

Movers and stayers

The previous chapter shared interview narratives from professional families living in rural and remote localities that told of the various motivations, complications and familial concerns behind their comings and goings. In this chapter, we continue to focus on this particular fraction of the middle class, given their importance to marginalised localities which must rely on the mobility of these credentialed professionals and their families to sustain human services and viable communities. In this more quantitative analysis, we engage with the broader potential pool of such professionals, not just those in situ, through an online survey. The online survey sought to understand the motivators and inhibitors that mediated professionals' motility and their resulting mobility in terms of family relocations over the years. The design of the survey was informed by the qualitative phase reported in Chapter 5, but sought to gauge the correlative effects of the various factors the interviews highlighted.

The online survey consisted of four components. The first component captured the demographic features of the participants. The second component plumbed their attitudinal responses to questionnaire items that operationalised constructs of 'public good', 'private good', 'neoliberalism', 'location range' and 'motility'. The third component documented up to eight previous family relocations and captured the broad-brush reasons behind their most recent and prior family relocations, as well as the reasons behind decisions to stay in the current location. The final component invited participants' open responses to hypothetical career opportunities in three rural/remote locations. Here we analyse data emerging from the first three components, while Chapter 8 considers their responses to the hypothetical rural/remote opportunities, and their role of place and space in their family mobility.

Introducing the sampled professionals

The professional groups were selected to offer a cline of educational investments – from the minimal higher education and in-house certification of the police officer to a doctor's long-term investment in higher education and high status qualifications. Despite this variation within our category of 'professional', all these groups share the common attribute of working in a closed occupation whose membership relies on licensed registration and formal credentialing. They also provide essential human services that are underwritten by the public purse.

The link to the online survey was distributed through professional organisations and employers in Queensland, namely the Queensland Teachers Union, the Queensland Nurses Union, the Queensland Police Service and the Australian Medical Association Queensland, inviting members with responsibility for school-aged children to participate. Eventually 278 professionals responded to the online survey. This sample included 27 doctors, 134 nurses, 45 police and 72 teachers, ranging in age between 23 and 60. There were 60 male and 217 female respondents, while one participant did not indicate gender. There were more females in the doctor, nurse and teacher groups, and more males among police respondents.

While the majority of participants (241, 87.1 per cent) indicated that they had a partner in their household, all participants had dependent children in their households as the criterion for participation. More than half (142, 51.1 per cent) had two children. One child (52, 18.7 per cent) and three child (67, 24.1 per cent) households were also common. The number of children for the remaining varied from four to eight. Some respondents indicated that they had a child or children with special needs (46, 16.5 per cent) in their households and some had a child with special talents (37, 13.3 per cent).

Of all the surveyed professionals, 161 (57.9 per cent) were working full-time, 103 (37.1 per cent) were working part-time, and 14 (5 per cent) were either working in a casual position, fully committed to home duties or seeking jobs at the time of the survey. Of all the professionals who were working (273, 98 per cent), 212 (77.6 per cent) were employed in a government sector, 51 (18.7 per cent) were employed in the private sector or were self-employed, and 10 (3.7 per cent) were employed across both sectors.

The vast majority (245, 91.4 per cent) of respondents had achieved a bachelor degree or higher qualification. Table 6.1 shows the spread of highest qualifications within and across professional groups. In addition, 57 (20.5 per cent) of the professionals reported that they were undertaking further study. Their studies varied from professional training certificates to doctoral degrees. This level of ongoing investment in further study is further explored in Chapter 7.

We were also interested in typifying the internal balance of projects within family units. This interest was premised on the expectation that a (male) breadwinner family mode, with one career accorded clear priority, would enhance motility, while family units with two high priority career projects would find relocation more difficult. In terms of how roles were organised within the family unit, many respondents with partners considered the careers of the couple equally important and the couple equally responsible for family demands (117, 42.1 per cent). Others reported a variety of different family models, such as one of the couple being the breadwinner and the other being the homemaker (34, 12.2 per cent), or one of the couple's careers given priority with the other's career accommodating more family demands (83, 29.9 per cent).

Table 6.1 Respondent profession by highest educational qualification

Respondent profession	Highest education qualification								Total
	Senior secondary certificate	Certificate	Diploma	Advanced diploma/ associate diploma/degree	Bachelor degree or equivalent	Bachelor honours degree/graduate certificate/ diploma	Masters degree	Doctoral degree	
Doctor	–	–	–	–	6 (22.2%)	1 (3.7%)	20 (74.1%)	–	27 (100.0%)
Teacher	–	–	–	–	36 (50.0%)	20 (27.8%)	15 (20.8%)	1 (1.4%)	72 (100.0%)
Nurse	–	–	8 (6.0%)	–	82 (61.2%)	28 (20.9%)	16 (11.9%)	–	134 (100.0%)
Police	1 (2.9%)	5 (14.3%)	5 (14.3%)	4 (11.4%)	14 (40.0%)	3 (8.6%)	3 (8.6%)	–	35 (100.0%)
Total	1 (0.4%)	5 (1.9%)	13 (4.9%)	4 (1.5%)	138 (51.5%)	52 (19.4%)	54 (20.1%)	1 (0.4%)	268 (100.0%)

The combined family income of the surveyed professionals differed dramatically, both across the sample, and within each professional group. Table 6.2 shows the distribution of the professional groups across income categories.

Beyond these demographic features, our survey revealed a rich history of family relocations over their careers. The respondents were asked to recall up to eight family relocations following their professional training. They reported receiving their initial professional preparation in more than 80 different cities and towns, then working in over 330 different cities and towns across Australia. These places differed dramatically in terms of socio-economic status and setting, varying from metropolitan areas (such as Brisbane, Sydney and Melbourne), through regional centres (such as Toowoomba, Cairns and Mackay) and inland rural towns, (such as Roma, Emerald and Warwick), to remote outback communities (such as Quilpie, Cunnamulla and Winton).

To capture a sense of the social affordances of each place we used the Index of Relative Socio-Economic Advantage and Disadvantage (IRSAD) developed by the Australian Bureau of Statistics (2013). IRSAD summarises information about the economic and social conditions of people and households within an area, including measures of both relative advantage and disadvantage. A low score indicates greater relative disadvantage and a lack of advantage in general. For example, an area could have a low score if there were (among other things) many households with low incomes or many people in unskilled occupations and few households with high incomes, or few people in skilled occupations. Conversely, a high score indicates a relative lack of disadvantage and greater advantage in general. For example, an area may have a high score if there were many households with high incomes, many people in skilled occupations and few households with low incomes, or few people in unskilled occupations. This information allowed us to ask how the family careers of these professionals intersected with less privileged places and their communities.

From the qualitative phase reported in Chapter 5, we can appreciate how the decision-making behind professionals' relocations is multifaceted, seeking to reconcile career opportunities and investments for adults with educational strategy for children, and strategically optimise all these projects over time and space. To explore the more general nature and dynamics of professionals' mobility and motility dispositions in the broader survey sample, we developed constructs of 'public good', 'private good', 'neoliberalism', 'location range' and 'motility'. These constructs are explained in the next section.

Introducing the constructs

We developed the construct of 'public good' from theoretical premises regarding the ethic of public service, which has been 'a core aspect of the majority of codes of professional associations' (Saks 1995: 3). It refers to 'a duty to improve not only the well-being of the client, but also that of the wider community' (p. 4), which the professions have historically embraced in exchange for a virtual

Table 6.2 Respondent profession by annual family income

Respondent Profession	Annual family income (Australian dollars)											Total
	$31,200–$41,599	$41,600–$51,999	$52,000–$64,999	$65,000–$77,999	$78,000–$103,999	$104,000–$129,999	$130,000–$155,999	$156,000–$181,999	$182,000–$207,999	$208,000–$259,999	$260,000 or more	
Doctor	–	–	–	2 (7.7%)	–	3 (11.5%)	2 (7.7%)	1 (3.8%)	3 (11.5%)	5 (19.2%)	10 (38.5%)	26 (100%)
Nurse	2 (1.5%)	7 (5.4%)	13 (10.0%)	15 11.5%	27 (20.8%)	24 (18.5%)	20 (15.4%)	11 (8.5%)	5 (3.8%)	2 (1.5%)	4 (3.1%)	130 (100%)
Police	–	–	1 (2.2%)	1 (2.2%)	7 (15.6%)	9 (20.0%)	15 (33.3%)	7 (15.6%)	5 (11.1%)	–	–	45 (100.0%)
Teacher	1 (1.5%)	–	5 (7.4%)	10 (14.7%)	15 (22.1%)	8 (11.8%)	14 (20.6%)	10 (14.7%)	2 (2.9%)	2 (2.9%)	1 (1.5%)	68 (100.0%)
Total	3 (1.1%)	7 (2.6%)	19 (7.1%)	28 (10.4%)	49 (18.2%)	44 (16.4%)	51 (19.0%)	29 (10.8%)	15 (5.6%)	9 (3.3%)	15 (5.6%)	269 (100.0%)

monopoly of a particular body of knowledge or practice. It also acknowledges the public investment that subsidises professional education as a common good, and in turn legitimates public demands made of certain professions to benefit society as a whole. In line with this ethic of public service, 'professional groups subordinate their own interests to the wider interest in carrying out their work' (Saks 1995: 3). More simply, it refers to the expectation and ethos of broad altruism. In this way, our construct 'public good' plumbed the degree to which the professional felt a sense of duty attached to their qualifications, knowledge and skills which impinged on career decisions.

In contrast, our construct of 'private good' plumbed the degree to which individuals seek to pursue and garner private rewards and personal advantage from their professional qualifications and career, and the prioritisation of such concerns over any sense or claim of public duty. Marginson (1997) argues that, with growing marketisation of educational sectors, the formal credential is shifting from being construed as a public good to serving more as a private, positional good. Accordingly, we would expect there to be some tension and shift underway between aspects of public good and private good in professional credentials that might impact on family mobility decisions.

Our third construct of 'neoliberalism' also pertained to marketisation, but more particularly to the professional's strategies as parents in the education market on behalf of their children. Here, neoliberalism pertains to the global policy wave that has fostered market logic and the exercise of consumer choice to drive innovation and quality improvements in public sector services. Thus, neoliberal attitudes are those that endorse and subscribe to this logic, and neoliberal dispositions are those that engage actively with markets of choice, to pursue consumer preferences. The narratives in Chapter 5 showed how school choice was a prominent factor in family mobility plans and decisions, and we would expect this to be reflected in high scores for neoliberalism in our sample.

The construct 'location range' captured how wide a range of locations families would entertain as possible household locations. Those with strong affiliations to one particular site, or type of site (e.g. urban, coastal, rural or remote) for whatever reason thus have a highly restricted location range. The 'optimising circuit' that emerged as a pattern in Chapter 5 illustrates this particularity. Those who are open to suggestion and opportunity, with few limitations about where they might move, entertain a very broad location range. The counter-narratives of the 'career movers' in Chapter 5 would exemplify this disposition.

Our construct of motility operationalises Kaufman's (2002) concept thereof which we have outlined in Chapter 2. He defines motility as 'the system of mobility potential ... the way in which an actor appropriates the field of possible action in the area of mobility, and uses it to develop personal projects' (p. 1). He points to different aspects contributing to an individual's motility: 'elements relating to access (i.e. available choice in a broad sense), the skills (the competence required to make use of this access), and appropriation (evaluation of the available access)' (p. 38). We developed attitudinal statements along these lines to tap such skills, resources and dispositions within family units that serve to heighten or deflate the collective's motility.

Measurement models of the constructs

Each of these constructs, 'public good', 'private good', 'neoliberalism', 'location range' and 'motility', was operationalised through a set of attitudinal items using a seven-point Likert scale (see Appendix 1). Responses could range from 1 (don't agree at all) to 7 (totally agree). This design allowed us to treat the range of responses as proxy interval levels of measurement in line with common practice in educational research (Lehman 1991; Tabachnick and Fidell 2007).

Subsequent to conducting descriptive analysis, internal consistency reliability tests, and exploratory factor analysis, we developed and validated measurement models for these constructs. Initially, single-factor congeneric models were fitted then tested against the more parsimonious equivalent and tau models. Where single-factor models could not be fitted to the data, higher order models were developed. Taking account of individual and joint measurement error, the scale score for each construct can be computed as a continuous variable by multiplying the individual's raw score on each indicator by the proportionally weighted factor score of each indicator and summing (Rowe 2002). The next section offers a succinct summary of the measurement model and the scale score index for each construct.

Public good

A single-factor tau measurement model[1] for the construct 'public good' was specified as a latent variable with four indicators (see Table 6.3 and Figure 6.1). The model fitted well ($\chi^2 = 4.87$, df = 5, $p = 0.433$; RMSEA = 0.000 (0.000, 0.082), GFI = 0.991, TLI = 1.001, CFI = 1.000). The CFI and TLI values of equal to or greater than 1 perhaps indicate model overfit. However, given that the p value for the absolute fit measure is close to 0.05 a decision was made to retain the current model. The Squared Multiple Correlations (SMCs) associated with the four indicators were 0.45, 0.36, 0.53 and 0.48 respectively, all higher than the recommended lower cut-off value of 0.30 (Jöreskog and Sörbom 1996). Construct reliability was calculated as 0.46, which was only marginally lower than the recommended cut-off value of 0.50 (Fornell and Larcker 1981). Variance extracted by the construct was 58.81 per cent, exceeding the lower recommended value of 50 per cent (Fornell and Larcker 1981). Coefficient H was calculated as 0.77, higher than the recommended cut-off value of 0.70 (Hancock and Mueller 2001). These measures were indicative of the high reliability of the model. In addition, the tau model also demonstrated a good level of validity, with the claim for construct validity being supported by the model fit measures and the claim for convergent validity being supported by the significant regression weights of the four indicators. The scale score of the public good construct, indicating the

Table 6.3 Item set for the construct 'public good'

Code	Item
Pub2	I feel a strong obligation to give back to society.
Pub3	I think governments have the right to expect professionals to work in underserviced communities.
Pub5	I think as a professional I have a duty to serve in disadvantaged communities.
Pub7	As a professional, I feel a strong commitment to ensure that all communities are well serviced.

degree to which each respondent demonstrated such a professional ethic, was then calculated as:

$$\text{Public Good construct score} = \text{Pub2} * 0.240 + \text{Pub3} * 0.165 + \text{Pub5} * 0.324 + \text{Pub7} * 0.271$$

Private good

A preliminary reliability test of internal consistency was run on the four items developed to map the construct 'private good' (see Table 6.4). Cronbach's α associated with the construct 'private good' was equal to 0.38, much lower than the suggested value of 0.80 indicative of adequate internal consistency reliability (Kline 1999). In addition, all corrected item-total correlations were lower than the suggested value of 0.33 (Ho 2006). Deleting any indicator would not increase the value of Cronbach's α. Moreover, correlations between any two indicators were all below the suggested value of 0.30 (Field 2009). Based on these measures, a decision was made to treat the four items as mapping four individual variables as the suggested construct 'private good' was not consistently accounting for shared item variance.

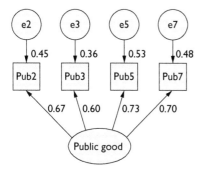

Figure 6.1 A single-factor tau model for public good (standardised estimates).

Neoliberalism

A single-factor tau measurement model for the construct 'neoliberalism' was specified as a latent variable with four indicators (see Table 6.5 and Figure 6.2). The model fitted the data well ($\chi^2(5)=5.78$, $p=0.328$; RMSEA$=0.024$ (0.000, 0.089); GFI$=0.990$, TLI$=0.985$, CFI$=0.987$). Construct validity was supported by the model fit and convergent validity was supported by the significant value of the regression weights. However, reliability measures were low (Cronbach's $\alpha=0.52$, SMCs<0.30, construct reliability$=0.21$, variance extracted$=41.15$ per cent, coefficient $H=0.52$). The low reliability scores may be a result of the items being mapped by a second unidentified construct other than the defined 'neoliberalism' construct. The 'neoliberalism' construct as defined did still account for approximately 41 per cent of the variance extracted in the items. Given this and the high level of model fit a decision was made to proceed with the construction of an index for the construct 'neoliberalism'. The scale score for the construct 'neoliberalism', indicating the degree to which each respondent demonstrated such attitudes as a parent, then became:

$$\text{Neoliberalism construct score} = \text{Neolib3} * 0.196 + \text{Neolib4} * 0.221 + \text{Neolib5} * 0.272 + \text{Neolib6} * 0.31$$

Table 6.4 Item set for the construct 'private good'

Code	Item
Priv1	I would only work in a remote community if there were strong financial incentives.
Priv2	I think an open competitive job market is the best way to encourage an equitable spread of professionals.
Priv3	I think professionals should be free to pursue their career opportunities as they choose.
Priv4	I think incentive payments are a good idea to attract professionals to hard-to-staff locations.

Table 6.5 Item set for the construct 'neoliberalism'

Code	Item
Neolib3	We strongly believe non-government schools offer a better education than government schools.
Neolib4	We choose where to live because of the quality of the schools in the area.
Neolib5	We think it's good if schools compete with each other in a market of choice.
Neolib6	The My School website plays an important role in informing our choice of school.

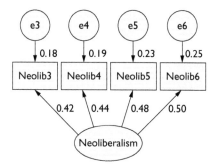

Figure 6.2 A single-factor tau model for neoliberalism (standardised estimates).

Location range

A one-factor congeneric measurement model for the construct 'location range' was specified as a latent variable with four indicators (see Table 6.6 and Figure 6.3). The data fitted the model well ($\chi^2(2)$ =2.68, p=0.262, RMSEA=0.035 (0.000, 0.130), GFI=0.995, TLI=0.989, CFI=0.996). Three out of four SMCs were above the cut-off value of 0.30; the construct reliability was calculated as 0.38; the variance extracted was 52.55 per cent; and the coefficient H was calculated as 0.74. These measures were indicative of an adequate level of reliability. Construct validity was supported by the model fit and the convergent validity supported by the significant value of the regression weights. The scale score for the construct 'location range' for each respondent then became:

$$\text{Location range construct score} = \text{LocRange1} * 0.160 + \text{LocRange3} * 0.362 + \\ \text{LocRange5} * 0.345 + \text{LocRange6} * 0.132$$

Motility

A higher-order congeneric measurement model with two factors for the construct 'motility' was specified as a latent variable with six indicators (see Table 6.7 and

Table 6.6 Item set for the construct 'location range'

Item code	Item
LocRange1	We are very open to the idea of working in rural or remote communities.
LocRange3	We are keen to experience life in a variety of settings.
LocRange5	We have an open mind about where we live.
LocRange6	We know where we want to raise our children. (Reverse)

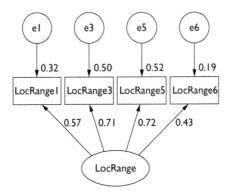

Figure 6.3 A single-factor congeneric model for location range (standardised estimates).

Figure 6.4). The higher-order factor was termed 'emergent motility' in Figure 6.4, with indicators two, three, four, and five loaded on the first factor 'Motility1' and indicators one and seven loaded on the second factor 'Motility2'. The model converged with a non-significant $\chi^2(8)$ value of 11.22 ($p=0.190$), a RMSEA value of 0.038 (0.000, 0.086), and GFI, TLI, and CFI values of 0.987, 0.989, and 0.994 respectively. These measures indicated good model fit.

The model demonstrated high reliability: all the SMCs were above 0.30. *Stratified* α was calculated as 0.85 following Cronbach *et al.* (1965) and the maximal reliability *H* was calculated as 0.95 following Li *et al.* (1996). The model also demonstrated high validity, with the construct validity confirmed by the model fit and the convergent validity confirmed by the significant values of

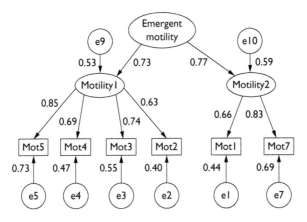

Figure 6.4 A higher-order congeneric measurement model with two factors for motility (standardised estimates).

Table 6.7 Item set for the construct 'motility'

Item code	Factor	Item
Mot2	Motility1	We often look for work opportunities outside the town we're in.
Mot3		We intend to stay in this location for the next ten years. (Reverse)
Mot4		We are prepared to move towns to get ahead in my/our career/s.
Mot5		We often talk seriously about moving to another town.
Mot7	Motility2	We would avoid moving our children while they are in school.
Mot1		We would be very reluctant to change schools once we've enrolled our children.

the regression weights. The scale score for the higher level construct 'motility' then became:

$$\text{Emergent Motility construct score} = \text{Mot2} * 0.082 + \text{Mot3} * 0.116 + \text{Mot4} * 0.095 + \text{Mot5} * 0.225 + \text{Mot7} * 0.326 + \text{Mot1} * 0.156$$

Characteristics and attitudes of the more motile and mobile professionals

In order to explore the characteristics and attitudes of more motile and mobile professionals, a multiple regression model was developed to analyse how selected demographic features and pertinent attitudinal propensities appear to impact dispositions of motility and impact on the number of family relocations. As such, demographic and attitudinal variables are treated as independent variables or predictor variables, while 'motility' and 'number of moves' are treated as dependent variables or outcome variables. Using the 'backward elimination'[2] strategy offered by SPSS, we were able to identify the most likely predictors of 'motility' and 'number of moves'.

The more motile professionals

On the basis of the previous qualitative phase, ten independent variables were selected to be entered into the regression model as the more meaningful predictors for 'motility'. As indicated in Table 6.8, the model suggests 'location range' to be the most powerful predicator for motility (Standardised Beta=0.66, $t = 12.68$, $p < 0.001$).

Table 6.8 also helps to portray the more motile professional family. They tend to: be younger in age; work in a non-full-time job; be currently studying; have a

Table 6.8 Significant predictors for motility

Predictors	Unstandardised		Std. Beta	t	p
	B	SE. B			
(Constant)	−49.10	24.60	–	−2.00	0.047
Year of birth	0.03	0.01	0.11	2.08	0.039
Work full-time or not	−0.26	0.15	−0.09	−1.76	0.080
Current study	0.58	0.19	0.16	3.11	0.002
Family income	−0.08	0.03	−0.12	−2.32	0.022
No. of moves	0.06	0.03	0.11	2.05	0.041
Public good	−0.12	0.06	−0.11	−2.07	0.039
Neoliberalism	−0.18	0.06	−0.15	−2.91	0.004
Location range	0.71	0.06	0.66	12.68	0.000
Priv3	−0.11	0.06	−0.09	−1.66	0.098
Priv4	0.13	0.06	0.10	2.06	0.041

lower family income; have experienced a greater number of family relocations; report a weaker sense of public good; be less swayed by neoliberal attitudes when selecting schools for their children; entertain a wider range of family household locations; and/or be more attracted by incentive payments to serve in hard-to-staff locations. These ten independent variables significantly contributed to 'motility', explaining 52 per cent of the variance (see Table 6.9). We could conjecture that this set of characteristics describes professionals in an earlier career and family phase, willing to contemplate a wide range of locations as a way to get a start or to get ahead.

The more mobile professionals

Similarly, we could identify characteristics and attitudes associated with more mobile professionals. 'Number of moves' was used as a measure of professional families' mobility. In general, professionals with a greater number of moves tended to: be older in age; have their first children younger in age; have no children with special needs; take their first career position in a more disadvantaged town; have higher family income; report a higher level of motility; be more attracted by incentive payments to serve hard-to-staff locations; and/or be in favour of an open competitive job market that encourages an equitable spread of professionals (see Table 6.10). Interestingly, police demonstrated a

Table 6.9 Model summary – dependent variable: motility

R	R square	Adjusted R square	SE of the estimate	R square change	F change	df1	df2	Sig. F change	Durbin–Watson
0.74	0.55	0.52	1.00	−0.004	1.63	1	185	0.204	2.03

greater number of moves than nurses, while there was no statistically significant difference between any other two professional groups in terms of number of moves.

Although we have a variety of meaningful predictors for professionals' mobility, these predictors only account for 26 per cent of the variance of number of moves (see Table 6.11). The bulk of the variance of mobility in our data remains unexplained. This might suggest professional family mobility to be a complicated biographical event. The current research design cannot capture this complexity completely but does offer some useful indicators for future research. The analysis also suggests that the social problem of underserviced communities stemming from professional families' selective mobility will not be amenable to simple policy solutions that attempt to address any single dimension.

Reasons behind the decisions for moving and staying

Our theoretical approach to family mobility outlined in Chapter 1 foregrounds the role of reflexivity in social processes: 'to consider themselves in relation to their (social) contexts and vice versa. Such deliberations are important since they form the basis upon which people determine their future courses of action – always fallibly and always under their own description' (Archer 2007: 4). In this

Table 6.10 Significant predictors for number of moves

Predictors	Unstandardised		Std Beta	t	p	Collinearity statistics	
	B	SE. B				Tolerance	VIF
(Constant)	141.35	67.48	–	2.09	0.037	–	–
Year of birth	−0.17	0.03	−0.41	−5.05	0.000	0.55	1.83
Year of birth (Child 1)	0.10	0.04	0.19	2.31	0.022	0.55	1.80
Family income	0.17	0.07	0.15	2.44	0.016	0.93	1.07
Priv2	−0.24	0.09	−0.17	−2.69	0.008	0.94	1.06
Priv4	0.30	0.13	0.14	2.25	0.025	0.95	1.05
Motility	0.43	0.11	0.24	3.92	0.000	0.95	1.05
Special needs	−0.68	0.40	−0.10	−1.69	0.092	0.94	1.06
Police vs nurse	1.95	0.44	0.27	4.41	0.000	0.94	1.06
IRSAD (first town)	0.00	0.00	−0.13	−2.08	0.039	0.98	1.02

Table 6.11 Model summary – dependent variable: number of moves

R	R square	Adjusted R square	SE of the estimate	R square change	F change	df1	df2	Sig. F change	Durbin–Watson
0.54	0.29	0.26	2.18	−0.007	2.03	1	197	0.16	2.10

frame, relocating families requires a conscious balancing of both risks and opportunities for family members. We were thus interested in what reasons respondents gave to explain and warrant their past moves.

In the online survey's third component, participants were asked to indicate the most important factor that motivated their most recent move and the prior move, as well as the second and third most important factors for each move if relevant. The 278 respondents provided data on a total of 405 moves by professional families. In addition, the same data also offered 183 paired sets of moves (the most recent and prior moves by the same family), sequenced over time to display any shift in priorities over time as children got older. Participants were also asked to recall whether they had ever considered an attractive career opportunity entailing a household move that they eventually chose not to pursue: that is, by making a decision to stay. Participants with such experience were further asked to indicate the most important factor behind their decision to stay, as well as the second and the next most important factors if relevant. We provided a broad set of factors that had been distilled from the earlier interview phase in the project. These factors were:

1   Requirements for your professional employment (for example, fulfilling bond or country service requirements, entry level posting).
2   To further your professional career (for example, a promotion, career opportunities, the professional experience available, professional development available, work satisfaction).
3   To further your partner's career (for example, a promotion, career opportunities, the professional experience available, professional development available, work satisfaction).
4   Financial incentives (for example, higher income, cost of living, housing subsidised or supplied).
5   For your children's education (for example, for the school choices on offer, children's extra-curricular opportunities).
6   For your own or partner's further study (for example, to undertake a course on campus at a selected university or institution).
7   For family reasons (for example, change of housing, forming a new household, medical services, proximity to extended family and social networks, child-care services, work/life balance).
8   For the location attributes (for example, climate, lifestyle on offer, recreational opportunities).
9   Sense of duty to serve where needed (for example, to go where my skills are needed most).

Participants could also provide further comment if they did not consider the nine provided factors relevant to their circumstances.

To investigate which factors emerged across the sample as the more important reasons behind these families' decisions for moving and staying, we developed a weighting strategy. Any factor ranked by any participant as the most important reason was allocated three points, while the second most important factor was allocated two points, and the third, one point. The points for each factor within each ranking were then summed. These summed scores were then used to rank each factor by level of importance across the prior move, most recent move and the aggregate of the two moves. The higher the ranking of a particular factor, the more frequently this factor was mentioned as more important by the participants with respect to the decision-making process underpinning professional family mobility. An indication of the degree and direction of the shift in rank between the prior move and the most recent move was calculated by subtracting the recent move ranking from the prior move ranking. The rankings are displayed in Table 6.12.

Reasons for moving

When factor weightings were aggregated across both moves (the first column in Table 6.12), family reasons emerged overall as the most important and compelling factor behind family moves. The location attributes factor was next most important overall, followed by consideration of both partners' careers. The close competition between the latter two factors highlights the complexity that double-career families negotiate in family mobility, plus the difference between individual professional itineraries and mobility within the intersubjective constraints of a family. In other words, any explanation of families' mobility decisions must attend to efforts to reconcile, harmonise or dovetail individuals' projects within the larger family project of being together over time. Alternatively, career trajectories need to be understood as shaped within this extended context of familial considerations.

Table 6.12 Rankings of the overall importance of factors in the two most recent moves

Factor	Rankings of overall importance factors			
	Over two moves	In prior move	In recent move	Ranking shift
For family reasons	1	2	1	1
For the location attributes	2	3	2	1
To further your professional career	3	1	3	−2
To further your partner's career	4	4	4	0
Requirements for your personal employment	5	5	6	−1
For your children's education	6	8	5	3
Financial incentives	7	6	7	−1
For your own or partner's further study	8	9	8	1
Sense of duty to serve where needed	9	7	9	−2

The shift in rankings (the fourth column in Table 6.12) gives us some sense of how priorities can change over time, as families were established as well as careers, and children got older. It becomes evident that considerations of the participants' own professional career shifted down in rank, becoming less important over time across the sample, while family reasons shifted up in ranking, becoming more important. We would highlight the relative importance and shift upwards in 'location attributes' over time, suggesting that these families could more actively select their location once careers were established, offset perhaps by the drop in importance given to a 'sense of duty'. Second, we would highlight that, over time, further study for adults and children's education also became more important factors motivating family mobility, as children get older. These trends are discussed further in Chapter 7.

Reasons for staying

We were equally interested in reasons behind respondents' decisions not to move, when faced with an attractive career opportunity elsewhere. In the survey, we asked participants to recall whether they had ever considered an attractive career opportunity entailing a household move that they eventually chose not to pursue. Participants with such experience (N = 146) were further asked to indicate the three most important factors behind their decision to stay, similar to the previous questions regarding decisions to move. We provided the same nine factors and applied the same weighting strategy detailed in the previous section. Scores for these factors and their respective rankings are illustrated in Table 6.13. Respondents only reported on one such decision to stay, so there is no ranking shift over time.

As indicated in Table 6.13, family reasons and children's education emerged as factors of high importance behind decisions to stay. Moreover, the scores associated with family reasons and children's education were remarkably higher than other factors, indicating the dominance of these two factors in decisions to stay. This outcome could be interpreted as reflecting normative preferences to

Table 6.13 Scores and rankings of the factors behind decisions to stay

Factor	Weighted score	Ranking
For family reasons	278	1
For your children's education	202	2
For the location attributes	93	3
To further your partner's career	61	4
Financial incentives	32	5
To further your professional career	27	6
For your own or partner's further study	8	7
Sense of duty to serve where needed	8	8
Requirements for your personal employment	5	9

be close to extended family and to avoid moving children while in school. Requirements for personal employment ranked as the least important reason behind family decisions to stay, where it had been a stronger factor behind reasons to move.

The social trajectories of family relocations

In Chapter 2, we situated our study in a 'politics of mobility' (Massey 1993: 63) whereby the selective mobility of the spatially autonomous is understood to impact on others. With this frame in mind, the documented history of moves from the sampled professionals allowed us to explore the mobility trajectories of the more mobile families through social strata of relative dis/advantage. Drawing on census data (Australian Bureau of Statistics 2013), we recoded the self-reported family locations over the years by their corresponding IRSAD scores. Figure 6.5 presents the recoded data associated with the subset of professionals who reported six family relocations after their professional training (N=28). For this exploratory analysis, we focused on families with a history of six relocations because there were very limited numbers of professionals who reported seven or eight family relocations. Figure 6.5 visualises how these professionals moved through locations according to their IRSAD values. It becomes evident that they typically undertook their training in places ('train town') associated with relatively higher IRSAD scores, and that the bulk of their moves stayed within a similar, relatively advantaged band. The marked departures from this norm are the 'V' moves into much less advantaged communities. These feature as 'one-off' experiences after which the professional and family return to the more advantaged band rather than continuing to work in such disadvantaged communities.

Further investigation revealed a significant mean negative difference between the IRSAD score of professionals' 'train town' and that of their first served

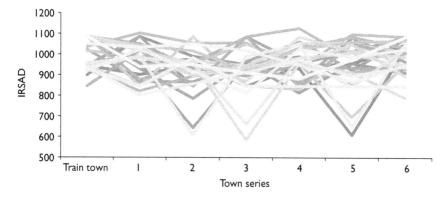

Figure 6.5 Shifting IRSAD scores over the past family relocations.

towns ($t=5.62$, $p<0.001$, $r=0.35$) and a mean positive difference between that of their careers' first town and that of their current town ($t=-4.33$, $p<0.001$, $r=0.27$). In other words, the towns where professionals undertook their professional training were regional or metropolitan centres with the requisite educational markets and relatively high IRSAD scores. The first towns in which these professionals served were by comparison less advantaged, as indicated by their lower IRSAD scores. Across their mobility histories, these professionals typically gravitated to more advantaged towns with higher IRSAD scores. Though this analysis has only explored the data of a subset of highly mobile professional families from our sample, these trends resonate with Chapter 5's narratives of taking the rural/remote posting to gain a professional start, then moving on to better resourced locations to optimise family projects.

Conclusion

This chapter has presented an analysis of survey responses from a broader sample of professionals with school-aged children as a way to scale up and contextualise the insights from the narratives presented in Chapter 5. While the narratives came from teachers, doctors, nurses and police officers living in regional, rural and remote locations, the survey sampled the same professional groups across the state of Queensland. In this way, it sought to tap the potential pool of professionals that might service such communities, in order to understand the reasons, priorities and patterning behind their selective mobility and behind the chronic shortage of such qualified professionals in these locations.

We designed attitudinal items aligned with theoretical constructs and informed by the qualitative research phase, to measure the strength and interplay of factors that might impinge on family mobility decisions. These included a professional ethic of public service, the pursuit of private interests, neoliberal dispositions when it came to their children's schooling, and the range of locations families would consider. These factors and respondents' demographic attributes were analysed as independent variables that could contribute to explaining variation in both motility, in terms of being open to the idea of moving, and mobility, in terms of the number of actual household relocations. We found that combinations of such factors could better account for variation in motility than for variation in mobility. While motility also accounted for some variation in mobility, there was much left unexplained. We would interpret this as reflecting the fact that these spatially autonomous professionals have multiple options at their disposal, including the option to stay.

Our visualisation of how a subset of high mobility professional families moved through social strata made evident how any relocation into areas of relative disadvantage was temporary, followed by a move back to more advantaged settings. These detours would align with the 'optimising circuit' described in Chapter 5 narratives, whereby families use the rural/remote location to achieve professional advantage, then gravitate back to larger, better resourced and more advantaged locations to optimise both career and education projects within the family.

Our design behind the survey questions about reasons behind the two most recent moves was sensitive to the dynamism of families and the fact that priorities change over time, as children get older and careers progress. Across the sample, the factors behind the earlier move with younger children were tipped towards addressing career progression for the adults, but the later move saw a shift in families' ballast to give more weight to family considerations. Children's education moved up in priorities, while the attributes of the location exerted more influence. In this way, professional families could be understood to impose more conditions on the subsequent move and could afford to be more selective. Family reasons and children's education exerted their greatest influence as factors behind decisions to stay. In this way, the tangle of projects within a family unit engenders an inertia that makes mobility less likely, converting potential movers to stayers.

Notes

1 The congeneric, tau, and parallel measurement models are examined in turn. In a tau model the factor loadings are constrained to be equal, while they are freely estimated in a congeneric model. In this respect, the tau equivalent model is nested within the less constrained congeneric model. The parallel model is identical to the tau model except that the error variances are set to be equal in the former model while freely estimated in the latter model. In this respect, the parallel model is embedded within the less parsimonious tau model. Therefore, the tau and parallel models will never have a better fit than the less parsimonious congeneric model. However, if the congeneric model does not present a significant better fit than the tau or the parallel model, the more parsimonious model is preferred.

2 All predictors are entered into the regression model. The program then calculates the contribution of each independent variable by looking at the t statistics and significance value corresponding to the t statistics of each predictor. If a predictor is not making a statistically significant contribution to how well the model predicts the outcome variable, it is removed from the model and the model is reassessed for the remaining predictors.

Chapter 7

Mobius markets

In Chapter 2 we reconceptualised credentialism as a mobility system: that is, as the social infrastructure that fosters and supports the portability of work experience, expertise and status, thus enabling mobility. This chapter concentrates on the other side of the coin to credentialism's role in mobility, given increasing pressure to invest in and upgrade educational credentials, and how such ongoing projects impinge on families' mobility decisions. We offer the concept of 'mobius markets' to capture the cyclical and intergenerational process of investing in educational capitals, maximising their value, then profiting from them before reinvesting.

A mobius strip is the topological anomaly of a single loop with one twist in it, whereby the loop becomes one continuous surface, not the double-sided shape it appears to be. We use this model as a metaphor to describe the imperative created within middle-class professional families to continually invest in educational capitals, for adults and children. We then explore how these projects can either motivate or curtail family mobility. This elaborated sense of educational markets extends the more usual sociological focus on educational markets as school choice within spatially defined markets, and illuminates the heightening anxieties around schooling and credentials in an increasingly uncertain and mobile labour market. Again, we seek to insert education more explicitly into treatments of work/family/education articulation.

The chapter builds a layered argument. First we provide a definition of the mathematically derived mobius strip and outline its metaphoric relevance to family projects and mobility. We then present a background to the broad scholarly arguments around credentialism, and its relationship to educational markets, occupational currency and the changing nature and structure of the labour market and career strategy therein. Next we clarify the nature of connections between credentialism and mobility in terms of specific social and educational policy in the Australian context, and changes to educational and professional development requirements to maintain membership of particular professional groups. Finally we explore the challenges and dynamics of these changes in the accounts of the middle-class professionals we interviewed in rural and remote communities, and those who responded to the broader survey.

Demystifying the mobius

The mobius strip or mobius band is a surface with only one side and only one actual boundary component. It has the mathematical property of being 'non-orientable' which Lury (2013: 131) explains as 'a surface in – not on – which consistent orientation – in the sense not only of fixed north and south, of positive and negative rotation, or left and right-handedness – is meaningless.' It was described independently by the German mathematicians August Ferdinand Möbius and Johann Benedict Listing in 1858 (Pickover 2006). It is often represented as a piece of paper that has been twisted 180 degrees with the ends taped together to create a continuous, one-sided surface. If a pencil line is drawn along the length of the strip from a starting point, it will traverse the entire piece of paper on 'both' sides and end up at the exact same starting point. The mobius strip has come to be associated with non-Euclidean geometry, science fiction, maths-related art, universal space–time theories and new age symbolism as an icon for endlessness. It also appears often as a spatial metaphor in literary criticism, for example with Lee (2011) focusing on its associations with interrelated notions of impasse, inaccessible meaning, collapsing binaries and narrative dead ends. The mobius metaphor has often been used in literature and mythology 'when a protagonist returns at a time and place with an alternative viewpoint, because a true mobius strip has the intriguing property of reversing objects that travel within its surface' (Pickover 2006: 26). This property allows us to metaphorically allude to the endless loop of formal study increasingly required to achieve then maintain the currency and value of a professional credential, and the recurrent reversal between competent professional and student roles on this loop.

More recently, and of particular relevance to our metaphor of mobius markets, Lury (2013) has emphasised that topological ideas (around geometrical shapes and their relationship to one another) have enabled the social sciences to pursue the notion of relational entities making their own space–time relationships – 'topological concepts have enabled social theory to move beyond a reliance on the mechanical and organic to include transductive and transitive modes of relating' (p. 128). This topological sense-making resonates with the new mobility paradigm, in particular Lury's suggestion that culture is becoming topological:

> in a topological culture, we no longer live in or experience 'movement' as the transmission of fixed forms in space and time but rather movement – organized in terms of the topological invariants of ordering and continuity of transformation – composes the forms of social and cultural life themselves.
>
> (p. 129)

The transformation in the etymology of 'market' exemplifies this shift, from its origins in a fixed place and time in the village square, to the fluid, dynamic and opportunistic reach of global markets and their constitutive effect on social and cultural life.

The concept of 'mobius market' thus seeks to capture the *perpetuum mobile* of the professional middle-class family's engagement with educational markets. They are constantly working to strategically invest in advantageous educational opportunities for both adults and children over time and space, to later derive profits in the labour market or enable further educational opportunities. These projects demand iterative cycles of reinvestment to maintain the currency and competitiveness of credentials. This concept brings us to consider credentialism as the broader social condition thus produced.

The social limits to credential society

Our title here plays on the titles of books by Collins (1979) and Hirsch (1976). Both writers present strong critiques of the notion that 'more credentials is a good thing'. They argue that the relations between individuals' education and work are often tense, ambiguous and contradictory. The relationship between education and socio-economic success, along with the meritocratic and credentialist aspects of this relationship, has long been discussed by sociologists, psychologists and labour economists. This section visits these debates as background to the conditions that underpin credentialism as a mobility system.

Early warnings that systemic credentialism and its inflation over time have little impact on intergenerational social mobility have remained pertinent. Collins's (1979) critique of credentialism as a 'system of barriers' (p. 200) argues that the pursuit of educational qualifications as a key medium of exchange enabled and sustained the 'educational discrimination' (p. 199) that serves to protect some groups' status: 'educational requirements have become a major basis of separating work into distinct positions and career lines, and hence in keeping labor markets fragmented' (p. 199). The professional fraction of the middle class most obviously benefit from such barriers. Collins offers a strong critique of the general view that an advanced technological society requires more formal education and that more education will provide for more social mobility. He asserts that the increase in credentialism has outstripped the increased demand in skill requirements, and that there is no evidence that better educated employees are more productive than those with less education because so many other variables are more relevant. He argues that education channels individuals into middle-class narrowness and pursuits of achievement through competition. Collins further argues that education serves more as the mechanism that sorts people into society's roles, to maintain social stratification. In addition, bureaucracies and elite 'old guard' structures continue to act as gatekeepers and limit entrance to the top end of the hierarchy, thus reproducing the embedded meritocracy and its maintenance of privilege. Collins argues that education is the key cultural medium of exchange which enables what he calls the 'political' job (p. 51) of controlling career entry and career channels. He asserts that educational credentialism fails to change social stratification – individuals typically continue in the same social strata as their forebears: 'What is learned in school has much more to do with conventional standards of sociability and propriety than with instrumental and cognitive skills' (p. 19). Further, Collins argues that 'A massively inclusive educational system has caused schools to become internally bureaucratic parts of an indefinitely lengthy sequence of obtaining a negotiable cultural currency. Hence the content of education has become increasingly irrelevant' (p. 130).

Brown (2001) updates and elaborates this argument in light of the continued rise in educational thresholds for entry to more jobs in the Western world: 'Historical credential inflation at the top of credentialing hierarchies drives educational expansion' (p. 20), resulting in an 'educational welfare state' (p. 29) and 'neocompulsory higher education' (p. 30). Echoing Collins's (1979) distinction between the material market (the work required by the level of technology) and the cultural market (where the nature of the work is specified through bureaucratic positions with strictly contested and defended ownership), Brown makes a distinction between the bureaucratic labour market (where the educational qualification is an individual pursuit, which serves as a marker of competence) and the more elite, self-regulating professional labour market where the educational qualification is a collective pursuit which serves 'to control the recruitment process (to recruit similar others) and to legitimate labour market monopolies' (p. 28). Collins (1979) argued strongly against the popular view that a 'knowledge economy' and the attendant pace of new knowledge creation, innovation and technologies require the worker's constant updating, while Brown (2001) suggests that this view speaks to the content of the qualification – learning that could be achieved by multiple means – not to what it symbolically signifies when credentialed, be it competence, disposition or trustworthiness (Brown 2001).

In economic theory, Hirsch (1976) outlines the systems dynamics view of connectedness between resources, population and environment, emphasising that there is a limit to growth as resources are finite and distribution among 'more' reduces that which is available to any. For example, an individual's demand for education to access a particular job actually alters the situation for others seeking to satisfy similar wants 'because the sum of such acts does not correspondingly improve the position of all individuals taken together' (p. 4). In this way, Hirsch (1976) outlines how the imperative to educate more of the population to higher levels effectively reduces the value of educational credentials as positional goods over time, though making them more socially necessary. He argues that the attraction (and perceived benefit) of higher educational qualifications increases demand for them in both the private and public sector, and their cost. Ironically, this demand is less about the content of the qualification (in agreement with Collins and Brown) than the symbolic value of the qualification, and its capacity to broaden access to higher strata of society. However, Hirsch reminds us that this:

> fails to allow for an important function education performs in modern society, that is, sorting or screening. In its own way education is a device for

controlling social scarcity ... improved performance by some worsens the position of those who would otherwise be ahead.

(p. 5)

Hirsch further asserts that the struggle between a resource provision, in this case education, is heightened by expectations of growth and advancement by more in the population – 'bluntly, where consumption or jobholding by others tends to crowd you out – then the key to personal welfare is again the ability to stay ahead of the crowd' (p. 7). In short, this drives market pressure to continually upgrade one's qualifications, to remain ahead of the pack.

Credentials for exchange value

These theoretical critiques of spiralling credentialism could be applied to recent policy initiatives in Australia (and their parallels elsewhere) which seek to increase mandatory levels of schooling and adopt OECD targets for the proportion of the population with completion of secondary school and university qualifications. In Australia, these policy efforts have been termed the 'widening participation agenda' (see Bradley *et al.* 2008). This policy push acknowledges that there remains a significant underrepresentation of those from low socio-economic groups in higher education in Australia (Karmel and Lim 2013), a fact which resonates with Collins's argument of education serving, not disrupting, social stratification.

Increasing education levels across the board is a policy goal derived from human capitalist assumptions. These connect more schooling or further education with economic productivity increases on the macro scale, and with an individual's meritocratic social mobility on the micro. However, ongoing changes in the nature of the workplace in a post-industrial economy, and the recent global financial challenges, have restricted career opportunities in many Western countries, thereby diminishing the expected returns on the meritocratic connection. Within Australia, the macro-economic impact of a better educated country is often cited as crucially important given that our small population cannot sustain large-scale manufacturing and related industries. Our international competitiveness is often seen to be dependent on the education level and status of our population. The critiques offered by both Collins (1979) and Hirsch (1976) remain relevant as an ongoing competition continues between private and public schools, older 'sandstone' and newer universities, and universities and providers of vocational education to credential the population. As Hirsch explains, even if an assurance could be made of equal quality of education provision and outcome, the edge of any degree from any institution would be diminished if more graduates from those institutions were delivered to the labour market. This view is often used to critique the 'widening participation' agenda and strategies.

Credentialism treats education foremost as an indicator of social class rather than a means of skill development (Evans and Kelley 2001). Dockery and Miller

(2012) define credentialism as 'an increase over time in the education standards for specific jobs ... which is not necessary for the effective achievement of tasks across positions in the labour market' (p. 7). Levels of education are read as proxy indicators of innate intellectual standing or ability rather than the particular human capital developed through the education. Moreover, credentialism can also be considered responsible for an actual reduction in productivity, if the cost of education and time out of the labour market does not produce a workforce with the required background for available jobs and with the skills required for the effective achievement of jobs. In the argument's strongest form, Collins (1979) asserts that there is no demonstrated correlation between education level and productivity.

While an extensive international body of empirical evidence affirms that there is a positive wage premium associated with each additional year of educational attainment, there are many critiques to this accepted view. Using Australian data from the International Adult Literacy Survey conducted in 2006, Barrett (2012) concluded that 'The mean return to an additional year of education is estimated to be 6.2 per cent, almost one-third of which may be attributed to the acquisition of cognitive skills' (p. 1). Using a more complex formula, Dockery and Miller (2012) concluded that, in Australia, 'a year of over-education still offers a positive return in terms of higher hourly wages, in the general magnitude of 3–6 per cent' (p. 41). However, these authors agree with others (for example, Hirsch 1976) that this refers to the wage premium at a point in time; it does not account for the time spent in education and out of the labour force, nor does it include the private and public cost of education. Similarly, it does not account for 'informal' costs or externalities such as impact on families. Dockery and Miller (2012) also caution that in some cases individuals may actually receive a lower return from years of education that are in excess of the requirements for the occupation in which they work.

Hirsch (1976) presented US data which showed an increase in students graduating with a high school diploma in the early 1970s to 70 per cent from under 40 per cent a generation earlier. Similarly the percentage with a college degree in the same time period had increased from 8 per cent to 25 per cent. Australian Bureau of Statistics (2012) data demonstrates a similar trend. In 1970, only three out of every 100 working age Australians had a higher education qualification; in 2011, this had increased to 25 out of every 100. In 2011, more than half of Australian men (57 per cent) and women (56 per cent) aged 15–64 years had a non-school qualification (Australian Bureau of Statistics 2012). In broad-brush comparison[1] with OECD countries, 34 per cent of Australian men and 40 per cent of Australian women aged 25–64 years had a tertiary qualification in 2009 compared with 29 per cent and 31 per cent respectively in OECD countries (Australian Bureau of Statistics 2012).

However, Hirsch (1976) asserted that increasing levels of attainment reduces 'the efficacy of a given unit of education in securing access to higher level jobs' (p. 49). In addition, the expansion of credentials faster than the number of jobs requiring them can actually intensify the employment screening process and reduce the individual benefits from obtaining the additional education. For example, Hirsch (1976) cited US data whereby the average mean income of male college graduates over high school graduates was reduced from 50 to 41 per cent between 1969 and 1973. While conventional wisdom assumes a return to the individual for additional education, Australian data mirrors Hirsch's US findings of a decline in such differentials. In 2001, the median gross weekly income of people aged 20–64 years who had higher education qualifications and were employed full-time was almost 50 per cent more than that of full-time workers without higher education qualifications. However, although people with higher education qualifications have had consistently higher incomes than those without, the relative difference has decreased. In 1976, the median gross weekly income of people with higher education qualifications was almost double that of those without. In 2001, it had fallen in relative terms to just under 50 per cent higher (Australian Bureau of Statistics 2004).

More recently, Karmel (in Matchett 2013) examined the correlation between skill level, income and social status using Australian data. He affirmed that while top jobs pay more and require higher skills, they are harder to get. He reported that in 1997, 80 per cent of higher degree graduates, 70 per cent of bachelor degree graduates and 40 per cent of diploma graduates had a job in the top quintile for skills and income. By 2011, these proportions had fallen to 60 per cent for higher degree graduates and 20 per cent for diploma graduates. Interestingly, 60 per cent of bachelor degree graduates were in the top quintile of skilled jobs and 45 per cent in the top quintile for income. Karmel asserted that the increase in education qualifications is greater than that required by the labour market, in both number and level. As Hirsch (1976: 52) asserted, as more attain higher levels of education, 'a kind of tax is imposed on those lacking such qualifications, while the bounty derived from possessing a given qualification is diminished.' However, the very growth in numbers obtaining higher qualifications increases the pressure on those who don't to join their ranks.

Thus pressure to enlist in the mobius market mounts on individuals and families, even though the eventual returns on one's investment may be diminishing. Credentialism leads to the public problem and private issue of over-education, when individuals have higher qualifications than required for a particular position. It is a form of skill-related underemployment, and its incidence appears to be rising (Linsley 2005; Miller 2007). It has also been associated with increasing job dissatisfaction and reduced productivity in overqualified employees (Green and Zhu 2010). In addition, Hirsch (1976) identified two forms of social waste through this increase: that of absorbing excess resources into the screening process, and that which will result from a collective disappointment and dissatisfaction of individuals not being employed in jobs commensurate with their educational and skill level. Linsley (2005) suggested that in Australia between 10 and 30 per cent of individuals are over-educated; and Miller (2007) has provided data which indicates that it is more of an issue for the university educated:

'Around one-half of workers with university degrees are categorised as over-educated' (p. 297). Miller also concluded that over-education is widespread, and more significant among recent graduates, while less the case as labour market experience increases. Dockery and Miller (2012) questioned whether over-education is a manifestation of credentialism, noting that the average years of schooling and post-schooling undertaken by 25–29 year olds has increased over time. They reported that strong evidence of credentialism is identified in that 'years of education associated with the cohort effect are found to provide a sub-stantially lower return (around 5.7 per cent) than years of required education (9.2 per cent)' (p. 41). They concluded that 'the rise in educational attainment over time has not increased mobility to higher paying occupations. Rather, the payoff is the same as returns from additional years of education within the one occupation' (p. 41).

For our purposes here, the mounting trends of more people pursuing more educational credentials despite the decreasing returns on such investment creates the widespread impetus to engage with the mobius market. As more people are doing it, then those who fail to engage will be more marginalised. This impera-tive will drive an important intergenerational agenda in professional families, with multiple projects around educational achievement and credentialing for both children and parents.

Credentials for use value

The section above has outlined how the pursuit and maintenance of formal credentials is gathering pace as a social phenomenon. This line of enquiry treats education as a symbolic, positional good (Hirsch 1976), foregrounding its exchange value. There are other more content-based or use value arguments fuelling the mobius market and its iterative investments in education. The changing world of work, its accelerating complexity and non-linearity have been well documented within vocational psychology organisational and socio-logical literatures (Arthur et al. 1999; Bills 2004; Poehnell and Amundson 2002). Competencies acquired for a job may now have a limited shelf life. Work is no longer characterised by a set of tasks which are mastered once and for all, and a career is no longer characterised by vertical advancement within the one organisation. Increasingly, 'career' needs to be understood as a series of periods within and outside paid employment, linked by experiences of learning and re-training.

In what has been termed the Knowledge Age by a number of authors (for example, Arthur et al. 1999; Jarvis 2003), workplaces demand more than techni-cal skills. Enterprises are aiming to be more fluid organisations structured around team and group arrangements, project- and portfolio-based work. As such, employees are expected to respond to and act on the changing work environ-ment, assume broader roles and responsibilities, and demonstrate a broad port-folio of generative capabilities as opposed to narrowly defined job skills.

The literature is replete with lists of enterprise skills, employability skills, generic capabilities, attributes and skills the Knowledge Age worker needs. These include what a number of writers have called core survival skills, such as resilience, the capacity for continuous learning and improvement, the ability to network and team, skill in using technology effectively, and willingness to take calculated risks and learn from setbacks. As the career patterns of individuals increasingly resemble a patchwork of work and learning experiences, of key importance is 'meta-competence', which cuts across occupational skills and can be universally applied. It is widely agreed that the most important type of meta-competence is the ability and the will to keep learning. Flexibility and the ability and willingness to continue learning have become much more important than specific occupational knowledge and skills. Thus the importance of lifelong learning has been championed by expanding literatures. The importance of ongoing learning in the knowledge economy was heralded by Perelman in 1992, in drawing a distinction between the core raw material of the industrial economy and that of the knowledge economy: 'Because knowledge is the steel of the modern economy – the essential commodity all else depends on – learning has become the strategically central enterprise for national economic strength' (Perelman 1992: 42). More succinctly, Mirvis and Hall (1996) asserted that workers need to *learn a living* rather than *earn a living*.

Inevitably related to these changes is a change in the work individuals need to undertake in their own career development. We are in an era of 'do-it-yourself career management' where individuals are being challenged to play a greater role in constructing and managing their own career development. Workers are encouraged to act as free agents, developing personal enterprises and marketing personal skills. This view resonates with Beck's individualisation thesis discussed in earlier chapters. Individuals increasingly need to focus on maintaining employability rather than job security, and learn the skills which will assist them in taking responsibility for the direction and evolution of their own careers. Security now lies in the individual's knowledge and skill currency, not the job itself. Developing necessary skills that enhance current performance and equip one for the next employment experience is an important underpinning of this focus. Savickas (1999) suggested that in preparing for such a dynamic working life, individuals need to constantly 'look ahead' and 'look around', with the focus not on unfolding careers but on actively constructing careers (Savickas 2002). These conditions and precepts will also drive investment effort in the mobius market.

As a result of this change in focus from linear/vertical career planning, Amundson *et al.* (2002) identify 'a continuing tension between leveraging past experience and positioning for future opportunity' (p. 27). In line with these other writers, they emphasise the imperative for individuals to learn to intentionally act on environments of change, drawing on an understanding of the individual as a self-organising, active system:

The common thread is that people make sense of the world of work through subjective interpretation of their own career experience. In living through the complexity of economic life, they draw new insights and formulate new strategies that make sense of this complexity.

(Amundson *et al.* 2002: 27)

This terrain is the same as Archer's treatment of reflexivity, fallible readings and projects, as discussed in earlier chapters.

Bernstein (2001) knits the credentialism pressure together with the constant work and strategy of updating knowledge and skills in his characterisation of current times as the 'second totally pedagogised society'.[2] By his description, this nexus involves an 'endless process of pedagogic forming and re-forming' (p. 365) of the subject typified by 'short-termism' (p. 365) and 'pedagogic inflation' (p. 367) in an accelerating cycle of training and re-training. The credentialed worker is thus increasingly enlisted in a recursive, mobius market to maintain occupational currency, promote prospects and protect employability. As return on this investment, the worker with the credentials that are in demand can choose the most desirable location or employer.

Professional currency on the mobius market

The previous section highlighted contextual factors that provide the impetus for family members to proactively invest in credentials; this section will focus more particularly on membership of particular professional groups and their growing requirements for demonstrating professional currency through documented professional development. These requirements for entry to, and ongoing membership of, these groups are another generative force behind the individual's mobius loop, and offer further fodder for Collins's (1979) critique of education for position and advantage rather than for learning. Indeed, Collins asserts that, 'It has been by the use of educational credentials that the lucrative professions have closed their ranks and upgraded their salaries, and it has been in imitation of their methods that other occupations have "professionalised"' (p. 189). It can be argued that the emphasis on currency requirements serves the professional group as much as the individual.

The expectation of ongoing professional development, represented through the accumulation, formal documentation and annual reporting of participation in approved activities to maintain professional status, is embedded in the professions. Although reports demonstrate the accepted responsibility of the employer for enabling this professional development (Hall and Las Heras, 2009), individual responsibility has also been emphasised (Clayton *et al.* 2013). For example, to maintain registration status, Australian nurses and midwives must participate in at least 20 hours of continuing professional development per year (www.nursingmidwiferyboard.gov.au/Registration-Standards.aspx, accessed 21 October 2013). Similar but more onerous requirements for continuing

professional development apply to Australian doctors (www.medicalboard.gov.
au/Registration-Standards.aspx, accessed 21 October 2013). To maintain registration with the Queensland College of Teachers, a teacher currently needs to
undertake and document at least 20 hours of Continuing Professional Development (CPD). This can include 'employer directed and supported, school supported and teacher identified CPD' (Queensland College of Teachers 2012: 6).

This effort is publicly subsidised while personally advantageous. Within the
Australian tax system, individuals can claim an annual tax deduction for ongoing
'self-education'. Recent moves by the Australian government to place a cap on
that amount have drawn protests from close to 70 professional groups across the
country. This tension between professional qualifications as both public good
and private good, and its relation to family mobility, is further explored in
Chapter 8.

We are interested in this work/education nexus for a number of reasons. The
pursuit of further credentials ties the adult, particularly the professional, to
educational institutions and opportunities beyond their initial qualifications.
While advocates of distance or online education would argue that place no
longer matters in the continuing education market, we suspect that urban centres
with their density of population and institutions will offer professionals both
quality and quantity of further education opportunities. In this vein, a doctor we
interviewed in a rural town described her frustration at the effort required to
access professional learning opportunities from her rural location:

> I currently have to leave (... to go to a bigger centre) to do it mostly which
> is very annoying. Oh you just – it's more like weekends and things ... like
> there's a lot of evening education in [city] and [regional centre] even, it's
> potentially hard to access from here. To travel to [regional centre], I just
> can't do it. I actually saw one today that's on Thursday nights that would be
> excellent. But the reality for us is it's an hour on top of that each way and
> the actual education finishes at 9.30. So I wouldn't get home until 10.30 at
> best – so no.
>
> (Beth, doctor family, two parents and three children)

At the other end of the occupational scale, another interviewee expressed his
frustration at trying to achieve the required credential for his work role at the
local council through university studies by distance mode:

> I hate distance education. I think it sucks ... I at 49 have a lot of difficulty in
> learning stuff and I would dearly love to be able to just go up to the teacher
> and say, 'Hey, sit me down, whack me around the head and show me how to
> do this,' but yeah, I just don't think that the support for distance education is
> as good as those that are on campus.... You will work and go home after work
> and put in a couple of hours hitting the books. I would dearly love to just
> throw them in the bin some days because currently I am doing physics and I

will never ever use physics in my career, never ever. It beats me why it is part of the course. My maths that I use is more trigonometry and there is none of that. So I have got to try and learn a subject that I will never ever use again.

(Josh, other occupation, two parents and three children)

A nurse working in a private practice in a remote town could access some but not all professional development offered through the public sector employer in her town, but reportedly relied on industry groups to facilitate professional training in other ways:

Just occasionally things come to [her remote town] and when they come to [remote town], we're usually there, too.... That's with [health department] bringing them out ... but because I work in the private sector, I don't always hear about what's coming.... Some of the things that are provided to [health department employees] are not really available to those who work in the private sector, because I don't do both. Some of the people in the private sector still have their foot in the door as a Queensland Health employee, and I don't. Whenever anything is provided for immunisation, it involves everyone who's got endorsement, so I have no problem at all being part of that. Then we – as private sector – have the support of the Division of Rural Practice. So the division through what we call Rhealth[3] puts on things for those of us who work in private surgeries, and that's a lot of our support. So it doesn't matter whether you're a receptionist or a practice manager or a practice nurse, there's quite a bit of support out there for us.... They have really come on board through the internet now.

(Kate, nurse family, two parents and three children)

In contrast, a nurse in a rural town described generous private employer support to travel to conferences to maintain her professional currency, but also her resistance to further credentialing in the interests of family demands:

I know at work they were wanting me to do my nurse practitioner's and I had a bit of pressure put on me to do that but I knew my limitations. I just don't have the time to do it. I wouldn't be able to do it.... Things are so busy at home. I'm certainly not keen on doing any further study as such ... I'm lucky, where I work the doctors are very good at allowing us to have ongoing education. They'll actually pay for most of our education. They pay for our flights sometimes to go down to some of the practice nurse conferences down in Melbourne.... You know you have to get your 20 points every year for your education to ensure that you're still updating your knowledge. So I can't complain. I'm happy that I'm maintaining my education and maintaining my skills as such and work's very rewarding. I'm very happy to just continue where I am at this stage.

(Ellen, nurse family, one parent and two children)

The common ground in these accounts is the pressure to stay engaged with formal education for reasons of credentialing or professional currency. These pressures exist regardless of where one lives; however, as we argued in Chapter 2, space is not a neutral backdrop and the educational affordances of different localities become an important feature in their gamekeeping capacity to recruit and retain professionals. In professional families, we would expect the adults' own ongoing educational projects to impinge on family mobility decisions. As the imperative to invest in the mobius market ramps up, we expect the magnetic pull of urban centres with their density of options to similarly grow in the absence of viable options. This gravitation to larger centres would constitute an ironic outcome, given that we have also argued that credentials, as a mobility system, make expertise increasingly portable.

Another ironic outcome was where state boundaries rendered one's credential invalid. Australia's history as a federation of states has produced state registration boards for many professional groups, which have at times chosen not to recognise parallel credentials from other Australian states. In this vein, an older nurse we interviewed in a remote town described having to re-do her credential to enable her move to another state:

> I did my child health all over again once I came to Queensland, so that they would recognise it and they would register me as a child health nurse.
>
> (Kate, nurse family, two parents and three children)

There is currently much work underway to up-scale professional registration bodies from state to national accreditation systems, to reduce this systemic viscosity. In 2010, a national registration and accreditation scheme was put in place for health professionals, to 'facilitate workforce mobility' (www.ahpra.gov.au/Support/FAQ.aspx, accessed 28 October 2013). Similarly, the teaching professions negotiated a nationally consistent approach to teacher registration in 2011 with the embedded principle of mutual recognition (www.aitsl.edu.au/teachers/registration/mutual-recognition.html, accessed 28 October, 2013).

Professional families moving in the mobius market

Our particular concern is Australia's many isolated communities and their capacity to recruit and retain qualified professionals, such as doctors, nurses and teachers. Maintaining a viable and equitable spread of such educational capital across space as a public good continues to be a challenge. Our argument above would suggest that the growing emphasis on credentialism and professional currency could exacerbate this problem. We now briefly revisit the survey responses gathered in the professional family project outlined in Chapter 3 and Chapter 6 to test the strength of such projects' role in family mobility. Here we draw on both qualitative and quantitative survey responses pertaining to families' investment in the mobius market to explore how these agendas might impinge on family mobility decisions. We then make connections with some of the interviews we collected with professional parents working in rural and remote locations.

Chapter 6's analysis of survey responses reported how various factors were reported to have contributed to professional families' decisions to move (see Table 6.12) and to stay (see Table 6.13). The analysis used weighted scores to aggregate the data across the sample to indicate the relative importance given to each factor, and rank shift to indicate generalised change in families' priorities over time. Of the nine broad factors, Factor 6 particularly referred to the pursuit of further qualifications by adult members of the family, while Factor 5 referred to children's educational pathways and opportunities as a key consideration. Together, these factors sought to capture the intergenerational facets of mobius market agendas in families.

As reported in Table 6.12, 'family reasons' emerged as the strongest overall factor, followed by 'attributes of the location', then 'professional career' and 'partner's career'. The mobius market factors, 'for your children's education' and 'for your own or partner's further study' were not as strong as other priorities across the sample, but nevertheless featured as important for some respondents.

We next considered respondents' paired moves as a time sequence, to consider how the ranking of factor's importance shifted over time as children got older. The factor 'for your children's education' showed the most marked shift in growing importance, at the expense of 'financial incentives', 'duty to serve', 'required for employment' and 'furthering the professional career'. 'For your own or partner's further study' also moved up in rankings, though more modestly.

We then divided survey respondents into two groups: those who ranked children's education as the top three most important reasons behind the most recent family moves (group one, $N=58$) and those who did not (group two, $N=164$). We were then able to compare the mean of the age of the oldest child at the time of the move in these two groups. For the group of participants who ranked children's education among the top three factors in their most recent family move, their first child was on average aged 6 years at the time of the move, while, for those who did not rank children's education in the top three factors in their most recent family move, their first child was on average aged 4 years at the time of the move. As illustrated in Table 7.1, the mean difference between these two groups is statistically significant ($t=2.92$, $p=0.004$) with a small to medium effect size ($r=0.20$). The result suggests that there is a typical tipping point in families' priorities as first children approach school age.

We also asked participants to recall an attractive career opportunity entailing a household move that they eventually chose not to pursue (reported in Table 6.13). Again, more diffuse 'family reasons' emerged as the dominant factor, but 'children's education' as a factor was shown to have exerted much more force in the sample's decisions to stay compared with their decisions to move. 'Your and

Table 7.1 Mean difference in the age of the oldest child at the time of the most recent move

	Levene's Test for Equality of Variances		t-test for Equality of Means						
	F	Sig.	t	df	Sig. (2-tailed)	Mean difference	Std error difference	95% confidence interval of the difference	
								Lower	Upper
Equal variances assumed	0.20	0.658	2.92	205	0.004	2.09	0.71	0.68	3.49
Equal variances not assumed	–	–	2.97	101.84	0.004	2.09	0.70	0.69	3.48

your partner's further study' ranked slightly higher in decisions to stay, suggesting that mobius market projects can serve to anchor families in localities.

This analysis is necessarily explorative, given the myriad of factors that ultimately contribute to mobility scenarios, but does assist in teasing out how educational projects might motivate or restrict family mobility and how such factors might impinge differently over time. We would suggest that the shift in family ballast over time towards considerations of children's education and adults' further study does reflect an escalation of stakes around educational investments and how professional families are engaged with an intergenerational mobius market of educational investment. We now turn to the qualitative data from open-ended survey responses and the interview phase of the research to give a richer sense of how educational investments for children and adults influence family mobility decisions.

The interplay of factors in moving/staying

In their open-ended responses, survey respondents could better explain how they adjudicated the claims of multiple factors over time. In these responses it becomes more evident that families are not making either/or decisions, addressing one priority at the expense of others. Rather, families described strategies to optimise the combination of factors in their choice of location, or reconcile them across a sequence of phases. In this way, Respondent #235, a female nurse, could clearly articulate where her investment phase in further career qualifications fitted with reference to her children's education:

It is impossible to be an excellent professional nurse and a devoted and committed mother. Therefore at different times you have to focus on one or the other. When my children were in primary school I worked less hours and just let my career 'tick over' – not doing any study or pursuing career opportunities.... Now that our children are in high school I have increased my work hours and completed post-graduate study. There is a time in life for everything.

(#235)

For Respondent #240, also a female nurse, a career investment was necessary earlier, and a strategic move helped later:

After having children I went back to study so I could move out of shift work and develop my career. My most recent move out of Brisbane was a deliberate one to reconcile my career, extended family support and educational choices for my family. I do not expect to move again during my working life, or at least with children at school.

(#240)

A third female nurse reported her family's more traditional breadwinner hierarchy of priorities, privileging the male career investments in their mobility decisions:

We go where the opportunities for my partner's training are and then we look for good educational choices for our children.

(#109)

Others reported more active conflict between priorities. The following interviewee, a female nurse, emphasised how the stability she valued for her child's education ultimately trumped other factors:

there must be a balance between getting ahead and enabling stability for my child. If I can manage self-education (via distance/on site) it would need to not emotionally, socially or physically disadvantage my child (as it stands, I have a good job, good pay, family close by and good residential location). The same could be said for relocation to further professional opportunities. If deemed to have too great a negative impact on my child or their education, it wouldn't be an option worth considering.

(#256)

Another female nurse highlighted how investments in further credentials entailed costs that had to be absorbed by families:

My career is important to me. However, attention to my family comes first, including decisions regarding financial outlay. The last course I did I received a scholarship so the burden was less, which made my experience more comfortable.

(#126)

A police officer we interviewed explained how proactive individual investment in further training was necessary to qualify for a promotion:

> There's no expectation, it's a personal decision. If you want to go climb through the ranks, you have to do what they call a constable development programme to progress, to get your senior constable rank, and then from then on you have to do a number of management development subjects to qualify for sergeant, and then there's another level for senior sergeant and there's another level for inspector … you've got to qualify to go up.
>
> (Ian, police family, two parents and two children)

Another male police officer as a survey respondent outlined the underlying conflict between different generations when it comes to investing in and profiting from such credentials:

> While career opportunities provide advancement to you and ultimately benefit your family monetarily, educational opportunities for you and your family and children can impact on their lives further down the track with limited opportunities potentially impacting upon their career opportunities and development.
>
> (#198)

The subtext here is that 'advancement' for police officers often entails both additional certified training and mobility across regions to fill vacancies at the desired level, while educational opportunities for children implies stability in larger urban centres. In these few lines, he has succinctly juxtaposed the differently scaled yet interconnected surfaces in families' mobius market agendas to describe the inherent tension for many between children's education and career advancement through mobility.

For teachers and police in particular, career investment and promotion were closely intertwined with a strategy of moving around rural and remote locations – their careers had spatial routes. In the following example, a police officer interviewee demonstrates the scanning described by Savickas (1999, 2002), exploring opportunities for, and the timing of, the next family move expressed as schooling stages:

> I don't mind moving around. No, moving around is fine. We were wondering what life would be like if we didn't; like there's a fellow here who doesn't move around at all and his kids are going into high school … as long as we move around a little bit while the kids are young, and then sort of stop looking at moving – stick to Queensland. Maybe one move at the transition from primary to high school.
>
> (Gill, police family, two parents and three children)

For others, both the timing and the placing of the career route were dictated by plans for children's education. One female doctor we interviewed living in a rural town described how she had her sons booked into three high status schools, two in the metropolitan centre and one in a regional centre, as both a strategic prediction of, and constraint on, her future career locations:

> they're booked into private schools for high school – or from Grade 7.... The timing is that [C1]'s booked into [school in regional centre]. Well, he's got a selection of schools on the off-chance we will end up in Brisbane or we may end up in [regional centre]. But that's for Year 7 and that will be maybe 2019 ... [school 1 in city], [school 2 in city] ... I guess it costs you a couple of hundred, maybe it costs you $1000 to book them into the three schools. But I think it's good to have that option, to have a choice and be able to choose the school which suits them the best. We'll go to [regional centre] or back to Brisbane, probably [regional centre].
>
> (Carol, doctor family, two parents and three children)

Taken together, these responses show how schooling choices, further study and career progression are woven together over time and space, as mutually impinging and compelling projects within these family units. The intersubjective work within the family is to negotiate a collective strategy that can dovetail and progress the multiple mobius market projects of both investing in educational credentials and profiting from them. This process involves scanning the landscape for opportunities and risks: timing a family move for career advancement before it interferes with high stakes schooling; booking into three schools of choice as risk management; and investing in further training to qualify for the next opportunity.

Conclusion

This chapter started with a consideration of credentialism and the growing emphasis it has placed on the symbolic or exchange value of formal education, while other use value arguments would point to the limited shelf life of knowledge in a changing world of work. Regardless of their contradictions, both arguments help explain the growing reliance on ongoing formally documented education to promote life chances in our 'totally pedagogised society' (Bernstein 2001: 365). We developed the concept of mobius markets to understand the ongoing work and iterative cycles of investing in educational credentials, deriving the profits thereof, then reinvesting to maintain the value and currency of the credentials in an increasingly crowded and credentialed labour market, despite diminishing returns. We have used the term 'mobius market agenda' to capture the way professional families are managing a number of such educational projects for both children and adults, simultaneously.

The mobius market ties adults as well as children to educational projects, and the capacity of different locations to feed this appetite will impact on their capacity to recruit and retain professionals, for better and for worse. The data profiled a number of strategies to meet this need of professionals working in more remote settings. These included the use of distance mode, industry-sponsored programmes both in situ and online, and employer-subsidised travel to access opportunities. However, the reports also displayed a degree of frustration and thirst for more. Credentialism – in play for both parents' career projects and with respect to their children's educational opportunities – may serve as a mobility system, but ironically the imperative to service such credentials to maintain their value could limit professional mobility.

The analysis of quantitative survey data explored patterning in how families ranked factors that prompted moves or underpinned decisions to stay. A shift to prioritising children's education as a reason behind family moves was evident as children approached school age. Children's education was also a major factor in decisions to stay, trumping attractive career opportunities. Professional families seemed prepared to move to optimise schooling choice, and once the goal is achieved the priority then becomes one of protecting stability, thus throwing out an anchor to moor the family where they perceive good educational opportunities.

The discussion of interview and open-ended survey responses demonstrated the importance placed by the participating families on protecting and progressing educational investments, and how families reconcile the claim of various projects in their strategies of whether, when and where to move. The particularities of each family's circumstances and their various designs to optimise their mobius market agenda defy broad-brush generalisations, except to highlight how maximising an adult career is rarely the prime consideration, despite its capacity to derive immediate profits. Rather, the intersubjectivity of family units means that potential profits in the far distant future from educational investments in the present have equal claim on family decisions in the present.

The next chapter continues to explore the selective mobility of professional families. It turns to questions of space and place, to explore how these families can encounter public/private dilemmas in rural and remote localities. It builds on the discussion in Chapter 2 about the social construction of places, and exemplifies the relations of competition between localities to attract and retain valuable human capital in terms of these skilled, credentialed professionals.

Notes

1 Comparing data is problematic as non-school may also include sub-tertiary as well as tertiary/higher education and even within Australia, data sources and naming can vary.
2 The first totally pedagogised society being the religious middle ages.
3 The government-funded services she is referring to here have since been restructured with a new model of tendering for regional delivery of such programmes.

Professionals' public/private dilemmas in rural service

Professional families and rural communities: a recursive im/mobility problem

In Chapter 1 we outlined the particular challenges posed by Australia's geography, and the ongoing challenge in recruiting and retaining professionals such as doctors, nurses, police and teachers to staff essential human services in rural and remote communities. Reports investigating this ongoing challenge repeatedly highlight family issues (for example, limited options for children's education and/or spouse employment), as well as limited access to ongoing professional development as key deterrents to professionals taking rural/remote employment, despite lucrative incentive schemes. While these factors make the rural/remote location less attractive, other relations make mobility in itself less likely, such as families being embedded in existing work and school contexts (Mitchell *et al.* 2001) and in social networks (Arnold and Cohen 2013). The scale of distance and population sparseness is extreme and exacerbated in Australia, but such rural professional workforce issues will resonate in many other national contexts.

Communities that cannot produce their own doctors, nurses, teachers and police inherently rely on the mobility of such professionals, while the mobility of such professionals inherently implicates their family members. In this chapter, we focus on how the professional families we surveyed and interviewed engaged with the 'no-go zones' that count on their mobility. This chapter reframes the national problem of recruiting and retaining professionals to service remote and rural communities through the public/private dilemmas these locations pose for the professional family, to understand more fully the terms and conditions under which professionals and their families might be prepared to move to such locations. In particular, the chapter probes further how family priorities interact with professionals' career decisions over time and space, and how amenable these interactions might be to policy interventions. Here, we are particularly interested in whether recent neoliberal policy encouraging more active school choice is constraining the mobility of professional families and undermining the implicit public service contract between professions and their client populations. In this way, we are interested in whether a policy solution pursued in one government sector is creating or exacerbating policy problems elsewhere.

Our thinking exploits the sociological gaze of the new mobilities paradigm (Sheller and Urry 2006) to understand various mobilities as a necessary and constitutive dimension of social relations and processes. Rural sociology often highlights the stability of rural populations, although more recently it has had to address the steady flow of young people out of such localities (for example, Carr and Kafalas 2009). Such a perspective renders invisible the inbound flow or churn of mobile professionals with trailing families in the sociological make-up of rural communities. In contrast, this same professional fraction of the middle class has become increasingly visible in the sociology of education, given the role of educational credentials in their own life opportunities and their intense investment in the school choice market to promote similar educational advantage for their children. This feature of professional families has been highlighted in previous chapters in this book and underpins our argument that, for professional families more so than others, education should be understood as an all-consuming primary concern about intergenerational status reproduction, not a mere secondary consideration. To date, the research around middle-class strategy in school choice has focused on metropolitan centres with deep educational markets. The missing link between rural sociology and the sociology of educational markets, which a mobility lens helps to identify, lies in understanding how professional families view the more limited educational choices available in smaller communities.

In addition, we enlist Honig's concept of dilemmatic space, as interpreted by Fransson and Grannas (2013). Rather than depicting dilemmas as atypical situations confronting the individual with an internal conflict of values, the concept of dilemmatic space refers to 'social constructions resulting from structural conditions and relational aspects in everyday practices ... how dilemmas emerge in a space between individuals and the context in which they find themselves' (p. 7). For Fransson and Grannas, dilemmatic space involves the dynamic between how people position themselves and are positioned by others. In this way dilemmas are not aberrant, singular events, but rather are 'ever-present spaces' (p. 14) in which identities and relations must be negotiated, creating tensions and dilemmas on both individual and social levels. Where they were interested in how new roles and responsibilities imposed by policy changes rubbed against professional identities and created metaphoric dilemmatic spaces for teachers' work, the same concept allows us to consider whether the rural/remote community creates a different sort of relational space for professionals whereby their public and private concerns cannot be held apart as they would be in larger population centres.

Professions and the public good

An altruistic commitment to the public good and an ethical code of public service have served to distinguish professions from other occupations in the past, and justified public subsidy of their extended preparation (Saks 1995). Saks, however, questions the strength of any commitment to the public service ethic in today's increasingly marketised societies: 'Do these elite occupational groups in fact embody a special moral standard based on the ideal of service? Or should such claims, which are often used in defence of professional privilege, be viewed with rather more cynicism?' (p. 6). In this frame, the common policy 'solution' of incentive schemes to attract professionals to rural and remote locations could be seen to contribute to the erosion of the public service ethic, by endorsing and institutionalising motives attached to private interests. These questions and the dilemmatic space they suggest informed our exploration of the constructs of 'public good' and 'neoliberalism' in Chapter 6.

Sciulli's (2009) assessment of the public service ethic is less critical than Saks's, concluding that 'norm-based, extra-economic behaviour' – that is, the altruistic service orientation – is as 'constitutive of any ongoing professionalism project as is providing expert services' (p. 295). For Scuilli, the professions remain an important intermediary institution for civil society, regardless of whether individual professionals themselves are motivated more by self-interest than the public good. In other words, society can still expect a service orientation from the profession, if not from the individual occupying that position.

These different treatments converge around the question of whether the public service ethic is under stress. For this reason, the tension between professionals' public duty and private interests playing out in underserviced rural and remote communities has broad policy and educational implications. Is professional socialisation managing to imbue an ethic of public service in the face of increasing individualisation and marketisation of the social fabric? Can smaller communities continue to call on the implicit contract underpinning public subsidy of professionals' lengthy and costly education?

With the survey data, we have been able to explore whether the level of the constructs 'public good' and 'neoliberalism' (explained in Chapter 6) were related in our sample. The Spearman correlation reported in Table 8.1 did not support any relationship between neoliberalism and public good ($r=-0.004$, one-tailed $p=0.476$).[1] The absence of a significant negative correlation offers a counterpoise to the concern about the gradual erosion of professionals' commitment to the public good by the pursuit of school choice for their children as encouraged by neoliberal policies.

Between the professional groups, the level of neoliberalism of police was statistically significantly higher than that of nurses and teachers, with a small to

Table 8.1 Spearman's correlation between 'neoliberalism' and 'public good'

Public good	Correlation coefficient	1.000	−0.004
	Sig. (1-tailed)	–	0.476
Neoliberalism	Correlation coefficient	−0.004	1.000
	Sig. (1-tailed)	0.476	–

medium effect ($t(177)$=3.38, p=0.001, r=0.25) and a large effect ($t(115)$=6.30, p<0.001, r=0.51) respectively. The level of neoliberalism of doctors and nurses was statistically significantly higher than that of teachers, with a medium to large effect ($t(97)$=4.20, p<0.001, r=0.39) and a small to medium effect ($t(204)$=3.67, p<0.001, r=0.25) respectively. Of particular interest, doctors reported relatively high levels for both neoliberalism and public good attitudes. We further tested whether a negative correlation between neoliberalism and public good existed within any particular professional group. No significant negative correlation was found. Again, this finding departs from Saks's thesis of eroding commitment to the public good in the face of marketisation.

From this exploration, we understand that it was not a case of either 'public good' or 'neoliberalism' in the professional families we sampled. Rather, they variably endorsed these two value sets independently of each other. In other words, it was not a case of pursuing one at the expense of the other, but more a case of accommodating both value sets in the family career, and how professional parents meshed diverse considerations. The analytical question then becomes how these families adjudicate public and private stakes in family mobility, and what tensions, contradictions or dilemmas arise from their concurrence.

This chapter adds two more layers to the empirical work reported in earlier chapters to explore such public/private tensions. In the next section, we focus on the teaching profession, to exemplify the dilemmatic space our teacher interviewees described in terms of how their public and private personas intersect problematically in the restricted education markets of smaller rural/remote community. The following section reports on survey responses from all four sampled professional groups to the hypothetical scenarios in terms of how respondents invoked public service and weighed it up against private rationales. The final section reflects on the findings and policy implications, and what it might mean for Australia when services in rural and remote communities are considered to be of insufficient quality to attract or retain the professionals needed to staff them.

Public/private dilemmas for teachers in rural and regional communities

Attracting and retaining qualified teachers to staff schools in regional, rural and remote communities is an important policy issue for the public good, of ongoing concern in both richer and poorer countries (see for example Voigt-Graf 2003; Mulkeen 2010). Much research about teachers in rural schools has focused on recruiting and retaining new teachers, highlighting factors such as pre-service rural experiences, incentives, mentorships, lifestyle, cultural values, infrastructure, employment conditions, and the pull of urban/coastal positions (Lunn 1997; Yarrow *et al.* 1999; Lock 2008; Sharplin 2009). A limited set of studies of teachers with families cite family reasons, such as spouse employment and children's education opportunities, as either disincentives for taking up rural positions or motivations for leaving such positions (Boylan *et al.* 1993; Roberts 2004; Lyons 2009; Sharplin 2009). While such family reasons remain self-explanatory and under-theorised in workforce reports (for example, Haslam McKenzie 2007), this book has sought to understand the deliberative processes of work/family/ education articulation behind professionals' selective mobility. Forsey (2010) similarly offers a qualitative account of two teachers working in metropolitan Western Australia, tracking their decisions to change which sector they work in and where, as family circumstances change. Under the phrase, 'publicly minded, privately focused' (p. 58), Forsey captures the contradictions for teachers caught between 'communitarian ideals' (p. 54) and ethical commitment to public education on one hand, and their choice of the independent or Catholic sector for their career or children.

Where the provision of public schools and registered teachers was once sufficient to attract middle-class professionals to less populated areas (Wells *et al.* 2005), the context has changed significantly. As discussed in Chapter 5, the ascendancy of neoliberal metapolicy (Rizvi and Lingard 2010) has encouraged the exercise of consumer choice and marketisation as mechanisms to improve public sector efficiency in Australia and elsewhere (Connell 2002; Pusey 2003; Wells and Crain 2000). In rural Australia, neoliberal economic restructuring has manifested as less protection for farmers, more exposure to global competition, and a gradual withdrawal of subsidised services. This restructuring marks a profound if gradual change in the economic and social footing of these communities:

> Regional towns were, to a limited extent, 'planned' by federal and state governments, which supported railways, roads, schools, law courts, police stations and other facilities and services. Such state involvement was consistent with ideologies of decentralisation, state-assisted economic growth and egalitarianism. Commitment to such ideals has now been replaced by a more narrow focus on free markets, 'user pays' and 'self help' – as part of what is known as neoliberalism.
>
> (Gray and Lawrence 2001: 9)

In the education sector, neoliberal policy is more obviously manifested in the MySchool website (www.myschool.edu.au). This was established by the Commonwealth government to publicly report on every Australian school's profile of achievements on standardised national tests, and thus inform parents' choices of school. Under this logic, the consumer learns to distrust public sector provision and the local school can no longer be presumed to satisfy parent demands. The 'good parent-citizen' (Campbell *et al.* 2009: 4) is thus encouraged and resourced to exercise prudent care in school choice. Campbell *et al.* (2009) pointed out that there are two sides to this cultivated choice disposition, 'aspiration and anxiety' (p. 3).

As demonstrated in Chapter 5's narratives of the optimising circuit, families' choice of school can undermine rural tenure. First, teachers are themselves middle-class professionals and likely to be closely engaged in educational markets as anxious parent-choosers at some stage. This makes teachers with children a special case positioned in a unique bind as both service providers and service choosers. Second, educational markets in smaller communities will offer more limited choice which may not satisfy the escalating aspirations of middle-class parents (Doherty *et al.* 2013). This concurrence of conditions constructs a dilemmatic space: teachers as skilled professionals are needed for hard-to-staff rural areas. However, while they provide the public solution for such localities, these same localities can present private problems for the teacher with family responsibilities, being a middle-class parent subject to the same aspirations and anxieties as others, whose disposition to exercise choice has been cultivated and legitimated by current policy. The following four brief vignettes from some of our teacher interviewees living and working in rural and remote localities show how unique public/private dilemmas can arise in the limited educational markets of rural/remote localities.

Case 1: Public service at private cost

Imogen, a teacher in a rural town, with two children and a partner, explicitly embraced country service as her professional duty. However, she told of an ongoing struggle balancing this responsibility with opportunities to achieve permanency in her chosen specialisation as student counsellor, and with health care for her family:

> When I was going to go back to work, I put in that form that said these are the places that I'd be interested in being relocated to, and [remote town] was one of them ... I knew that it was part of my teacher responsibilities that we had to do the out west thing.... When an expression of interest came up in [rural town 1] for six months I was like, 'Yes, pick me, please pick me!' ... because I was just getting really disgruntled with [remote town's] services. My children were very sick in the first year.... We could never get into a doctor, like three-week waiting list ... [Child 1] should have had grommets put in ... so his speech started to get affected and his hearing.... So we picked up the whole family and went to [rural town 1].... It was great career-wise and it was great for [husband]'s health ... he needed surgery immediately.... The day that he was admitted ... I had to have my interview for my classified appointment for the following year ... I had the interview and then by November I think we had found out that I had won the position in [rural town 2], and I didn't want to come to be quite honest because of [husband]'s health ... but [husband] said, 'Well, we need to have permanency ...' I'd be looking at moving probably at the end of the year if I could

so that [Child 1] could go to a different school. Not just for his education, but so that I can be closer to my mother.

This vignette wove a tangled web of mobility considerations involving critical health issues, professional responsibility, permanency, promotion, family ties and school choice, pulling her family in different directions. All these factors jostled simultaneously for priority in the family, not as neatly compartmentalised domains. The underserviced remote town that satisfied her public service responsibility did not offer adequate health services for the young family, and the rural town that offered a permanent position in her chosen field did not offer the desired school choice.

Case 2: Professional allegiance and private choice

Yvonne, a teacher with three school-aged children and a partner working in a remote township, expressed a strong allegiance to the government sector as both parent and professional. She had attended government schools for her own education and then invested her career in that sector across a number of rural and remote towns. When Yvonne's eldest child was ready to start preschool, there was only ever one choice in her mind: 'Well, it's difficult to be working in one system and promoting it as the best and then sending your child up to another.' Her comment captures the visibility of teachers' private choices and their professional resonance in small communities. Notwithstanding this principled stance, Yvonne told how she quickly capitulated when her daughter encountered problems in the remote town's only government school:

> She was going to come here until Year 10. What happened there is … she was treated quite poorly … and she just said to me, one day she came home and she said, 'I'm going away to boarding school.' I said, 'Okay. Off you go'…. In [previous rural town], a number of families send their girls to [independent boarding school], so I had heard about it from the teachers…. People from [independent school] would come out during show days and things like that and advertise the school. I knew they had a good cross-country programme, which is what [Child 1] was interested in at the time…. But I also knew musically speaking, they had programmes there, as well … I knew that it would give her the opportunity to take part in that stuff, if she wanted it, but it would also, academically speaking, I knew she'd be right where she was.

Like other middle-class parents, Yvonne was alert to her child's academic prospects and extra-curricular enrichment. Despite a professional loyalty to the government sector, her daughter's wellbeing and happiness were immediately considered more important, thus the private issue trumped the professional principle.

Case 3: Professional insider knowledge in private choices

Nancy taught in another remote township that offered a choice between government and Catholic primary schools. Working on casual contracts in both schools over time had provided Nancy with intimate, comparative knowledge of the two schools. Despite being strong advocates of government schooling, she and her husband chose the Catholic primary school for both children, not for religious reasons but because of the social environment Nancy had observed:

> I was working at the state [government] school as well as [Catholic school]. I based my decision at the time on where he would go purely on the nature of the school.... At the time I just felt that the state school couldn't offer the positive family environment that I wanted my kids to be in. So I chose [Catholic school] purely because ... it was a nice family school ... I was 100 per cent sure my kids would go to a state school. I've always said that and it was very difficult for me to not send them to a state school because I was teaching.... It's very difficult being a teacher in a small town of a state school and being seen to be sending your child to another school.

Elsewhere Nancy had summarised the limited educational market in her community: 'We don't have a lot of choice so we basically have to pick the best of what's available at the time for our kids.' Nevertheless, Nancy also expressed her willingness to change schools if necessary, a disposition which casts her as the anxious middle-class parent closely monitoring each child's progress and exercising what choice she had. In this way, teachers as parents can emerge as uniquely well-informed, assertive educational consumers in these small markets. The public/private dilemma for Nancy lay not in choosing what she felt was best for her child, but in wearing her private choice professionally, 'being seen to be sending your child to another school'. In this way teachers become conspicuous consumers in limited educational markets. Being held professionally accountable for one's private choices is a stress particular to teachers-as-parents, and their unique dilemmatic space given their heightened if not inescapable visibility in small communities.

Case 4: Private risks in public service

When Helen and her partner moved to their rural town to fulfil her required country service, they had a choice between the government primary school (where Helen was working) and the Catholic school for their four children:

> Well, at first, we thought we might send them to the private [Catholic] school, because I didn't know how – they'd never been at the same school as me before ... and it was like, 'Oh, I don't know. This is a bit scary, them

being there.' So when we moved here, I thought, 'No, I'll put them with me and we'll see how it goes'.... My first year, I was actually in his year level ... I made sure I said straight up, 'Please don't put him in my class.' But I was still a bit worried that he would have to still interact with me as a teacher, not as a mum. He didn't mind, so I thought – the first time he said to me, 'I don't like this,' it would have been, 'All right, let's go' ... I wasn't sure how kids would react. Will they tease him? Will they pick on him? Will they bully him because he's my son? I wasn't sure.

In this vignette, Helen reflects on the limited choices, anxieties and fears particular to the teacher-as-parent in these smaller communities, and the possible consequences emanating from her professional role that would be borne by her children.

In such ways, the teachers we interviewed described the dilemmatic space of working in rural and remote communities. The concerns these teachers reported were exacerbated by factors ostensibly common to small towns: limited schooling choices; teachers' visibility in the community that risked conflating their parent and professional roles; and being privy to insider knowledge of one's limited options. These vignettes make evident how the teachers were mindful of school choice, similar to the middle-class parents reported in other studies. However, they were distinguished from such parents in other ways, being differently resourced with sectoral allegiances and insider knowledge, and being differently positioned by the duty of public service, and by the ensuing interaction between their public role as teacher-as-professional and their private concerns as teacher-as-parent. We would argue that such conflation of roles, though still possible, would be much less likely in larger, more diffuse communities with deeper educational markets. In this way, we can understand how these social attributes of rural/remote places might distinguish them in the professional imaginary and impact on the professional family's mobility therein. The next section takes this point further with a consideration of how professionals responded to hypothetical opportunities in rural and remote locations in the online survey.

Reconciling neoliberal and public good value sets

As outlined in Chapter 6, respondents to the online survey were given the following hypothetical scenario and invited to share their reaction in an open-ended prose response to the following question:

In this question, we ask you to consider different places as hypothetical locations for you and your current family household. Imagine you are offered very attractive positions at the following locations: Roma, Bowen and Cunnamulla. What would be your reaction to such options, and what considerations would guide your decision?

The three nominated locations were the rural town of Bowen on the tropical coast, inland regional hub Roma and more remote and disadvantaged Cunnamulla (see Figure 8.1). As an indication of the difficulty these communities have had attracting professionals, the Queensland Department of Health currently offers medical officers an 'inaccessibility incentive' allowance of $41,400 for a year's service in Cunnamulla and $20,700 per annum in Roma or Bowen (Queensland Government 2013). With this range, we sought to explore how professionals with school-aged families engaged with these rural and remote communities, and on what terms. The question received 275 responses ranging from a few words to a paragraph.

A thematic analysis of the responses highlighted repeated mentions of private considerations, including: lifestyle attributes of the locations; school quality; access to medical services; proximity to extended family; remuneration and incentives; disruption to children's education; opportunities for spouse employment; career prospects. These concerns resonate strongly with the narratives presented in Chapter 5, and are well documented in the literature around rural workforce and regional sustainability (for example, Cameron 1998; Humphreys *et al.* 2002; OECD 2005; Miles *et al.* 2006; Australian Government Department of Health and Ageing 2008; Owen *et al.* 2008). However, here we are more interested in exploring how these predictable concerns were weighed and balanced against any call to public duty. In other words, we were interested in the relations constructed between public service and private family considerations, and the logic that governed their ordering.

Figure 8.1 Locations in survey's hypothetical scenarios.

There were only seven unconditional positive responses indicating that the respondent would entertain any location offered: 'If I was transferred I'd go. I joined a statewide organisation, not a southeast Queensland organisation' (#19, police); 'would move to all three, rural nursing is my passion' (#83, nurse). There were also ten unconditional rejections of the idea: 'no, not going' (#64, teacher): 'have no interest in changing work locations. Am not interested in uprooting myself and the family' (#124, nurse). These responses mark polar opposites, with the public service ethic dominating mobility decisions at one extreme and private concerns dominating at the other.

In between these two poles, the vast majority of respondents outlined multi-faceted decisions that integrated a number of work, family and education considerations. The responses invoked a variety of conditions across a number of institutional fronts, which needed to align and be satisfied to make such a move thinkable. For example:

> I am happy to try a move and living in a rural/remote location given consideration to the following: minimal or no impact on husband's career opportunities. Opportunity to excel in given career. Opportunity to increase family's financial position. Opportunity to school kids in an excellent learning environment including curricula, sports, social and cultural opportunities.
>
> (#239, nurse)

Such lists of conditions reference the multiplicity of risks involved in moving a family unit and how any relocation decision in the public interest implicates managing private risk on a number of fronts. This professional's response seeks a guarantee that no family member's life projects will be compromised by the move. It is also evident that the response sets a high benchmark in terms of 'excellence' and extra-curricular enrichment that the limited educational markets of small communities could find hard to satisfy. Conditions over which a prospective employer has some influence, such as remuneration, feature as only one facet in this multifaceted complex.

Other respondents stipulated a single necessary condition, though the nature of the dominant factor differed across respondents:

- 'If our religious beliefs were strong in that area' (#16, police);
- 'If a location does not have good health facilities and schools, I would not consider moving' (#12, police);
- 'Would have to be significant career and financial reward to get me to move '(#34, police); and
- 'We would not be prepared to go because of the educational choices for our children would not be there and we would not like to send them to a boarding school' (#217, nurse).

More subtly, some responses engaged with the hypothetical locations only on the assumption that they as professionals would travel in and out, leaving the family home and its associated spouse employment and schooling projects in place:

- 'Would only consider if fly-in fly-out[2] on a four week on, one week off at the employer's expense' (#256, nurse); and
- 'Depending on pay rise and work conditions, flexibility of holidays to go back and visit family eight-plus weeks of paid leave, having a set roster to allow for family to visit me' (#216, nurse).

For other respondents, the necessary condition would be placing their children in boarding school, thus assuming the need to transcend the local educational market in these localities: 'I would consider Roma as a possibility as it is only a four-hour drive away – my daughter could board at her current school' (#172, nurse). These responses that considered de-aggregating family units to progress individual projects give some indication of the middle-class family's intense dedication to children's education in a school of choice as the priority.

Some responses indicated that although the professional opportunity appealed, other family circumstances trumped any such possibility: 'Fantastic, but I cannot move there because my children need the stability of attending the same school' (#219, nurse); 'My husband is in his "perfect job" … and the kids love their schools and social life. I personally love rural and remote nursing but cannot do it until a later time' (#227, nurse). Gamekeeping strategies of offering financial incentives addressed to the individual worker can fail to offset such family considerations, as one respondent explained: 'Kids very stable at current school main reason not to leave. I earn enough. Not greedy and financial reasons not enough incentive to move' (#21, doctor).

Other responses brought to the surface the constraining circumstances of more complex and extended family forms. As a stark example, family units negotiating shared custody arrangements had other more pressing accountabilities which temporarily overruled any public service claim:

> I would refuse due to family reasons. I have already indicated to the department that I will not be able to do 'country service' until my current school-aged children have finished school and no longer require custodial access to their father.
>
> (#189, teacher)

Twelve responses mentioned past remote/rural service. Two of these respondents indicated that they had already worked in remote/rural settings and had not ruled out further, but now faced additional considerations given family responsibilities. Nine of these respondents invoked past service in rural/remote or disadvantaged communities as the reason why they would not, or should not have to, consider the locations suggested: 'have done western service' (#295, teacher). In other words, past service in rural/remote communities was proffered as evidence of having satisfied any claim such duty could make on them as professionals, and hence their right to legitimately prioritise other needs. One respondent was very clear about how public service and family priorities had been purposefully addressed and staged sequentially: 'I have done six years in a rural location – I chose to do this before having my children so I could give them a stable home environment surrounded by extended family' (#305, teacher). Commitment to a public service ethic thus impinged explicitly on these professionals' decision making to some degree, but within limits.

This section has exemplified the qualitative responses to an open-ended survey question regarding hypothetical professional opportunities in three purposefully selected rural/remote locations. In the mindsets of these professional parents, family considerations, in particular school choice, repeatedly trumped the professional ethic of public service in rural/remote localities. While the public service ethic was evident in many responses, it was typically circumscribed and mitigated by family conditions and phases. Thus across the sample, both value sets were present, but not exercising equal impact on family mobility decisions.

Conclusion: the private limits to public service in small communities

This chapter has explored tensions in the relationship between public and private considerations of professional parents to better understand their chronic shortage in Australia's rural and remote communities. We have approached this social problem as a family mobility issue. We recognised professionals as a distinct category of worker, given their membership in closed occupations which entail implicit contracts of altruistic service with the public, in particular the responsibility to service rural/remote communities. This duty of 'country service' creates a mobility imperative peculiar to professionals, which in turn implicates the mobility of their families. Literature from the sociology of the professions warns that this traditional service ethic could be eroding in today's more marketised times with the emphasis now on private interests and risk management. The same professionals were further identified as a distinct group of middle-class parents with vested interests in their children's education to protect the intergenerational reproduction of advantage. This chapter has been concerned with whether such educational dispositions, fanned by the current zeitgeist of neoliberal policy, have further compromised and undermined professional mobility into rural/remote localities. These towns must rely on a flow of qualified professionals, but cannot promise the quality of services these professionals might aspire to for their families.

Following this line of thinking, we expected a negative correlation between our survey constructs of 'public good' and 'neoliberalism', but the analysis revealed no statistically significant correlation to support the argument that neo-liberal values worked to erode professionals' public service ethic. In other words, there was no either/or binary operating between these two values sets. This led us to ask how these professional families managed to dignify and reconcile both in their mobility decisions.

We appropriated the concept of dilemmatic space (Fransson and Grannas 2013) to capture how social relations within the limited educational markets of these smaller communities can precipitate unique dilemmas for the professionals who work there. Vignettes from teachers with school-aged children working in rural and remote communities illustrated how the professional's public and private interests could rub uncomfortably against each other in ways that would not happen in larger population centres. Then we turned to the broader survey data to enquire how the two value sets compete or cohere in family mobility deliberations using the ploy of a hypothetical scenario of attractive career opportunities in particular rural/remote settings. The analysis of responses highlighted how the professional parents in general acknowledged the public service duty of country service but subjugated its claim on their career path in the interest of family considerations, in particular the education of their children. Such ordering was evident in the conditions respondents required to make such a career move thinkable, or the temporal ordering of an early country service phase to fulfil such duty before prioritising family considerations.

The interplay between family, educational strategy, career opportunities and locality implicates multiple institutions, which makes the problem less amenable to simple policy levers. Workforce policy solutions to promote recruitment and retention of professionals in rural and remote communities often pursue an individualised 'carrot' approach of additional remuneration or incentive schemes (Health Workforce Australia 2012), and thus gloss over this complex family interface in mobility decisions. Other policy solutions, such as bond schemes attached to university places in medicine, forced postings for teachers in government sectors, minimum service periods for police promotion, and visa or registration restrictions for overseas trained doctors, resort to more forceful stick tactics. Neither approach fosters or dignifies the ethical commitment to altruistic public service that has underpinned the professions.

By virtue of the ongoing need for these services and the closed nature of their registration systems, professionals have been largely protected from the changes in the nature of work and the workplace of recent times (Billett 2006). However, there are no such guarantees for the next generation, so these professional parents will exercise their relative advantage in risk-management strategies in order to prioritise their children's educational chance. Metropolitan and regional centres with deeper educational and labour markets offer these families the capacity to address educational priorities. However, this private solution will continue to re-create the public issue of underserviced rural and remote communities. The problem is not static but will spiral and worsen over time — as a community's services erode, local housing prices can fall then attract a welfare-dependent population with higher service needs (Hugo and Bell 1998).

In a nutshell, these communities that rely on professional mobility will need not just viable services, but services of sufficient quality to attract and retain the professionals needed to staff them. The benchmark of 'sufficient quality' is getting higher. However, under market logic, 'declining communities frequently face a policy environment that views developing their services as a poor investment' (Larson 2010: 309). We suggest that policy discussions about the recruitment and retention of professionals to sustain services in rural and remote communities could benefit from reconsidering the intrusion of market logic and dynamics into public institutions and professional sensibilities. These mindsets are likely to promote proactive, risk-managing strategy by those in a position to do so, in order to protect current and future life opportunities for family members. As spelt out throughout this book, the risks, opportunities and dilemmas within such a policy landscape are increasingly left for family units to resolve through their intersubjective negotiations over time and place. Given their chronic maldistribution across the communities that rely on their mobility, there is a growing concern that the private decisions and selective mobilities that protect and advantage these professional families will increasingly disadvantage others less fortunate at a distance.

Notes

1 We reported the 'one-tailed' significance level because we posed a directional hypothesis and employed a Spearman correlation because of the non-parametric nature of the data.
2 'Fly-in fly-out' is a mode of employment that has developed around remote mine sites in Australia, whereby the worker leaves the family home to travel to the work site, living on site temporarily to work an extended, intensified roster, then travel home for an extended break.

Chapter 9

Families moving on to get ahead

> R: If you can bear with me, this is the sort of story I want to document.
> P1: Oh okay.
> R: The whole complexity...
> P2: Oh, we've got complexity.
> P1: We've got complexity up the Wazoo!
>
> (Robyn and Rob, military family, two parents)

Our exploration of family mobility throughout this book has purposefully courted complexity. We have demonstrated how family life, career decisions, educational strategy and geographic mobility interact. Rather than treat each of these aspects in a separate analytic container, we have grappled with the messiness (Pocock 2003), dilemmas and contingencies involved in how family, education and work articulate over time and space. This multifocal gaze contrasts with the oversimplification evident in calls for a more mobile and responsive workforce within and beyond the nation. Such business-oriented discourse fails to dignify workers' other social roles, and the intersubjective complications these roles entail. Nevertheless, families are not immune to the lure of opportunities elsewhere and can be mobile under a variety of conditions and logics, as our previous chapters have demonstrated. By unpacking the narratives and reasoning behind the mobility histories of two different groups of families – the hypermobile military family and the selectively mobile professional family – this book starts to refract such overly simplistic rhetoric into a consideration of different families and their differently textured mobilities.

Family mobility is both prosaic and profound as a social phenomenon. It may not foreground the sleek technologies and funky urban spaces popular in other mobility studies, but its intersection of public and private vectors offers fertile ground for social science. Family mobility provides an empirical window on how this most ubiquitous and meaningful social unit juggles duties, aspirations, anxieties, risks and opportunities to produce problems and/or solutions on a micro scale. These private outcomes in their aggregated patterns in turn produce social problems, solutions or both on a macro scale. In this chapter we reflect on what the work of the previous chapters can tell us more generally about the family, mobility, careers, education and the social fabric in these more mobile times. We revisit some of the earlier theoretical discussion regarding the social construction of space and place, and the growing mobility imperative to consider how the profits available in moving on to get ahead are unevenly distributed across social groups. We also sketch some practical implications that might redress this imbalance. The conclusion considers possible further lines of enquiry, and whether mobility in itself is necessarily a desirable thing.

Mobility as a lens on family

Across the book's chapters, we have maintained our focus on the whole family as the unit of analysis, concentrating on the intersubjectivity of this social unit and in particular the intense family phase of caring for school-aged children. As the object of study, the family implicates additional forces and intergenerational dynamics that impinge on actors' strategies, practices and actions. It is this whole-of-family explanatory stratum that studies using the individual worker as the unit of analysis tend to overlook or underestimate. Our interest in family mobility has brought these generative forces and their complications to the empirical surface. In im/mobility decisions, families are forced to explicitly negotiate priorities. These moments of collective reflexivity expose then weigh up the variety of projects and institutional fronts family members are engaged in, and their nesting within the meta-project of being a family. The sacrifices, mitigations and compromises our participants reported have shown how the strength of intersubjective claims that distinguish familial relations from other social relations serve to decentre adults' career projects. This decentring has been shown to be the case for male parents as much as female parents. While not every adult will build a family, the vast majority of people do, so it becomes an analytical conceit to conceptualise workers as untrammelled individuals, or to treat family considerations as an afterthought.

Our conceptualisation of family highlighted its active and reactive processes at the interface between public and private domains: that is, families as 'the arena where macro- and micro-forces come together' (Sherif-Trask 2010: vii). Chapter 8's exploration of how the professionals' ethic of public service was filtered and diluted through family considerations of school quality serves as an example of this public/private nexus. We suggested that the family will increasingly serve as the social institution of last resort in that it is left to assess, integrate and resolve the multiple demands made by the variety of external institutions family members are engaged with. Narrative 4.1, 'I do the corridor thing', in Chapter 4 exemplifies this through its story of parents mapping routes between child-care centres, schools and workplaces to ensure their choice of housing can make getting to work on time possible. It is left to the family to make the combination of disparate institutional regimes work. Again, our lens on family mobility events has allowed us to capture these processes in action, as families describe their work to strategically coordinate and re-place their variety of projects.

It also made evident how some members absorbed the externalities of certain decisions on behalf of other members in order to make im/mobility possible. For example, children in the military families had to manage discontinuities in their education to facilitate the military career; professionals dampened career aspirations to protect stability in their children's education. These are relations like no other – being part of a family decentres the individual and requires that their various projects take account of effects on other members. These intersubjective processes of subsidising and accommodating others' projects are not necessarily free of conflict or friction, as poignantly illustrated in Chapter 4's Narrative 4.27, 'Moving time at our house is extremely stressful'. Thus a lens on mobility can expose how family relations can become attenuated, as well as the possible fracture line at the point where the individual refuses to continue absorbing the intersubjective claims made of them.

While intersubjective subsidy may serve as a distinctive feature of family relations, it should not be taken for granted. There is growing improvisation in how families respond to the risky freedoms of institutional individualisation (Beck and Beck-Gernsheim 2004). In particular, social scripts around women's employment are changing, troubling past assumptions and templates. Chapter 4's exploration of military families' narratives offered snapshots of such social change underway, whereby the ADF's presumptions about how families work rubbed against the hopes and aspirations of the non-ADF partners. In a reflective moment that captures this tension between individual and family projects, one mother in a military family explained how she habitually subjugated her individual interests to enable others' projects, but this workable solution had not extinguished her own aspirations:

> and you know always in the back of my mind – not that that's been a huge issue for me since the kids because my career has really taken a back step in that I've chosen to be at home with the kids and stuff like that – but always in the back of my mind is what opportunities are going to come for me and are they going to fit in with what's happening with everybody else.
>
> (Pat, military family)

We would expect family mobility to get harder, not easier, as women's career projects come to exert more weight and priority in family equations, and women become less willing to absorb intersubjective costs on behalf of other family members. Family mobility events bring such underlying assumptions, bargains and dispositions to the surface for overt reassessment. When we understand how such internal equations allow families to be together over time and place, we can also understand how family units can become tenuous and liable to break.

While there is a growing literature concerned with the interface between family and work, our mobility lens has highlighted how education is an equally pivotal concern shaping family processes that warrants more explicit treatment. Chapter 7 provided the background to the context of spiralling credentialism and provided evidence of intergenerational educational projects contributing to im/mobility decisions, in particular the decision to stay put. In this way, the mobility lens makes visible how intergenerational educational projects are core and ongoing business in families. Such focal endeavours demand more than social science's habitual treatment of education as demographic background. For this reason, we have coined the term 'work/family/education articulation' to boost the profile of educational matters in such fields of research.

Family as a lens on mobility

If a mobility lens can help develop our understanding of family, how might studies of families develop our understanding of mobility? By locating the actor in a sticky web of familial relations, a family focus can offer a counter-weight to the individualism evident in much mobility research to date. Family settings may not reflect the cutting edge of social change, but they present very real and resilient complications that have largely resisted the best efforts of social policy, employer incentives and labour market strategy. We have concentrated on familial relations within the immediate family household, but repeated references to extended family considerations across our data indicate a second layer of familial relations complicating or constraining mobility decisions. The intrusion of family considerations in career mobility was most obvious in narratives concerning children with special needs which emphatically trumped other family members' projects to become the focal priority. In this way, a focus on family offers a timely corrective on overstated claims celebrating mobility as the new lifestyle. It's not that families don't move, but that there are more considerations and social forces at play.

By concentrating on the larger biographical event of domestic relocations, it becomes evident that such mobility events do not feature as a constant potential in people's reflexivity, but rather as an intermittent potential that stutters and starts over family phases. In this way, the family has its own more and less motile phases, which are closely related to the normative preference for stability around educational projects. This suggests that the dimension of time in terms of life course phase would enrich any understanding of mobility. One of our teacher interviewees used the phrase 'window of opportunity' to project where mobility might fit in their family career:

> I've sort of looked at windows of opportunity. I thought this year or next year was a window where the eldest one was going into Year 10, the second one was going into Year 8, but if we were heading back to [regional centre], she'd be going back in with her friends that she still maintains from there.... So we looked at this year, next year was a possible, even the year after when the eldest one goes into Year 11 and then the second one into Year 9. We

figure that it's probably not too bad to move then because, again, if we're moving we'd be going back to [regional centre] where they'll have that support. Then after that we figure, we'd have to stay put for a few years. If we don't move then we'll stay put and then, depending on what the eldest one does, we'd come up to another window where we could move again.

(Alex, teacher family in rural town with partner and three children)

Such windows of opportunity offer the potential of moving, but whether or not mobility eventuates will depend on multiple other forces and conditions.

To conceptualise such conditions, we developed the concept of viscosity in Chapter 2 to describe the varying degrees of resistance or enablement the structural context can offer the mobile agent. This concept derived from the military family narratives and the various treatments they reported receiving from the many schools their children passed through, for better and for worse. We showed how the motility of families waxes and wanes over time, according to the experiences, troubles and learning accrued as various members pass through a variety of institutions. In particular, children accrued educational complications from institutional discontinuities and these could compound over their family's mobility history. Families engage with many social structures including health services, education systems, labour markets and child-care markets. It will be the lived outcome of the interactions between family members' motility and the institutional viscosity they encounter that primes their outlook on future mobility. This process was evidenced in the codas of family narratives, which folded past mobility events into future plans and dispositions.

Though derived from family mobility narratives, we suggest that the concept of viscosity can add a valuable analytical dimension to mobility studies more generally, and augment its treatments of agentive motility. The concept of viscosity will also help organisations and policies concerned with managing mobility to better assess and operationally tweak the institutional conditions they have at their disposal.

Family mobility as a lens on career/work studies

Our focus on whole-of-family relocation has also illuminated the extended context that contributes to adult career decisions. Our lens has emphasised the fact that family members form an interconnected system. Therefore, any relocation decisions prompted by education and/or career opportunities of one family member will necessarily take into account the goals and projects of all family members. Though both sampled groups (military personnel and professionals) were shown to use the strategy of moving on to get ahead in their chosen careers, they experienced very different conditions for career decision-making. Military career progression was conditional on mobility. Relocations by these families privileged that consideration, and protected its continuity, while other family members' projects wrestled with discontinuities. For the family as a whole, this game plan typically worked until children reached critical junctures in their education. At this point, the family balance of priorities tipped, sometimes at the expense of military career advancement, other times at the expense of the military career itself.

The professional families could approach mobility for career advancement very differently. In their interview narratives and survey responses, mobility was a popular strategy to achieve a professional start or fulfil country service obligations, but subsequent mobility typically had to meet the condition that it would improve the prospects for all family member projects. The dual samples also served to contrast the non-negotiable mobility requirements of the military career, with the more negotiable, and therefore more compromised, expectation of mobility in the professional career as public service. The new mobility paradigm invites more consideration of the role mobility plays in career trajectories, while the consideration of families invites more exploration of how different occupations move on to get ahead, on whose terms and at what cost within the family unit. This multifaceted lens could profitably be applied to emergent modes of working such as 'fly-in fly-out' rosters and expatriate postings.

The book has also identified credentialism as a mobility system that makes occupational status and expertise more portable. Credentialism thus underpins horizontal/geographic mobility as well as vertical mobility in terms of career progression. In Chapter 7 we connected past debates about spiralling credentialism with current concerns about maintaining professional currency. We developed the concept of mobius markets to capture the ongoing and iterative work that individuals and families undertake to invest in advantageous educational credentials, derive the profits thereof, then reinvest to maintain the value and currency of the credentials in an increasingly crowded and credentialed labour market. The focus on family points to the way mobius markets tie adults, as well as children, to educational projects. We have used the term 'mobius market agenda' to highlight the way professional families in particular are managing a number of such educational projects for both children and adults, simultaneously.

There was evidence in our analysis of survey responses that adults' further study and children's education could motivate family moves, but these factors could also anchor families in a location that served these projects well. Credentialism – in play for both parents' career projects and their children's educational opportunities – may serve as a mobility system, but ironically the mobius market imperative can deter mobility into rural and remote locations given more limited opportunities there to continue to develop such credentials.

More broadly, our explorations demonstrate that families, whatever their circumstances, sought to optimise mobius market agendas for all family members. This meant the career of the adult, at times the sole breadwinner, was rarely the prime consideration, and that potential profits in the far distant future from educational investments in the present carried considerable weight in family decisions in the present. We understand this outcome in two ways. First, it reflects the rising stakes around credentialing in the 'totally pedagogised society' (Bernstein 2001: 365). Second, and perhaps more importantly, it demonstrates how family commitments decentre the adult career project and mitigate more material motives. One of the non-professional council workers we interviewed in a rural town explains how this commitment works.

Narrative 9.1 'But why would you?'

Dave: non-professional council worker family, two parents, two children

Abstract	R: Any prospects of moving?
Orientation	As soon as they do, well see, [C2] at the moment, he's in Grade 2 ... so we've got a while till he finishes school and then, so long as they stay in [rural town], well we'll stay in [rural town].... Family first ... I don't look [for other job opportunities].
Complication	There was all the talk with all the mines and that that came around,
Evaluation	but why would you leave a stable job to go and work for one of them? They keep saying big money in the mines and everything, but to do it you're doing 12-hour shifts or more. By the time you drive out there and back you're doing sort of 14 hours.... Yeah, and you got no lifestyle then.
Resolution	Not for me.
Coda	I got a family.

Dave did not work in a well-paid profession and received no incentive payments or allowances to live in his rural setting, yet the 'big money' available within the booming mining industry could not compete with the value and satisfactions of settled family life. This narrative and similar ones from professional families in Chapter 5 suggest that gamekeeping tactics that offer financial incentives to individual workers can miss the point somewhat.

Family mobility as a lens on educational markets

Sociological treatment of educational markets has tracked the global spread of neoliberal policy discourses and described the associated practices of institutions and strategies of parents, in particular the highly invested professional fraction of the middle class. Empirical studies of educational marketisation have focused on school choice as the manifestation of such policy and the expression of the dispositions it cultivates. As reported in Chapter 1, such studies have also documented across a number of countries the strategy of residential moves into the catchment zone of the school of choice within cities. Our study has taken this line of enquiry to another level by asking what role school choice plays in family mobility between towns and across rural/remote space. By scaling up the school choice issue we were able to ask how families reconciled career mobility with educational strategy over time and space, then what larger effect market choice at this scale produced on smaller localities offering limited choice.

The narratives from both military and professional families included detailed accounts of parents' careful consideration of school quality and their encounters with marketisation practices in the schooling sector such as zoning regulations, booking fees and waiting lists. The short notice that military families received regarding when and where they were to be posted made it difficult for them to use the same strategies the professional families had at their disposal. Through the military family narratives, we were privy to the informal trade in school reputations and intense research phase that informed these families' housing choices. These were strategies and routines that this community had developed to play their role as parent/consumer in educational markets, and to sustain their motility under challenging circumstances. While restricted to their allocated town, these families were keen to exercise what choice they could within the means at their disposal, but they were poorly served by the viscous assumption of an immobile local population built into such school practices.

The professional families we interviewed along the regional to remote transect were differently resourced – they had more control of the timing and placing of their mobility, more choice, and some had more resources at their disposal. A few had booked places for children in high status schools years well in advance, on the assumption that they would make their way back to larger centres. Narrative 5.19, 'If, if, if – if I get promoted, if we move, if you go to this school' in Chapter 5 gave some sense of the stress in how that strategy might later play out. Others had the material resources to consider boarding schools as a way to achieve the notional quality and status they aspired to. The casualties by this strategy were those families caught in the trap between middle-class aspirations and the price of boarding options (for example, Chapter 5's Narrative 5.16, 'If we lived down there', and Narrative 5.24, 'We've got to find 20-odd grand').

Boarding school featured in both military family and professional family narratives as an ambivalent affordance for family mobility. As a solution, it could assure the stability many families sought regardless of where the military family was posted or where the promotional opportunity arose. The boarding school choice could also transcend the perceived drawbacks of limited local school markets, thus avoiding a whole-of-family move. In this way, it became a more normalised choice the further we travelled along the transect into remote communities. For professionals with the means, the boarding school option also allowed for a quick intervention when problems arose in the local school (see Yvonne's case in Chapter 8). However, the same choice posed a problem by exacting significant financial and emotional costs that left families in a quandary (as exemplified in Narrative 5.17, 'That's happening a lot', in Chapter 5). Interviewees who themselves had experienced boarding school were more comfortable with it as a solution, but others were very wary of the family separation it entailed.

Our participants outlined other possible 'solutions' to reconciling career mobility and educational strategy that entailed breaking up the family unit.

These included unaccompanied postings for military personnel, leaving their families in the previous location, or mothers relocating to larger centres with school-aged children, leaving the father in the family home (as described in Narrative 5.17, 'That's happening a lot'). These are all intriguing scenarios because they highlight points in the family career at which work interests and educational strategy cannot be reconciled in the same location, and the family unit's meta-project of togetherness in time and space is sacrificed. Only a small number among our interviewees had reportedly made this choice at one stage or other. For others, it was a last resort choice they were reluctantly considering. In Beck and Beck-Gernsheim's words, the 'risks are distributed so that they are … shifted on to individuals and families' (2004: 502). As such solutions become more thinkable and doable in an increasingly mobile society, we suggest that employers take pause to consider what they are asking the family unit to absorb on their behalf.

By encouraging schools to differentiate and distinguish themselves under a market logic, neoliberal policy has reversed earlier commitments to delivering a uniform standard across the board: that is, 'the view, deeply enshrined in the Australian system, that location is of no consequence to the delivery of education, that distance can be effectively annulled, and that space simply doesn't matter' (Green and Letts 2007: 61). From our exploration of family narratives, we would highlight the growing distrust in the local school as a default school choice. This mindset has been legitimated and cultivated by educational marketisation. We would suggest that it is becoming a major complication in efforts to attract professionals into the smaller communities that need them. Narrative 5.14, 'Seventeen years later we're still here' in Chapter 5, talks back to this mindset. However, a more general issue lies in how the narrator was initially 'devastated' about being sent to the rural town she later celebrates. In this vein, reputations and suppositions of what a rural/remote place might offer can precede any lived experience thereof and can shape families' fallible readings of possible locations from a distance. Following Lefebrve (1991), the chimera of discursively conceived space can become disconnected from the experientially lived space, but nevertheless the former travels ahead and exerts causal force in family deliberations.

The nature and competitiveness of the educational market offered is becoming a major attribute in the social construction of place in professional families' mobility deliberations. It has become an important aspect of locations that contributes to the 'politics of mobility' (Massey 1993) and the relational competition between 'here' and 'there'. One location's reputation for high quality schools can leach that value and spatially autonomous families from other locations. It is in this way that government efforts to energise parental choice in educational markets are having unanticipated effects beyond the purview of that policy domain. The rural/remote location with limited educational choices is vulnerable in this competition, caught in a conundrum of having to offer human services of a quality that can attract and retain the professionals needed to staff them.

Family mobility as a lens on the mobile society

Throughout the book, we have drawn on Archer's (2007) concepts of reflexivity and project to highlight the work of conscious strategy in family mobility deliberations. While Archer's work extends further to explore how modes of reflexivity produce social change, we have used these two concepts to make visible the calculative weighing up of risks and opportunities between 'here' and 'there', and the weighing up of various members' projects against each other. By taking the family as the unit of analysis, the 'internal conversation' (Archer 2007: 2) of reflexivity within the individual is drawn out to resource the intersubjective conversation within the collective. Archer argues that more aspects of life are demanding reflexivity given the 'decline and fall of routinisation' (p. 5). The concepts of protean career in Chapter 2 and mobius market investments in Chapter 7 capture this effect with regard to the workplace. The onus on parents to exercise choice in educational markets rather than trust in the local school offers another example. We would connect this work of reflexivity with Appadurai's (1996) description of imagination as 'the quotidian mental work' (p. 5) that fuels mobilities on a global scale:

> Ordinary people have begun to deploy their imaginations in the practice of their everyday lives.... More people than ever before seem to imagine routinely the possibility that they or their children will live and work in places other than where they were born: this is the wellspring of the increased rates of migration at every level of social, national, and global life.
>
> (Appadurai 1996: 5–6)

Family mobility relies on this mental work of imagination: to project lives into new places of possibility; to make plans beyond the here and now; to conjure strategies from fears, anxieties, hopes and aspirations. Local and global imaginaries intermingle across the map. We interviewed doctors with overseas qualifications working in rural Australia and officers from the British armed forces who had transferred to the Australian forces. Our interviewees described the research phase and word-of-mouth knowledge that informed their strategies. Archer pointed out that these self-generated readings are necessary, but will be inherently fallible. In other words, there can be no guarantees. Archer (2007) also highlighted that the deliberative processes of reflexivity are more than the rational choice of economics, given the constitutive play of emotions. By inviting our interviewees to tell the story surrounding their history of family household moves we could dignify the emotional links and complications in their thinking. Under this theory and methodology, emotions are not qualitative colour, but rather, they exert causal force within the family unit's deliberations.

Family mobility as a lens on workforce mobility policy

Geographic mobility has continued to be an important goal for economic policy. For example, a recent inquiry and draft report by the Productivity Commission

(2013), a key Australian government advisory body, starts from the premise that labour mobility is an important element of a well-functioning, efficient and flexible labour market. Its authors argue that, by improving the match between employers and workforce, geographic labour mobility can contribute to economic efficiency and ultimately to community wellbeing through higher incomes. A more mobile workforce makes every sense in that frame. Moving on is associated with getting ahead at both macro and micro scales, and solutions such as long-distance commuting that separate family members for extended periods emerge as cost-efficient propositions.

Our study, however, has demonstrated that families often bear the brunt of such mobility and that the mobility of some can create complications for others, at both macro and micro scales. By following our participants' narratives and their sequence of moves, our study has offered a richer understanding of what family mobility achieves and entails, beyond delivering the worker to a new worksite. The Productivity Commission notes that many government policies aiming to influence where people live and work in regional and remote areas have achieved limited effect. Our findings help illuminate the report's conclusion that personal factors will win over government efforts to incentivise mobility to achieve equitable services across our vast geography. A lens on family as the object of study rather than the worker exposes how gamekeeping the professional or worker in rural/remote places is a 'wicked' policy problem (Head 2008) that resists simple interventions, because families are engaged with multiple institutions, each with its own demands.

There are 'public' levers such as transport infrastructure, housing, employment conditions and tax incentives that are amenable to public or corporate policy to encourage geographic mobility, but these will not necessarily address the private concerns and priorities of families. Policy makers should equally recognise that there are other policy effects that work against worker mobility, such as educational marketisation practices, and institutional discontinuities that underpin the normative preference for immobility in certain family phases. Then there are private factors that make mobility more or less thinkable and doable. These will not be amenable to such policy, because its dominant economic frame offers no way to measure and factor the value of family life.

Our discussion in Chapter 2 juxtaposed the variables of family motility and institutional viscosity. The former refers to how the family, as a collective, is disposed towards, and resourced for, potential mobility; the latter refers to how easy any institution makes it for people to move through its processes. A high viscosity context could be likened to swimming through treacle, while a low viscosity setting could be likened to swimming through water with less resistance and more support. A high motility family has ample strategies and supports to cope with a move, with an optimistic outlook. A low motility family, by contrast, would have concerns, misgivings or complications that make any prospect of moving stressful. Table 9.1 breaks these variables down to degrees of high (+) and low (−), then cross-tabulates them to describe four possible combinations of

Table 9.1 Cross-tabulating motility and viscosity

V+/–, M +/–	Low motility M– (Dislikes moving and lacks the skills to cope with demands of moving)	High motility M+ (Willing to move and has the skills to cope with the demands)
Low viscosity V– (institutional culture facilitates and supports mobility)	V–M– Helpful combination if family has to move	V–M+ Well matched and mutually supportive
High viscosity V+ (institutional culture hinders or ignores mobility)	V+M– Not a problem if not moving Highly problematic if family has to move	V+M+ Might move on if not happy

circumstances. This schema might help policy makers, institutions and systems think about the variety of factors at play in family mobility, and how they might work with and for the mobile family.

Cell 1 (V–M–) is the combination of the low motility family or member moving through a low viscosity setting. This combination is potentially helpful. The supportive attributes of the institution could help the family cope better by removing institutional obstacles, enabling continuity across settings and facilitating the necessary articulation processes. Cell 2 (V–M+) describes a high motility family moving through a low viscosity setting. This is an optimal scenario for family mobility – they are well resourced themselves and also well supported by institutional systems to move on to get ahead. Cell 3 (V+M–) is a highly problematic combination: the low motility family that does not cope well moving through a high viscosity setting that has not developed a culture or systems that normalise and support mobility. Not only is the family ill equipped to cope themselves, but the institution will also fail to actively support, if not hinder, their mobility. Of course, on the flipside, if the family does not move, there is no problem and the two attributes are well matched. This scenario might describe the circumstances for many immobile families in schools with low turnover. In Cell 4 (V+M+), a high motility family in a high viscosity setting will make for a critical customer who will not hesitate to move on to a better, more supportive context if warranted. Current marketisation policies in education would actively encourage such behaviour.

To summarise, not all families will be equally disposed to take up an opportunity to move on to get ahead. However, if corporations and governments have vested interests in workforce mobility, then they could look at normalising mobility and lowering the viscosity of the range of institutions and systems that families have to deal with to re-place members' projects. When child-care centres and schools reserve a proportion of places for mobile families, and schools share information with students' previous and next schools as a matter of routine, then families may find that moving is not as onerous as feared.

Urry (2007: 12) posed the question, 'Is it good to be mobile?' to challenge more celebratory accounts of mobile society. Government and corporate interests in workforce mobility might argue that it is, given the economic profits and efficiencies it could produce, and the public good that could flow as positive externalities from these. However, such market logic fails to account for negative externalities that will be absorbed by intersubjective subsidy within the private domain of the family. If mobility is an inherently good thing, policy to maximise mobility would aim for highly motile, spatially autonomous individuals moving through low viscosity institutions, in an unregulated market that pits localities against each other in a competition to attract the required human capital. This workforce would be one that could flow effortlessly from opportunity to opportunity. Such a frictionless model, however, reduces the worker to one dimension and one social role. In contrast, fostering an element of stickiness that engenders binds, mutual responsibilities and multivalent stakes in localities over more time has value too. Gamekeeping the professional is not just about recruitment, but equally about retention over time to build expertise in enterprises, services and communities. In this frame, mobility is not a good thing in and of itself but needs to be tempered in terms of its pace and its intersubjective terms. In this light, social institutions need to consider not just how they respond to growing mobility, but what they might do to manage mobility by judiciously encouraging and discouraging mobility over time.

Conclusion

This book grew from two very real social problems – the educational challenges for children in hypermobile military families, and chronic professional workforce shortages in rural and remote localities. We have explored the tangle of dimensions around these family mobility issues in the unique geographic conditions of Australia, with its isolated communities and sparse population. However, neither problem is limited to Australia. The same issues and dynamics will exist elsewhere as a matter of degrees.

There are many other forms and types of family mobility that could do with similar scrutiny, so their particularities are not lost in statistical averages. The two populations we sampled had the benefit of secure employment. Other families are moving in much less secure conditions: for seasonal employment; to seek employment; in the wake of war or natural disaster; after divorce; and so forth. While mobility is increasingly visible and captures the attention of researchers, there are equal and opposite forces within families that seek continuity and institutions that privilege stability, so the mobility imperative will always be incomplete, mitigated and unevenly distributed. Any account of mobility must consider these counter forces.

Within a world where career opportunities increasingly implicate mobility, this book has inserted thinking around mobility in careers studies, in particular in the applicability of mobilities studies to career development and organisation studies. It is evident that, despite a focus on boundaryless and protean careers, the significance of mobilities for career and organisation studies has not been explored. Similarly we have brought the mobilities paradigm into dialogue with the sociology of the family and the sociology of education. Our omnivorous gaze will inevitably mean thin treatment at points. We hope other researchers can bring their expertise to do these aspects better. Inevitably there will be blind spots, but we hope we have started a more complex, nuanced conversation by crossing boundaries between fields of research.

To close, we share one more narrative of family mobility. On a recent long-haul international flight one of us (Doherty) was travelling alone, while seated next to four-year-old twins and their Australian-accented father, while their Canadian-accented mother was seated across the next aisle with an infant. They were making their way to Sydney to visit the Australian grandparents. With my headphones on, I watched how mother and father juggled the constant and various demands of their small charges with good humour and conscientious patience. They maintained this demeanour despite long delays at one fuel stop-over adding hours to what was already a very long flight. There were other family parties elsewhere on the plane doing essentially the same trip and, given global migrations, there will be more. Our point in this story is twofold: to high-light the arduous and ongoing work that families take on board to make the mobility imperative a reality; and to demonstrate how family mobility exposes the intersubjective work that families do.

Appendix I

Original item sets for their corresponding constructs

Appendix I Original item sets for their corresponding constructs

Code	Item
Public good	
Pub1	I'm prepared to go wherever my profession is needed.
Pub2	I feel a strong obligation to give back to society.
Pub3	I think governments have the right to expect professionals to work in underserviced communities.
Pub4	I'm prepared to put duty before self-interest in my career.
Pub5	I think as a professional I have a duty to serve in disadvantaged communities.
Pub6	I think governments should have the means to require professionals to serve in remote areas as needed.
Pub7	As a professional, I feel a strong commitment to ensure that all communities are well serviced.
Private good	
Priv1	I would only work in a remote community if there were strong financial incentives.
Priv2	I think an open competitive job market is the best way to encourage an equitable spread of professionals.
Priv3	I think professionals should be free to pursue their career opportunities as they choose.
Priv4	I think incentive payments are a good idea to attract professionals to hard-to-staff locations.
Neoliberalism	
Neolib1	We get very stressed deciding which school to send our children to.
Neolib2	We are prepared to change our child's school if not satisfied.
Neolib3	We strongly believe non-government schools offer a better education than government schools.
Neolib4	We choose where to live because of the quality of the schools in the area.
Neolib5	We think it's good if schools compete with each other in a market of choice.
Neolib6	The My School website plays an important role in informing our choice of school.

Location range

LocRange1   We are very open to the idea of working in rural or remote communities.

LocRange2   We want to be close to our extended family. (Reverse)

LocRange3   We are keen to experience life in a variety of settings.

LocRange4   Boarding school is an option for our children at some stage.

LocRange5   We have an open mind about where we live.

LocRange6   We know where we want to raise our children. (Reverse)

LocRange7   We really treasure the community where we live. (Reverse)

Motility

Mot1   We would be very reluctant to change schools once we've enrolled our child. (Reverse)

Mot2   We often look for work opportunities outside the town we're in.

Mot3   We intend to stay in this location for the next ten years. (Reverse)

Mot4   We prepared to move towns to get ahead in my/our career/s.

Mot5   We often talk seriously about moving to another town.

Mot6   There is plenty of support available to help our family move.

Mot7   We would avoid moving our children while they are in school. (Reverse)

Mot8   We would all cope well with a move to another town.

Mot9   One of us would be prepared to do long-distance commuting between towns rather than move the family. (Reverse)

Mot10   We get 'itchy feet' and want to move after a few years in one place.

Bibliography

Abraham, M., Auspurg, K. and Hinz, T. (2010) 'Migration decisions within dual-earner partnerships: a test of bargaining theory', *Journal of Marriage and Family*, 72: 876–892.

ADF Recruitment Centre (n.d.) *Recruitment Centre. Frequently Asked Questions (FAQ)*. Online. Available: www.defencejobs.gov.au/recruitmentCentre/supportAndDownloads/FAQs/Postings/ (accessed 13 September 2013).

Amundson, N., Parker, P. and Arthur, M. (2002) 'Merging two worlds: linking occupational and organisational career counselling', *Australian Journal of Career Development*, 11: 26–35.

Appadurai, A. (1990) 'Disjuncture and difference in the global cultural economy', *Public Culture*, 2: 1–24.

Appadurai, A. (1996) *Modernity at Large: Cultural dimensions of globalisation*, Minneapolis: University of Minnesota Press.

Apple, M. (2001) *Educating the 'Right Way': Markets, standards, god and inequality*, New York and London: RoutledgeFalmer.

Archer, M. (2007) *Making Our Way through the World: Human reflexivity and social mobility*, Cambridge: Cambridge University Press.

Archer, M. (2012) *The Reflexive Imperative in Late Modernity*, Cambridge: Cambridge University Press.

Arnold, J. and Cohen, L. (2013) 'Careers in organisations', in W.B. Walsh, M.L. Savickas and P. Hartung (eds) *Handbook of Vocational Psychology: Theory, research and practice*, 4th edn, Hoboken, NJ: Taylor & Francis.

Arthur, M. B. (1994) 'The boundaryless career: a new perspective for organizational inquiry', *Journal of Organizational Behavior*, 15: 295–306.

Arthur, M.B. and Rousseau, D.M. (1996) *The Boundaryless Career: A new employment principle for a new organizational era*, New York: Oxford University Press.

Arthur, M.B., Hall, D.T. and Lawrence, B.S. (eds) (1989) *Handbook of Career Theory*, Cambridge: Cambridge University Press.

Arthur, M.B., Inkson, K. and Pringle, J.K. (1999) *The New Careers: Individual action and economic change*, London: SAGE.

Australian Bureau of Statistics (2004) *Australian Social Trends* 4102.0, Canberra: ABS.

Australian Bureau of Statistics (2012) *Australian Social Trends* 4102.0, Canberra: ABS.

Australian Bureau of Statistics (2013) *2033.0.55.001 – Census of Population and Housing: Socio-economic Indexes for Areas (SEIFA), Australia, 2011*. Online. Available: www.abs.gov.au/ausstats/abs@.nsf/Lookup/2033.0.55.001main+features100042011 (accessed 30 December 2013).

Australian Curriculum Assessment and Reporting Authority. (2012) *Australian Curriculum*. Online. Available: www.acara.edu.au/curriculum/curriculum.html (accessed 13 June 2013).

Australian Government Department of Health and Ageing (2008) *Report on the Audit of Health Workforce in Rural and Regional Australia*, Canberra: Australian Government Department of Health and Ageing.

Australian Health Practitioner Agency (AHPRA) (n.d.) *FAQ*. Online. Available: www. ahpra.gov.au/Support/FAQ.aspx (accessed 28 October 2013).

Australian Health Practitioner Agency (AHPRA) (n.d.) *Registration Standards*. Online. Available: www.medicalboard.gov.au/Registration-Standards.aspx (accessed 21 October 2013).

Australian Health Practitioner Agency (AHPRA) Nursing and Midwifery Board (n.d.) *Registration Standards*. Online. Available: www.nursingmidwiferyboard.gov.au/ Registration-Standards.aspx (accessed 21 October 2013).

Australian Institute for School Leadership Limited (AITSL) (n.d.) *Mutual Recognition*. Online. Available: www.aitsl.edu.au/teachers/registration/mutual-recognition.html (accessed 28 October 2013).

Ball, S. (1993) 'Education markets, choice and social class: the market as a class strategy in the UK and the USA', *British Journal of Sociology of Education*, 14: 3–19.

Ball, S. (2003) *Class Strategies and the Education Market: The middle classes and social advantage*, London: RoutledgeFalmer.

Ball, S. and Vincent, C. (1998) ' "I heard it on the grapevine": "hot" knowledge and school choice', *British Journal of Sociology of Education*, 19: 377–400.

Ball, S., Bowe, R. and Gewirtz, S. (1996) 'School choice, social class and distinction: the realization of social advantage in education', *Journal of Educational Policy*, 11: 89–112.

Ball, S., Vincent, C., Kemp, S. and Pietikainen, S. (2004) 'Middle class fractions, child-care and the "relational" and "normative" aspects of class practices', *The Sociological Review*, 52: 478–502.

Bansel, P. (2007) 'Subjects of choice and lifelong learning', *International Journal of Qualitative Studies in Education*, 20: 283–300.

Barrett, G. F. (2012) 'The return to cognitive skills in the Australian labour market', *The Economic Record*, 88: 1–17.

Baum, S., O'Connor, K. and Stimson, R. (2005) *Fault Lines Exposed: Advantage and disadvantage across Australia's settlement system*, Melbourne: Monash University.

Bauman, Z. (2000) *Liquid Modernity*, Cambridge: Polity Press.

Baxter, J. and Alexander, M. (2008) 'Mothers' work-to-family strain in single and couple parent families: the role of job characteristics and supports', *Australian Journal of Social Issues*, 43: 195–214.

Beck, U. (1992) *Risk Society: Towards a new modernity*, London: SAGE.

Beck, U. and Beck-Gernsheim, E. (2004) 'Families in a runaway world', in J. Scott, J. Treas and M. Richards (eds) *Blackwell Companion to the Sociology of Families*, Malden, MA: Blackwell.

Beck, U. and Willms, J. (2004) *Conversations with Ulrich Beck*, trans. M. Pollak, Cambridge: Polity Press.

Bell, C. (2009) 'Geography in parental choice', *American Journal of Education*, 115: 493–521.

Berger, B. (2002) *The Family in the Modern Age: More than a lifestyle choice*, New Brunswick & London: Transaction Publishers.

Bernstein, B. (1990) *The Structuring of Pedagogic Discourse – Class, Codes and Control, Volume IV*, London: Routledge.

Bernstein, B. (2001) 'From pedagogies to knowledges', in A. Morais, I. Neves, B. Davies and H. Daniels (eds) *Towards a Sociology of Pedagogy: The contribution of Basil Bernstein to research*, New York: Peter Lang.

Billett, S. (2006) *Work, Change and Workers*, Dordrecht: Springer.

Bills, D. (2004) *The Sociology of Education and Work*, Malden, MA: Blackwell.

Blustein, D.L. (2001) 'Extending the reach of vocational psychology: toward an inclusive and integrative psychology of working', *Journal of Vocational Behavior*, 59: 171–182.

Blustein, D.L. (2006) *The Psychology of Working: A new perspective for career development, counseling, and public policy*. Mahwah, NJ: Erlbaum.

Bonnet, E., Collet, B. and Maurines, B. (2008) 'Working away from home: juggling private and professional lives', in W. Canzler, V. Kaufmann and S. Kesselring (eds) *Tracing Mobilities: Towards a cosmopolitan perspective*, Abingdon, UK: Ashgate Publishing Group.

Booth, B., Segal, M., Bell, D.B., Martin, J., Ender, M., Rohall, D. and Nelson, J. (2007) *What We Know About Army Families: 2007 update*, Family and Moral, Welfare and Recreation Command, US Army. Online. Available: www.army.mil/fmwrc/documents/research/WhatWeKnow2007.pdf (accessed 20 December 2013).

Boulding, E. (1983) 'Familia faber: the family as maker of the future', *Journal of Marriage and Family*, 45: 257–266.

Bourdieu, P. (1986) 'The forms of capital', in J. Richardson (ed.) *Handbook of Theory and Research for the Sociology of Education*, New York: Greenwood Press.

Boylan, C., Sinclair, R., Smith, A., Squires, D., Edwards, J., Jacob, A., O'Malley, D. and Nolan, B. (1993) 'Retaining teachers in rural schools: satisfaction, commitment, and lifestyles', in C. Boylan and M. Alston (eds) *Rural Education Issues: An Australian perspective*, Wagga Wagga, Australia: Society for the Provision of Education in Rural Australia.

Bradley, D., Noonan, P., Nugent, H. and Scales, B. (2008) *Review of Australian Higher Education: Final report*, Canberra: Commonwealth of Australia.

Brown, D. (2001) 'The social sources of educational credentialism: status cultures, labor markets and organizations', *Sociology of Education*, 74: 19–34.

Bruner, J. (2002) *Making Stories: Law, literature, life*, New York: Farrar, Straus and Giroux.

Butler, T. and van Zanten, A. (2007) 'School choice: a European perspective', *Journal of Education Policy*, 22: 1–5.

Byram, M. and Dervin, F. (eds) (2008) *Students, Staff and Academic Mobility in Higher Education*, Cambridge: Cambridge Scholars.

Cameron, I. (1998) 'Retaining a medical workforce in rural Australia', *Medical Journal of Australia*, 169: 293–294.

Campbell, C. (2005) 'Changing school loyalties and the middle class: a reflection on the developing fate of state comprehensive high schooling', *Australian Education Researcher*, 32: 3–24.

Campbell, C. (2007) 'Schools and school choice', in R. Connell, C. Campbell, M. Vickers, A. Welch, D. Foley and N. Bagnall (eds), *Education, Change and Society*, Melbourne: Oxford University Press, pp. 211–238.

Campbell, C., Proctor, H. and Sherington, G. (2009) *School Choice: How parents negotiate the new school market in Australia*, Sydney: Allen & Unwin.

Carr, P. and Kafalas, M. (2009) *Hollowing out the Middle: The rural brain drain and what it means for America*, Boston, MA: Beacon.

Castaneda, L. and Harrell, M. (2008) 'Military spouse employment: a grounded theory approach to experiences and perceptions', *Armed Forces and Society*, 34: 389–412.

Clark, T.R., Freedman, S.B., Croft, A.J., Luscombe, G.M., Brown, A.M., Tiller, D.J. and Frommer, M.S. (2013) 'Medical graduates becoming rural doctors: rural background versus extended rural placement', *Medical Journal of Australia*, 199: 779–782.

Clayton, B., Jonas, P., Harding, R., Harris, M. and Toze, M. (2013) *Industry currency and professional obsolescence: what can industry tell us?* Adelaide, SA: NCVER.

Cocklin, C. and Alston, M. (2003) *Community Sustainability in Rural Australia: A question of capital?* Wagga Wagga: Charles Sturt University.

Collin, A. and Patton, W. (2009) 'Towards dialogue and beyond', in A. Collin and W. Patton (eds) *Vocational Psychological and Organizational Perspectives on Career: Towards a multidisciplinary dialogue*, Rotterdam: Sense Publishers.

Collins, R. (1979) *The Credential Society: An historical sociology of education and stratification*, New York: Academic Press.

Collins, R. (1990) 'Changing conceptions in the sociology of the professions', in R. Torstendahl and M. Burrage (eds) *The Formation of Professions*, London: SAGE.

Commonwealth Department of Education Science and Training and Department of Defence (2002) *Changing Schools: Its impact on student learning*, Canberra: Commonwealth of Australia.

Connell, J. (2010) *Migration and the Globalisation of Health Care: The health worker exodus?* Cheltenham, UK: Edward Elgar.

Connell, R. (2002) 'Making the difference, then and now', *Discourse: Studies in the Cultural Politics of Education*, 23: 319–327.

Connell, R. (2003) 'Working-class families and the new secondary education', *Australian Journal of Education*, 47: 235–250.

Connell, R., Ashenden, D., Kessler, S. and Dowsett, G. (1982) *Making the Difference: Schools, families and social division*, Sydney: Allen & Unwin.

Costas, J. (2013) 'Problematizing mobility: a metaphor of stickiness, non-places and the kinetic elite', *Organization Studies*, 34: 1467–1485.

Coulter, R., van Ham, M. and Feijten, P. (2012) 'Partner (dis)agreement on moving desires and the subsequent moving behaviour of couples', *Population, Space and Place*, 18: 16–30.

Crompton, R. (2006) *Employment and the Family: The reconfiguration of work and family life in contemporary societies*, Cambridge: Cambridge University Press.

Cronbach, L.J., Schönemann, P. and McKie, D. (1965) 'Alpha coefficients for stratified-parallel tests', *Educational and Psychological Measurement*, 25: 291–312.

Crossley, N. (1996) *Intersubjectivity: The fabric of social becoming*, London: SAGE.

Danaher, P., Danaher, G. and Moriarty, B. (2007) 'Subverting the hegemony of risk: vulnerability and transformation among Australian show children', *Educational Research*, 49: 211–224.

Defense Manpower Data Center. (2009) *2008 Survey of Active Duty Spouses: Tabulations of responses*, Report No. 2008–041, Arlington, VA: Defense Manpower Data Center. Online. Available: http://prhome.defense.gov/Portals/52/Documents/RFM/MCFP/docs/2008%20Military%20Spouse%20Survey.pdf (accessed 20 December 2013).

Directorate of Strategic Personnel Policy Research. (2009) *A Picture of Australian Defence Force Families: Results from the first survey of Australian Defence Force families. General Report*, Canberra: Directorate of Strategic Personnel Policy Research.

Dockery, A.M. and Miller, P.W. (2012) *Over-education, Under-education and Creden-tialism in the Australian Labour Market*, DIISRTE: NCVER Monograph Series 10.

Doherty, C. and Lassig, C. (2013) 'Workable solutions: the intersubjective careers of women with families', in W. Patton (ed.) *Conceptualising Women's Working Lives: Moving the boundaries of our discourse*, Rotterdam: Sense.

Doherty, C., Rissman, B. and Browning, B. (2013) 'Educational markets in space: choice and its effects on professionals across Australian communities', *Journal of Education Policy*, 28: 121–152.

Dougherty, J., Harrelson, J., Maloney, L., Murphy, D., Smith, R., Snow, M. and Zannoni, D. (2009) 'School choice in suburbia: test scores, race and housing markets', *American Journal of Education*, 115: 523–548.

Drago, R. (2007) *Striking a Balance: Work, family, life*. Boston: Dollars & Sense.

Edin, K. and Kefalas, M. (2005) *Promises I Can Keep: Why poor women put motherhood before marriage*, Berkeley: University of California Press.

Ehrenreich, B. (1990) *Fear of Falling: The inner life of the middle class*, New York: Harper Perennial.

Elder, G. and Giele, J. (eds) (2009) *The Craft of Life Course Research*, New York: Guildford Press.

Elliott, A. and Urry, J. (2010) *Mobile Lives*, London: Routledge.

Ender, M. (ed.) (2002a). *Military Brats and Other Global Nomads*, Westport: Praeger.

Ender, M. (2002b) 'Beyond adolescence: the experiences of adult children of military parents', in M. Ender (ed.) *Military Brats and Other Global Nomads*, Westport: Praeger.

Evans, A. and Gray, E. (2005) 'What makes an Australian family?' in S. Wilson, G. Meagher, R. Gibson, D. Denemark and M. Western (eds) *Australian Social Attitudes: The first report*, Sydney: UNSW Press.

Evans, M. and Kelley, J. (2001) *Australian Economy and Society: Education, work and welfare*, Leichardt, NSW: Federation Press.

Evetts, J. (2006) 'Short note: the sociology of professional groups: new directions', *Current Sociology*, 54: 133–143.

Field, A. (2009) *Discovering Statistics Using SPSS*, 3rd edn, London: SAGE.

Flamm, M. and Kaufmann, V. (2006) 'Operationalising the concept of motility: a qualitative study', *Mobilities*, 1: 167–189.

Florida, R. (2005) *The Flight of the Creative Class: The new global competition for talent*, New York: HarperCollins.

Fornell, C. and Larcker, D.F. (1981) 'Evaluating structural equation models with unob-servable variables and measurement error', *Journal of Marketing Research*, 18: 39–50.

Forsey, M. G. (2010) 'Publicly minded, privately focused: Western Australian teachers and school choice', *Teaching and Teacher Education*, 26: 53–60.

Fransson, G. and Grannas, J. (2013) 'Dilemmatic spaces in educational contexts – towards a conceptual framework for dilemmas in teachers work', *Teachers and Teaching: Theory and Practice*, 19: 4–17.

Garrett, P. (2010) 'More mobile students need a national curriculum', *The Australian*, 29 November. Online. Available: www.theaustralian.com.au/national-affairs/more-mobile-students-need-a-national-curriculum/story-fn59niix-1225962379374 (accessed 20 December 2013).

Gilding, M. (1997) *Australian Families: A comparative perspective*, Melbourne: Longman.

Gray, I. and Lawrence, G. (2001) *A Future for Regional Australia: Escaping global misfortune*, Cambridge: Cambridge University Press.

Green, B. and Letts, W. (2007) 'Space, equity and rural education: a "trialectical" account', in K. Gulson and C. Symes (eds) *Spatial Theories of Education: Policy and geography matters*, New York: Routledge.

Green, F. and Zhu, Y. (2010) 'Overqualification, job dissatisfaction, and increasing dispersion in the returns to graduate education', *Oxford Economic Papers*, 62: 740–763.

Gubrium, J. and Holstein, J. (1998) 'Narrative practice and the coherence of personal stories', *The Sociological Quarterly*, 39: 163–187.

Hall, D.T. (1996) *The Career is Dead – Long Live the Career: A relational approach to careers*, San Francisco: Jossey-Bass.

Hall, D.T. and Las Heras, M. (2009) 'Long live the organizational career', in A. Collin and W. Patton (eds) *Vocational Psychological and Organizational Perspectives on Career: Towards a multidisciplinary dialogue*, Rotterdam: Sense Publishers.

Hancock, G.R. and Mueller, R.O. (2001) 'Rethinking construct reliability within latent variables systems', in R. Cudeck, S.D. Toit and D. Sörbom (eds) *Structural Equation Modeling: Present and future – a festschrift in honor of Karl Jöreskog*, Lincolnwood: Scientific Software International.

Hannam, K., Sheller, M. and Urry, J. (2006) 'Editorial: mobilities, immobilities and moorings', *Mobilities*, 1: 1–22.

Harrell, M., Lim, N., Castaneda, L. and Golinelle, D. (2005) 'Working around the military: challenges to military spouse employment and education', *The Leadership Quarterly*, 21: 20–32.

Harvey, D. (1993) 'From space to place and back again: reflections on the condition of postmodernity', in J. Bird, B. Curtis, T. Putnam, G. Robertson and L. Ticknew (eds) *Mapping the Futures: Local cultures, global change*, London: Routledge.

Haslam McKenzie, F. (2007) *Attracting and Retaining Skilled and Professional Staff in Remote Locations*, DKCRC Report 21, Alice Springs: Desert Knowledge Cooperative Research Centre.

Haslam McKenzie, F. (2010) 'Fly-in fly-out: the challenges of transient populations in rural landscapes', in G. Luck, D. Race and R. Black (eds) *Demographic Change in Australia's Rural Landscapes*, Dordrecht: Springer.

Head, B. (2008) 'Wicked problems in public policy', *Public Policy*, 3: 101–118.

Health Workforce Australia (2012) *Australia's Health Workforce Series: Doctors in focus 2012*, Adelaide: Health Workforce Australia.

Healy, K. and Hillman, W. (2008) 'Young families migrating to non-metropolitan areas: are they at increased risk of social exclusion?' *Australian Journal of Social Issues*, 43: 479–497.

Henderson, R. (2001) 'Student mobility: moving beyond deficit views', *Australian Journal of Guidance and Counselling*, 11: 121–129.

Henderson, R. (2002) 'Student mobility and school literacy performance: what does research suggest for classroom practice?' paper presented at Australian Indigenous Education Conference, Townsville, Australia, 2–4 July 2002.

Henderson, R. (2004) 'Educational issues for children of itinerant seasonal farm workers: a case study in an Australian context', *International Journal of Inclusive Education*, 8: 293–310.

Henderson, R. (2005) 'An invasion of green-stained farm workers from outer space(s)? or a rural community struggling with issues of itinerancy', *Education in Rural Australia*, 15: 3–16.

Hirsch, F. (1976) *Social Limits to Growth*, Cambridge, MA: Harvard University Press.

Ho, R. (2006) *Handbook of Univariate and Multivariate Data Analysis and Interpretation with SPSS*, Boca Raton: Chapman & Hall/CRC.

Hodgson, H. (2008) 'More than just DNA – tax, welfare and the family. An examination of the concept of family in the Tax Transfer system, with particular reference to family benefits', *Australian Journal of Social Issues*, 43: 601–641.

Holdsworth, C. (2013) *Family and Intimate Mobilities*, Houndmills, Basingstoke: Palgrave Macmillan.

House of Representatives Standing Committee on Health and Ageing (2012) *Lost in the Labyrinth: Report on the inquiry into registration processes and support for overseas trained doctors*, Canberra: Commonwealth of Australia.

Hugo, G. and Bell, M. (1998) 'The hypothesis of welfare-led migration to rural areas: the Australian case', in P. Boyle and K. Halfacree (eds) *Migration into Rural Areas: Theories and issues*, Chichester: John Wiley & Sons.

Humphreys, J., Jones, M., Jones, J. and Mara, P. (2002) 'Workforce retention in rural and remote Australia: determining the factors that influence length of practice', *Medical Journal of Australia*, 176: 472–476.

Inkson, K. (2007) *Understanding Careers: The metaphors of working lives*, Thousand Oaks, CA: SAGE.

Inkson, K. and Elkin, G. (2008) 'The context of careers in developed nations', in J.A. Athanasou and R. Van Esbroeck (eds) *International Handbook of Career Guidance*, Dordrecht: Springer Science and Media.

Jarvis, P. (2003) *Career Management Paradigm Shift: Prosperity for citizens, windfall for governments*. Online. Available: www.lifework.ca/papers.htm (accessed 23 January 2004).

Johnson Jr, O. (2012) 'Relocation programs, opportunities to learn, and the complications of conversion', *Review of Educational Research*, 82: 131–178.

Jöreskog, K.G. and Sörbom, D. (1996) *LISERAL 8 User's Reference Guide*, Mooresville, IN: Scientific Software International.

Karmel, T. and Lim, P. (2013) *Socioeconomic Disadvantage and Participation in Tertiary Education: Preliminary thoughts*, Adelaide, SA: National Centre for Vocational Education Research.

Kaufmann, V. (2002) *Re-thinking Mobility: Contemporary sociology*, Aldershot: Ashgate.

Kaufmann, V., Bergman, M. and Joye, D. (2004) 'Motility: mobility as capital', *International Journal of Urban and Regional Research*, 28: 745–56.

Kelley, M. (2002) 'The effects of deployment on traditional and nontraditional military families: navy mothers and their children', in M. Ender (ed.) *Military Brats and Other Global Nomads*, Westport: Praeger.

Kenny, M. and Danaher, P. (2009) 'Editorial introduction: three dimensions of changing schools', in P. Danaher, M. Kenny and J. Leder (eds) *Traveller, Nomadic and Migrant Education*, Hoboken: Routledge.

Kesselring, S. (2006) 'Pioneering mobilities: new patterns of movement and motility in a mobile world', *Environment and Planning*, 38: 269–279.

King, R. and Kendall, G. (2004) *The State, Democracy and Globalization*, Houndmills, UK, and New York: Palgrave Macmillan.

Kingma, M. (2001) 'Nursing migration: global treasure hunt or disaster-in-the-making?' *Nursing Inquiry*, 8: 205–212.

Kline, D. (2003) 'Push and pull factors in international nurse migration', *Journal of Nursing Scholarship*, 35: 107–111.

Kline, P. (1999) *The Handbook of Psychological Testing*, 2nd edn, London: Routledge.

Knight, J. and de Wit, H. (eds) (1997) *Internationalisation of Higher Education in Asia Pacific Countries*, Amsterdam: European Association for International Education (EAIE).

Labov, W. (1997) 'Some further steps in narrative analysis', *Journal of Narrative and Life History*, 7: 395–415.

Labov, W. and Waletzky, J. (1997) 'Narrative analysis: oral version of personal experience', *Journal of Narrative and Life History*, 7: 3–38.

Lareau, A. (2003) *Unequal Childhoods: Class, race and family life*, Berkeley: University of California Press.

Lareau, A. (2011) *Unequal Childhoods: Class, race and family life*, 2nd edn, Berkeley and Los Angeles: University of California Press.

Larson, A. (2010) 'Doing more for fewer: health case for declining rural communities', in G. Luck, D. Race and R. Black (eds) *Demographic Change in Australia's Rural Landscapes*, Dordrecht: Springer.

Leander, K., Phillips, N. and Taylor, K.H. (2010) 'The changing social spaces of learning: mapping new mobilities', *Review of Research in Education*, 34: 329–394.

Lee, S. (2011) 'Madame Bovary and the Mobius strip: Mapping a "monde a part"', *Nineteenth Century French Studies*, 40: 96–111.

Lefebvre, H. (1991) *The Production of Space*, trans. D. Nicholson-Smith, Oxford: Blackwell.

Lehman, R. (1991) *Statistics and Research Design in the Behavioral Sciences*, Belmont, CA: Wadsworth Publishing.

Lent, R.W., Brown, S.D. and Hackett, G. (1994) 'Toward a unifying sociocognitive theory of career and academic interest, choice, and performance', *Journal of Vocational Behavior*, 45: 79–122.

Lesthaeghe, R. (1995) 'The second demographic transition in Western countries: an interpretation', in K. Oppenheim Mason and A.M. Jensen (eds) *Gender and Family Change in Industrialized Countries*, Oxford: Oxford University Press.

Levin, I. (2004) 'Living apart together: a new family form', *Current Sociology*, 52: 223–240.

Li, H., Rosenthal, R. and Rubin, D.B. (1996) 'Reliability of measurement in psychology: from Spearman-Brown to maximal reliability', *Psychological Methods*, 1: 98–107.

Linsley, I. (2005) 'Causes of over-education in the Australia labour market', *Australian Journal of Labour Economics*, 8: 121–143.

Littleton, S.M., Arthur, M.B. and Rousseau, D.M. (2000) 'The future of boundaryless careers', in A. Collin and R.A. Young (eds) *The Future of Career*, Cambridge: Cambridge University Press.

Lock, G. (2008) 'Preparing teachers for rural appointments: lessons from Australia', *The Rural Educator*, 29: 24–30.

Lubienski, C. and Dougherty, J. (2009) 'Mapping educational opportunity: spatial analysis and school choices', *American Journal of Education*, 115: 485–491.

Luck, D. and Ruppenthal, S. (2010) 'Insights into mobile living: spread, appearances and characteristics', in N. Schneider and B. Collet (eds) *Mobile Living across Europe II*, Opladen and Farmington Hills: Barbara Budrich Publishers.

Lunn, S. (1997) *Rural Strategies Project: Report*, Brisbane, Queensland: Priority Country Area Program.

Lury, C. (2013) 'Topological sense-making: walking the mobius strip from cultural topology to topological culture', *Space and Culture*, 16: 128–132.

Lyons, T. (2009) 'Teachers' motivations for working in rural schools', paper presented at the Innovation for Equity in Rural Education Symposium, University of New England, Armidale, NSW Australia, February 2009.

MacArthur, J. and Higgins, N. (2007) *Addressing the Needs of Transient Students: A collaborative approach to enhance teaching and learning in an area school*, Wellington, NZ: Teaching and Learning Research Initiative.

McIlveen, P. and Schultheiss, D. (2012) *Social Constructionism in Vocational Psychology and Career Development*, Rotterdam: Sense Publishers.

McLachlan, D. (2007) 'Global nomads in an international school', *Journal of Research in International Education*, 6: 233–249.

Mahoney, M. J. (2003) *Constructive Psychotherapy*, New York: Guildford.

Maloutas, T. (2007) 'Middle class education strategies and residential segregation in Athens', *Journal of Education Policy*, 22: 49–68.

Marchal, B. and Kegels, G. (2003) 'Health workforce imbalances in times of globalization: brain drain or professional mobility?', *International Journal of Health Planning and Management*, 18: 89–101.

Marginson, S. (1997) *Markets in Education*, St Leonards, NSW: Allen & Unwin.

Massey, D. (1993) 'Power-geometry and a progressive sense of place', in J. Bird, B. Curtis, T. Putnam, G. Robertson and L. Ticknew (eds) *Mapping the Futures: Local cultures, global change*, London and New York: Routledge.

Matchett, S. (2013) 'High Wired update: degrees don't deliver like they used to', *The Australian*, 12 July. Online. Available: www.theaustralian.com.au/higher-education/high-wired-update-degrees-dont-deliver-like-they-used-to/story-e6frgcjx-1226677869892 (accessed 9 January 2013).

Meil, G. (2009) 'Balancing job mobility and family life: effects on household division of labour', paper presented at IX ESA Congress, Lisbon, 4 September 2009.

Miles, R., Marcheall, C., Rolfe, J. and Noonan, S. (2006) 'The attraction and retention of professionals to regional areas', *Australiasian Journal of Regional Studies*, 12: 129–152.

Miller, P. W. (2007) 'Overeducation and undereducation in Australia', *The Australian Economic Review*, 40: 292–299.

Mirvis, P. H. and Hall, D.T. (1996) 'New organizational forms and the new career', in D.T. Hall (ed.) *The Career is Dead – Long Live the Career*, San Francisco, CA: Jossey-Bass.

Mitchell, T.R., Holtom, B.C., Lee, T.W., Sablynski, C.J. and Erwz, M. (2001) 'Why people stay: using job embeddedness to predict voluntary turnover', *Academy of Management Journal*, 44: 1102–1121.

Mulkeen, A. (2010) *Teachers in Anglophone Africa: Issues in teacher supply, training and management*, Washington, DC: The World Bank.

Mulkeen, A. and Chen, D. (eds) (2008) *Teachers for Rural Schools: Experiences in Lesotho, Malawi, Mozambique, Tanzania and Uganda*, Herndon, VA: World Bank Publications.

Nicholson, N. and West, M. (1989) 'Transitions, work histories and careers', in M.B. Arthur, D.T. Hall and B.S. Lawrence (eds) *Handbook of Career Theory*, Cambridge: Cambridge University Press.

Noreisch, K. (2007) 'School catchment area evasion: the case of Berlin, Germany', *Journal of Education Policy*, 22: 69–90.

OECD (2005) *Teachers Matter: Attracting, developing and retaining effective teachers*, Paris: OECD.

Owen, S., Kos, J. and McKenzie, P. (2008) *Staff in Australia's Schools: Teacher workforce data and planning processes in Australia*, Canberra: Department of Education Employment and Workplace Relations, ACER, Australian College of Educators.

Perelman, L.J. (1992) *School's Out: Hyperlearning, the new technology, and the end of education*, New York: William Morrow.

Pickover, C.A. (2006) *The Mobius Strip: Dr August Mobius's marvellous band in mathematics, games, literature, art, technology, and cosmology*, New York: Thunder's Mouth Press.

Pocock, B. (2003) *The Work/Life Collision: What work is doing to Australians and what to do about it*, Annadale, NSW: Federation Press.

Pocock, B. (2005) 'Work–life "balance" in Australia: limited progress, dim prospects', *Asia Pacific Journal of Human Resources*, 43: 198–209.

Poehnell, G. and Amundson, N. (2002) 'CareerCraft: engaging with, energizing, and empowering career creativity', in M. Peiperl, M. Arthur and N. Anand (eds) *Career Creativity: Explorations in the remaking of work*, New York: Oxford University Press.

Polkinghorne, D. (2007) 'Validity issues in narrative research', *Qualitative Inquiry*, 13: 471–486.

Poupeau, F., Francois, J.C. and Couratier, E. (2007) 'Making the right move: how families are using transfers to adapt to socio-spatial differentiation of schools in the greater Paris region', *Journal of Education Policy*, 22: 31–47.

Power, S., Edwards, T., Whitty, G. and Wigfall, V. (2003) *Education and the Middle Class*, Buckingham: Open University Press.

PriceWaterhouseCoopers (2010) *Talent Mobility 2020: The next generation of international assignments*, Online. Available: www.pwc.com/gx/en/managing-tomorrows-people/future-of-work/pdf/talent-mobility-2020.pdf (accessed 9 January 2014).

Productivity Commission (2013) *Geographic Labour Mobility: Draft report*, Canberra: Australian Government.

Prout, S. (2009) 'Policy, practice and the "revolving classroom door": examining the relationship between Aboriginal spatiality and the mainstream education system', *Australian Journal of Education*, 53: 39–53.

Pusey, M. (2003) *The Experience of Middle Australia*, Cambridge: Cambridge University Press.

Queensland College of Teachers (2012) *Continuing Professional Development Framework*, Brisbane: Queensland College of Teachers.

Queensland Government (2013) *SMO and Resident Medical Officer Inaccessibility Incentive Scheme*. Online. Available: www.health.qld.gov.au/rural/docs/remote_allowance. pdf (accessed 15 January 2014).

Richardson, M.S. (1993) 'Work in people's lives: a location for counseling psychologists', *Journal of Counseling Psychology*, 40: 425–433.

Richardson, M.S. (2000) 'A new perspective for counsellors: from career ideologies to empowerment through work and relationship practices', in A. Collin and R.A. Young (eds) *The Future of Career*, Cambridge: Cambridge University Press.

Richardson, M.S. and Schaeffer, C. (2013) 'Expanding the discourse: a dual model of working for women's (and men's) lives', in W. Patton (ed.) *Conceptualising Women's Working Lives: Moving the boundaries of discourse*, Rotterdam: Sense Publishers.

Riessman, C. (1993) *Narrative Analysis*, Newbury Park, CA: SAGE.

Riessman, C. (2008) *Narrative Methods for the Human Sciences*, Thousand Oaks, CA: SAGE.

Rizvi, F. and Lingard, B. (2010) *Globalizing Education Policy*, London: Routledge.

Roberts, P. (2004) *Staffing an Empty Schoolhouse: Attracting and retaining teachers in rural, remote and isolated communities*. Online. Available: www.parliament.nsw.gov. au/prod/parlment/committee.nsf/0/ccd8bea3f266c355ca256fe0007bdc01/$FILE/ sub%2042%20Attachment%201.pdf (accessed 22 May 2013).

Robertson, S. and Keeling, R. (2008) 'Stirring the lions: strategy and tactics in global higher education', *Globalisation, Societies and Education*, 6: 221–240.

Rosen, H. (1988) 'The irrepressible genre', in M. Maclure, T. Phillips and A. Wilkinson (eds) *Oracy Matters: The development of talking and listening in education*, Milton Keynes: Open University Press.

Rowe, K. (2002) 'The measurement of latent and composite variables from multiple items or indicators: applications in performance indicator systems', paper presented at the Royal Molbourne Institute of Technology Statistics Seminar Series, Melbourne, 11 October 2002.

Saks, M. (1995) *Professions and the Public Interest: Medical power, altruism and alternative medicine*, London: Routledge.

Savickas, M.L. (1999) 'The transition from school to work: a developmental perspective', *The Career Development Quarterly*, 4: 326–336.

Savickas, M.L. (2002) 'Career construction: a developmental theory of vocational behavior', in D. Brown and Associates (eds) *Career Choice and Development*, 4th edn, San Francisco, CA: Jossey-Bass.

Schmid, C. (2008) 'Henri Lefebrve's theory of the production of space: towards a three-dimensional dialectic', in K. Goonewardena, S. Kipfer, R. Milgrom and C. Schmid (eds) *Space, Difference, Everyday Life: Reading Henri Lefebvre*, New York: Routledge.

Schneider, N. and Limmer, R. (2008) 'Job mobility and living arrangements', in W. Canzler, V. Kaufmann and S. Kesslring (eds) *Tracing Mobilities: Towards a cosmopolitan perspective*, Aldershot: Ashgate.

Schultheiss, D.E. (2009) 'To mother or matter: can women do both?', *Journal of Career Development*, 36: 25–48.

Schultheiss, D.E. (2013) 'A relational cultural paradigm as a theoretical backdrop for considering women's work', in W. Patton (ed.) *Conceptualising Women's Working Lives: Moving the boundaries of discourse*, Rotterdam: Sense Publishers.

Sciulli, D. (2009) *Professions in Civil Society and the State: Invariant foundations and consequences*, Leiden and Boston: Brill.

Scott, A., Witt, J., Humphreys, J., Joyce, C., Kalb, G., Jeon, S.H. and McGrail, M. (2012) *Getting Doctors into the Bush: General practitioners' preferences for rural location*, Melbourne: Melbourne Institute of Applied Economic and Social Research.

Segal, M. (1986) 'The military and the family as greedy institutions', *Armed Forces and Society*, 13: 9–38.

Sennett, R. (1998) *The Corrosion of Character: The personal consequences of work in the new capitalism*, New York: W. W. Norton.

Shah, C., Webb, S., Nicholas, A., Beale, D., Devos, A. and Faine, M. (2012) *Geographic Dimensions of Social Inclusion and VET in Australia: An overview*, Adelaide: National Centre for Vocational Education Research (NCVER).

Sharplin, E. (2009) 'Quality of worklife for rural and remote teachers: a model of protective and risk factors', paper presented at the International Symposium for Innovation in Rural Education: Improving Equity in Rural Education. Online. Available: www.une.edu.au/ simerr/ISFIRE/pages/ISFIRE_proceedings.pdf#page=212 (accessed 30 December 2013).

Sheller, M. and Urry, J. (2006) 'The new mobilities paradigm', *Environment and Planning A*, 38: 207–226.

Sherif-Trask, B. (2010) *Globalization and Families: Accelerated systemic social change.* New York: Springer.

Shortland, S. (2012) 'Women's participation in expatriation: the contribution of organisational policy and practice', unpublished PhD thesis, University of Westminster.

Snider, G. (1991) 'Australia's largest family: institute conducts Defence Force Census', *Family Matters*, 30: 28–29.

Sullivan, O. (2006) *Changing Gender Relations, Changing Families: Tracing the pace of change over time*, Lanham: Rowman & Littlefield.

Sullivan, S.E. and Arthur, M.E. (2006) 'The evolution of the boundaryless career concept: examining physical and psychological mobility', *Journal of Vocational Behavior*, 69: 19–29.

Super, D.E. (1957) *The Psychology of Careers*, New York: Harper and Row.

Super, D.E. (1980) 'A life-span, life-space approach to career development', *Journal of Vocational Behavior*, 16: 282–298.

Super, D.E., Savickas, M.L. and Super, C.M. (1996) 'The life-span, life-space approach to careers', in D. Brown and L. Brooks (eds) *Career Choice and Development*, 3rd edn, San Francisco: Jossey-Bass.

Tabachnick, B.G. and Fidell, L.S. (2007) *Using Multivariate Statistics*, 5th edn. Boston: Allyn and Bacon.

Taylor, C. (2007). 'Geographical information systems (GIS) and school choice: the use of spatial research tools in studying educational policy', in K. Gulson and C. Symes (eds) *Spatial Theories of Education: Policy and geography matters*, New York: Routledge.

Teese, R. (2000) *Academic Success and Social Power: Examinations and inequality*, Melbourne: Melbourne University Press.

Teese, R. and Polesel, J. (2003) *Undemocratic Schooling: Equity and quality in mass secondary education in Australia*, Melbourne: Melbourne University Press.

Tyler, M. (2002) 'The military teenager in Europe: perspectives for health care providers', in M. Ender (ed.) *Military Brats and Other Global Nomads*, Westport: Praeger.

United Nations, Department of Economic and Social Affairs, Population Division (2011) *World Population Prospects: The 2010 revision*, New York: United Nations. Updated: 22 October 2010.

Urry, J. (2000a) *Sociology Beyond Societies: Mobilities for the twenty-first century*, London: Routledge.

Urry, J. (2000b) 'Sociology of time and space', in B. Turner (ed.) *The Blackwell Companion to Social Theory*, Malden, MA: Blackwell.

Urry, J. (2007) *Mobilities*, Cambridge: Polity Press.

Urry, J. (2008) 'Mobilities and social theory', in B. Turner (ed.) *The New Blackwell Companion to Social Theory*, Hoboken: Wiley-Blackwell.

van der Klis, M. and Karsten, L. (2009) 'The commuter family as a geographical adaptive strategy for the work–family balance', *Community, Work and Family*, 12: 339–354.

Vannini, P. (2010) 'Mobile cultures: from the sociology of transportation to the study of mobilities', *Sociology Compass*, 4: 111–121.

Voight, A., Shinn, M. and Nation, M. (2012) 'The longituding effects of residential mobility on the academic achievement of urban elementary and middle school students', *Educational Researcher*, 41: 385–392.

Voigt-Graf, C. (2003) 'Fijian teachers on the move: causes, implications and policies', *Asia Pacific Viewpoint*, 44: 163–175.

Vondracek, F.W., Lerner, R.M. and Schulenberg, J.E. (1986) *Career Development: A life-span developmental approach*, Hillsdale, NJ: Erlbaum.

Wang, D. and Gao, M. (2013) 'Educational equality or social mobility: the value conflict between preservice teachers and the Free Teacher Education Program in China', *Teaching and Teacher Education*, 32: 66–74.

Weiss, A. (2005) 'The transnationalization of social inequality: conceptualizing social positions on a world scale', *Current Sociology*, 53: 707–728.

Wells, A. and Crain, R. (2000) 'Do parents choose school quality or school status? A sociological theory of free market education', in S. Ball (ed.) *Sociology of Education: Major themes*, London and New York: Routledge Falmer.

Wells, J., Dewar, M. and Parry, S. (2005) 'Introduction', in J. Wells, M. Dewar and S. Parry (eds) *Modern Frontier: Aspects of the 1950s in Australia's Northern Territory*, Darwin: Charles Darwin University Press.

Widegren, P. and Doherty, C. (2010) 'Is the world their oyster? The global imagination of pre-service teachers', *Asia-Pacific Journal of Teacher Education*, 38: 5–22.

Williams, K. and Mariglia, L. (2002) 'Military brats: issues and associations in adulthood', in M. Ender (ed.) *Military Brats and Other Global Nomads*, Westport: Praeger.

Williams, R. (1973) *The Country and the City*, London: Chatto & Windus.

World Bank (2013) *Data*. Online. Available: http://data.worldbank.org/indicator/EN. POP.DNST (accessed 11 April 2013).

Yarrow, A., Ballantyne, R., Hansford, B., Herschell, P. and Millwater, J. (1999) 'Teaching in rural and remote schools: a literature review', *Teaching and Teacher Education*, 15: 1–13.

Index

Page numbers in *italics* denote tables.

a-mobile theory 62
Aboriginal populations 18
Abraham, M. 4
access, axis of 27, 137
accreditation of professions 32, 161–2, 164
agency/structure binary 27, 28, 29
Alexander, M. 6
Amundson, N. 159, 160–1
Appadurai, A. 2, 195
Apple, M. 14
appropriation, axis of 27, 28, 137
Archer, M. 8–9, 28, 34, 47, 53, 56, 96, 145, 161, 195
Arnold, J. 171
Arthur, M.B. 10, 11, 159
Arthur, M.E. 11
Australian Bureau of Statistics 135, 149, 157, 158
Australian Institute or Family Studies 60
autonomy 7; spatial 2, 97–8, 126, 129

Ball, S. 14, 47
Bansel, P. 15
Barrett, G.F. 157
Baum, S. 25, 26
Bauman, Z. 2
Baxter, J. 6
Beck, U. 6, 9, 12, 14, 160, 188, 194
Beck-Gernsheim, E. 6, 14, 188, 194
Bell, C. 15, 31
Bell, M. 26, 185
Berger, B. 5, 6
Bernstein, B. 14, 15, 169, 192
Billett, S. 184
Bills, D. 159
Blustein, D.L. 11

boarding schools 41–2, 84, 114, 115, 123–4, 126, 177, 182, 193
Bologna Accord (1999) 30
Bonnet, E. 12
Booth, B. 59, 60
Boulding, E. 5
boundaryless careers 11–12, 199
Bourdieu, P. 14
Boylan, C. 175
Bradley, D. 156
brain drain 17, 98
Brown, D. 155
Bruner, J. 34, 35
bureaucratic labour market 155
Butler, T. 14
Byram, M. 30

Cameron, I. 180
Campbell, C. 14, 31, 66, 99, 175
care work 10–11, 12, 20–1
career 10–13, 23, 190–2, 198; boundaryless 11–12, 199; as complex, non-linear 159; defined 10; do-it-yourself management of 160–1; family 12; and identity 11; linear/vertical 159, 160; military spouses 59–60, 87–90, 95; protean 11, 195, 199; rural/remote professionals 100–31, 146, 147, 148, 191
Carr, P. 172
Castaneda, L. 59
Chen, D. 98
child-care services 12, 64, 65, 66, 104
citizenship 6
class differences 7; in educational strategies 14, 99; *see also* middle-class; working-class

Clayton, B. 161
coda: mobility in the 45–6; as section in narrative 35, *36*
Cohen, L. 171
collective mobility 7
Collins, R. 13, 15, 16, 154–5, 156, 157
commuting 63, 64; long-distance 3, 7, 196
complication: mobility as 42–3; as section in narrative 35, *36*
Connecting People with Jobs initiative 3
Connell, J. 3, 17
Connell, R. 9, 14, 99, 175
continuity, manufacturing 81–7
Costas, J. 3, 29
Coulter, R. 4
country service 17, 51, 98, 106, 111, 128, 146, 176, 183, 184, 191
Crain, R. 99, 175
credentialism *see* educational credentials
Crompton, R. 12
Crossley, N. 5, 9
cultural capital 14, 99
cultural market 155

Danaher, P. 30, 58
de Wit, H. 30
Defence School Transition Aides (DSTAs) 80
Dervin, F. 30
dilemmatic space 172, 173, 176, 184
distance education 162–3
Dockery, A.M. 156–7, 159
doctors *see* health sector professionals
Doherty, C. 17, 87, 99, 176
Dougherty, J. 15, 31
Drago, R. 6
drive-in drive-out arrangements 3
duty, sense of 146, *147*, 148, 165

economic regionalisation 3
Edin, K. 4
education 6, 60; differences across state/territory jurisdictions 61, 69–77, 95; distance 162–3; higher 30, 156, 157; institutional contradictions/discontinuities 60–3, 69–77, 95; institutional viscosity in 30–1, 61, 79–81, 95, 190, 196–7; and learning trajectories 62, 77–9, 95; and national curriculum 30, 61, 95; over- 158–9; and sedentary assumption 58; widening participation

agenda 156; *see also* educational credentials; educational strategies; school choice; schools
educational credentials 13–14, 15–16, 22, 23, 31, 172, 189, 191–2; exchange value 156–9, 169; and income 158; and labour market 13–14, 15, 21; as mobility system 17, 31–2, 34, 97, 152, 170; and mobius markets 153, 154–70; and over-education 158–9; overseas, recognition of 32; and productivity 154, 157, 158; and professional development 161–4; as public versus private good 137; social limits to 154–6; state recognition of 164; symbolic value 155; use value 159–61, 169; and wage premium 157
educational marketisation 14–15, 66, 95, 98, 99, 137, 192, 194, 196
educational strategies 13–16, 188–9, 192–4; financial considerations 123, 124–5, 126; middle-class 14–15, 98, 99; military families 60, 61–2, 69–85, 193; rural/remote professionals 98, 99, 100–2, 105–7, 108–9, 112–26, 127–8, 129–31, 146, *147*, 148, 151, 165, 166, 167–70; working-class 14, 99; *see also* school choice
Ehrenreich, B. 15
Elder, G. 6
Elkin, G. 11
Elliott, A. 23
emotions 195; and mobility decisions 53–5, 56
employability 160, 161
employment, military spouses 59–60, 87–90, 95
Ender, M. 59
evaluation, as section in narrative *36*
Evans, A. 4 156
extended family 103, 130, 149

fallible readings 9, 20, 34, 47, 55, 127, 161, 194, 195
family: extended 103, 130, 149; forms of 4–5; individualization of 6; as a lens on mobility 189–90; nuclear 5; as process 4–8
family career 12
family leave 12
family orchestration score 38–9, 55
family reasons for moving/staying 146, *147*, 148–9, 151

Fidell, L.S. 138
Field, A. 139
financial incentives 3, 20, 144, 146, *147*, *148*, 165, 182, 192
Flamm, M. 27
flexible working 12
Florida, R. 3
fluidification 28, 29
fly-in fly-out arrangements 3, 7, 191
Fornell, C. 138
Forsey, M.G. 175
Fransson, G. 172, 184

'gamekeeping' strategies 3, 17, 25, 32, 34, 98, 126, 129, 182, 192, 196, 198
Gao, M. 17
'gardening' strategies 17
Garrett, P. 61
gender differences 7
Giele, J. 6
Gilding, M. 4
globalisation 2
Grannas, J. 172, 184
Gray, E. 4
Gray, I. 175
Green, B. 25, 194
Green, F. 158
Gubrium, J. 37, 38

Hall, D.T. 11, 160, 161
Hancock, G.R. 138
Hannam, K. 17
Harrell, M. 59
Harvey, D. 25, 26
Haslam Mckenzie, F. 3, 7, 16, 98, 175
Head, B. 131, 196
health sector professionals 17, 32, 98; neoliberalism 173, 174; professional development and registration 161–2, 163, 164; public good attitudes 174
Healy, K. 26
Henderson, R. 30, 58, 60, 62, 81
Higgins, N. 62, 81
higher education 158–9; and incomes 158; increased participation in 156, 157; viscosity of 30
Hillman, W. 26
Hirsch, F. 13, 15, 154, 155–6, 157–8, 159
Ho, R. 139
Hodgson, H. 4
Holdsworth, C. 7, 8, 15, 58
Holstein, J. 37, 38
Honing, B. 172

house choice, military families 63, 65, 66, 68, 193
house prices, and school catchment areas 15
Hugo, G. 26, 185
human capital 157, 170; just-in-time 3; maldistribution of 98
Humphreys, J. 180

identity, career and 11
imagination 195
immobility 2, 7, 8, 10, 16, 66, 115, 196
incentive systems 20, 32, 131, 174, 180, 184, 189, 196; financial 3, 20, 144, 146, *147*, *148*, 165, 182, 192
income: and higher education 158; military families 59; professionals 135, *136*, 144; and skill level 158
Index of Relative Socio-Economic Advantage and Disadvantage (IRSAD) 135, 149, 150
individual mobility 7
individualization 6, 12, 160, 173, 188
Inkson, K. 11
institutional contradictions/discontinuities 60–3, 69–77, 95
institutional individualization 6, 188
institutional structures 27
institutional viscosity 21, 30–1, 32, 61, 79–81, 95, 190, 196–7
International Adult Literacy Survey 157
intersubjectivity 5, 20–1, 23, 188, 198

Jarvis, P. 159
Johnson Jr, O. 31
Jöreskog, K.G. 138
just-in-time human capital 3

Karmel, T. 156, 158
Karsten, L. 7
Kaufmann, V. 26, 27, 28, 29, 137
Keeling, R. 30
Kefalas, M. 4, 172
Kegels, G. 17, 98
Kelley, J. 156
Kelley, M. 59
Kendall, G. 99
Kenny, M. 30, 58
Kesselring, S. 28
King, R. 99
Kingma, M. 98
Kline, D. 17
Kline, P. 139

Knight, J. 30
knowledge about spatial options 47–53,
    55–6; informal 'hot' 47, 48, 56; local
    knowledge 48–9, 51, 52; official/
    institutional 47, 56
Knowledge Age 159–60
knowledge-based economy 15, 155, 160

labour: domestic division of 6, 7; mobility
    policy 195–8
labour markets 3, 6; bureaucratic 155;
    credentialed 13–14, 15, 21; fragmented
    154; professional 155
Labov, W. 35, 37, 55
Larcker, D.F. 138
Lareau, A. 14, 99
Larson, A. 185
Las Heras, M. 11, 161
Lassig, C. 87
Lawrence, G. 175
Leander, K. 62
learning trajectories 62, 77–9, 95
Lee, S. 153
Lefebvre, H. 24, 194
legal system 6
Lehman, R. 138
Lesthaeghe, R. 6
Letts, W. 25, 194
Levin, I. 7
Li, H. 142
lifelong learning 15, 160
Lim, P. 156
Limmer, R. 3, 7
Lingard, B. 30, 98, 175
Linsley, I. 158
liquid modernity 2
Lisbon Recognition Convention 32
Listing, J.B. 153
Littleton, S.M. 11
local knowledge 48–9, 51, 52
location attributes 146, 147, 148, 151
location range construct 132, 137, 138,
    141, 142, 143, 144
Lock, G. 174
Lubienski, C. 31
Luck, D. 7
Lunn, S. 174
Lury, C. 153
Lyons, T. 175

MacArthur, J. 62, 81
McLachlan, D. 62
Maloutas, T. 31

Marchal, B. 17, 98
Marginson, S. 137
Mariglia, L. 59
marketisation 98–9, 173, 174, 175;
    educational 14–15, 66, 95, 98, 99, 137,
    192, 194, 196
marriage: breakdown of 115; redefinition
    of 6
Massey, D. 2, 24–5, 46, 56, 97–8, 149,
    194
material market 155
Meil, G. 3, 7
meritocracy 154
meta-competence 160
middle-class 22, 24, 154, 172; educational
    strategies 14–15, 98, 99; see also
    professionals
Miles, R. 98, 107, 180
military families 24, 31, 37, 57–96, 100,
    103, 130, 188, 190–1; and child-care
    services 64, 65, 66; and continuity,
    manufacture of 81–7; educational
    strategies 60, 61–2, 69–85, 193, see also
    school choice; house choice 63, 65, 66,
    68, 193; household income 59;
    managing space and time 63–5; motility
    65–9, 91–4, 95; research literature on
    58, 59–60; school choice 49, 63, 64,
    65–9, 95, 193; spouses employment/
    career 59–60, 87–90, 95
Miller, P.W. 156–7, 158–9
Mirvis, P.H. 160
mobile culture 28, 158
mobility imperative 2–4
mobility system(s) 29–30; credentialism as
    17, 31–2, 34, 97, 152, 170; defined 29;
    efficiency of 29
Möbius, A.F. 153
mobius markets 15–16, 22, 152–70, 191,
    195
mobius strip 152, 153
motility 21, 31, 32, 34, 190, 196–7; axes of
    access, skills and appropriation 27–8,
    137; construct 132, 137–8, 138, 141–4;
    defined 26–7, 137; military families
    65–9, 91–4, 95; predictors of,
    professionals 143–4, 150; as a
    prerequisite 26–8
movement capital 27
moves, number of 143, 144–5
moving, reasons for 146–8, 151, 165–6
Mueller, R.O. 138
Mulkeen, A. 98, 174

MySchool website 30, 175

narratives 21, 34–56; construction of place in 46–53; structural elements of 35, *36*, 37
national curriculum 30, 61, 95
neoliberal policies 14, 98, 99, 173, 175, 183, 192, 194
neoliberalism construct 132, 137, 138, 140, *141*, 144, 173–4; and public service values 173, 179–84
network capital 29
networks, formal/informal 48
new mobilities paradigm 1–2, 6–7, 17, 29, 62, 94, 153, 172
Nicholson, N. 10
Noreisch, K. 14, 31
normalisation of mobility 197
nuclear family 5
nurses *see* health sector professionals

optimising circuit strategy 100–8, 130, 150–1; variations on 108–19, 130
orientation: mobility in the 40–2; as section in narrative 35, *36*
over-education 158–9
overseas qualifications, recognition of 32
Owen, S. 180

Perelman, L.J. 160
Pickover, C.A. 153
place 21, 22; construction of in narratives 46–53; interactive constructions of 24–6, 34; progressive, relational sense of 24–5, 46–7, 56, 97–8
Pocock, B. 12–13, 186
Poehnell, G. 159
Polesel, J. 13
police service 32, 98, 115–16, 128–9, 173–4
politics of mobility 24, 97, 149, 194
Polkinghorne, D. 37
population 18
Poupeau, F. 14–15, 31
Power, S. 14, 99
PriceWaterhouseCoopers 3
private good construct 132, 137, 138, 139, 140
productivity, and educational levels 154, 157, 158
Productivity Commission 195–6
professional currency/development 161–4, 171, 191

professional labour market 155
professionals 16–17, 31, 37–8, 154; accreditation and registration of 32, 161–2, 164; educational strategies 98, 99, 100; maldistribution of 16, 98; public service ethic 129, 135, 137, 150, 172–3, 187, 191 (and neoliberal values 173, 179–84); school choice 14–15, 99, 106, 107, 169, 170, 171, 172, 173, 176, 183; spatial autonomy 97, 126, 129; *see also* rural/remote professionals
projects, reflexive 8–10, 195
protean career 11, 195, 199
Prout, S. 58
psychological mobility 11–12
public good construct 132, 137, 138–9, 144, 172–4, 179–83
public service ethic 129, 135, 137, 150, 172–3, 187, 191; and neoliberal values 173, 179–84
public/private dilemmas in rural service 171–85
Pusey, M. 99, 175

reflexive projects 8–10, 23, 195
reflexivity 8, 46, 52, 55–6, 99, 145, 161, 187, 189, 195
regional, as a term 25
registration of professions 32, 161–2, 164
Relocations Grants Scheme 3
remote, as a term 25
researching, to inform mobility decisions 47–8, 50–1, 55, 193
resolution: mobility as 43–5; as section in narrative 35, *36*
Richardson, M.S. 10–11, 12
Riessman, C. 35, 37, 38
Rizvi, F. 30, 98, 175
Roberts, P. 175
Robertson, S. 30
Rosen, H. 34, 38
Rousseau, D.M. 11
Rowe, K. 138
Ruppenthal, S. 7
rural, as a term 25
rural/remote professionals 16, 17, 22, 24, 32, 97–131; career 100–31, 146, 147, 148, 191; educational strategies 98, 99, 100–2, 105–7, 108–9, 112–26, 127–8, 129–31, 146, *147*, 148, 151, 165, 166, 167–70, *see also* school choice; extended family 103, 130, 149;

rural/remote professionals *continued*
and mobius market 164–9; motility,
predictors of 143–4, 150; number of
moves 143, 144–5; optimising circuit
strategy 100–8, 130, 150–1 (variations
on 108–19, 130); public/private
dilemmas 171–85; recruitment and
retention strategies 16, 32, 171, 174,
184, 185 ('gamekeeping' policies 3, 17,
25, 34, 98, 126, 129, 183, 192, 196;
sidestepping 126–9); school choice 106,
107, 169, 170, 171, 172, 173, 176, 183,
193; survey of 132–51, 164–9
(educational qualifications of sample
134; income categories of sample 135,
136, 144; location range construct 132,
137, 138, 141, *142*, 143, 144; motility
construct 132, 137–8, 138, 141–4;
neoliberalism construct 132, 137, 138,
140, *141*, 144, 179–83; private good
construct 132, 137, 138, 139, *140*;
public good construct 132, 137, 138–9,
144, 179–83

Saks, M. 135, 137, 172–3, 174
Savickas, M.L. 160, 168
-scapes 2
Schaeffer, C. 10–11, 12
Schmid, C. 24
Schneider, N. 3, 7
school choice 30–1, 137, 175, 192–3;
boarding schools 41–2, 84, 114, 115,
123–4, 126, 177, 182, 193; financial
considerations 123, 124–5, 126; military
families 49, 63, 64, 65–9, 95, 193;
professional/middle-class 14–15, 99,
106, 107, 169, 170, 171, 172, 173, 176,
183, 193
schools: boarding 41–2, 84, 114, 115,
123–4, 126, 177, 182, 193; booking
systems 6, 15, 95, 193; catchment areas
14–15 (zoning boundaries 49, 66, 192,
193); high 83, 84, 95; institutional
viscosity 30–1, 61, 79–81, 95, 190,
196–7; starting age and year placement
issues 69–77; waiting lists 15, 66, 95,
193
Schultheiss, D. 12
Sciulli, D. 173
'score' representation of family projects
38–9, 55
Scott, A. 16
seasonal workers 58, 62, 95, 198

sedentary practices 2, 58, 63
self-concept 11
Sharplin, E. 174, 175
Sheller, M. 1, 2, 7, 16, 62, 94, 172
Sherif-Trask, B. 5, 187
Shortland, S. 3
skill level, and income/social status 158
skills, axis of 27–8, 137
Snider, G. 60
social mobility: and educational
credentials 31, 154–6; and spatial
mobility interface 28
social security 6
social stratification 154–5, 156
social structures 27, 28
social theory 2
social trajectories 149–50
Sörbom, D. 138
space 6–7, 21; dilemmatic 172, 173, 176,
184; interactive constructions of 23–6,
34; managing 63–5
spatial autonomy 2, 97–8, 126, 129
spouse employment/career, military
families 59–60, 87–90, 95
staying, reasons for 146–7, 148–9, 151
strategies 8–10, 23
structural conditions 27, 28
Sullivan, O. 6
Sullivan, S.E. 11
Super, D.E. 11

Tabachnick, B.G. 138
talent 3
Taylor, C. 31
teachers 17; country service 17, 51, 98,
111, 176; neoliberalism 173, 174;
professional development and
registration 162, 164; in rural/remote
communities (public/private dilemmas
174–9; recruiting and retaining 174)
Teese, R. 13
time 6, 63–5, 189
topological culture 153
Torres Strait Islander populations 18
transportation 28, 29
Tyler, M. 59

unpaid care work 10–11, 12
Urry, J. 1–2, 3, 7, 16, 23, 25, 28, 29, 62,
94, 172, 198

van der Klis, M. 7
van Zanten, A. 14

Vannini, P. 17, 23, 28
Vincent, C. 47
viscosity 28–33, 34, 61, 79–81, 95, 190, 196–7
Voight, A. 3
Voight-Graf, C. 17, 98, 174

wage premium, and educational credentials 157
Waletzky, J. 35, 37, 55
Wang, D. 17
Weiss, A. 2, 26, 97
Wells, A. 98, 99, 175
Wells, J. 175
West, M. 10
Widegren, P. 17
Williams, K. 59
Williams, R. 25

Willms, J. 9
women's status 6, 188
work 10–13; defined 10
work/family/education articulation 13, 21, 23–33
work/life articulation 12
work/life balance 6, 12, 21
work/life collision 12
work/life imbalance 12
work/life strain 6
workforce mobility policy 195–8
working-class families, educational strategies 14, 99

Yarrow, A. 174

Zhu, Y. 158

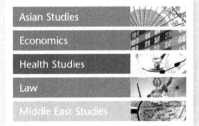
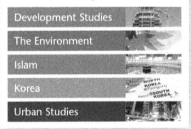

For Product Safety Concerns and Information please contact our EU
representative GPSR@taylorandfrancis.com
Taylor & Francis Verlag GmbH, Kaufingerstraße 24, 80331 München, Germany